Technologies of Sexiness

Sexuality, Identity, and Society Series

Series Editors
Phillip L. Hammack and Bertram J. Cohler

The purpose of this series is to foster creative scholarship on sexuality, identity, and society that integrates an appreciation for the historical grounding of sexuality research, seeks to transcend or integrate the boundaries constructed by disciplinary approaches, and takes theoretical and methodological risks to move the field forward. As such, the books presented here identify with a new kind of inquiry in sexuality research—one that moves us beyond questions of "origins" and "categories" toward the *meaning* of desire, experience, and identity in particular contexts. They are designed to be useful in both teaching and research.

BOOKS IN THE SERIES

The Story of Sexual Identity: Narrative Perspectives on the Gay and Lesbian Life Course
Phillip L. Hammack and Bertram J. Cohler

The Monogamy Gap: Men, Love, and the Reality of Cheating
Eric Anderson

The Declining Significance of Homophobia: How Teenage Boys are Redefining Masculinity and Heterosexuality
Mark McCormack

Technologies of Sexiness: Sex, Identity, and Consumer Culture
Adrienne Evans and Sarah Riley

Technologies of Sexiness

Sex, Identity, and Consumer Culture

ADRIENNE EVANS AND SARAH RILEY

OXFORD
UNIVERSITY PRESS

Oxford University Press is a department of the University of
Oxford. It furthers the University's objective of excellence in research,
scholarship, and education by publishing worldwide.

Oxford   New York
Auckland   Cape Town   Dar es Salaam   Hong Kong   Karachi
Kuala Lumpur   Madrid   Melbourne   Mexico City   Nairobi
New Delhi   Shanghai   Taipei   Toronto

With offices in
Argentina   Austria   Brazil   Chile   Czech Republic   France   Greece
Guatemala   Hungary   Italy   Japan   Poland   Portugal   Singapore
South Korea   Switzerland   Thailand   Turkey   Ukraine   Vietnam

Oxford is a registered trademark of Oxford University Press
in the UK and certain other countries.

Published in the United States of America by
Oxford University Press
198 Madison Avenue, New York, NY 10016

Library of Congress Cataloging-in-Publication Data
Evans, Adrienne.
Technologies of sexiness : sex, identity, and consumer culture / Adrienne Evans and Sarah Riley.
    pages cm.—(Sexuality, identity, and society series)
Includes bibliographical references and index.
ISBN 978–0–19–991476–0
1. Gender identity.   2. Sex in popular culture.   3. Feminism.   4. Consumption (Economics)
I. Riley, Sarah.   II. Title.
HQ1075.E9293 2014
305.3—dc23
2014010224

9 8 7 6 5 4 3 2 1
Printed in the United States of America
on acid-free paper

CONTENTS

When Bert Cohler and I first conceived the Oxford Series on Sexuality, Identity and Society, we envisioned a forum for interdisciplinary, theoretically rich works that would challenge and provoke. We envisioned works that would defy easy categorization in the knowledge production industry, works of social and political significance that would do more than *describe* a particular phenomenon or empirical reality. We envisioned, rather, works that would *prescribe* a world of alternative empirical realities, works that skirted traditional boundaries of academic disciplines as well as the traditional aims of a knowledge production industry that denies its place in social and political change.

This compelling, theoretically and empirically rich volume by Adrienne Evans and Sarah Riley embodies our vision for a science of sexuality that is rigorous in its analysis and bold in its aspirations. The volume captures the way in which two generations of women construct identity in the historical moment of present-day neoliberalism, consumer capitalism, and postfeminism. Evans and Riley interrogate the way in which women of distinct generation-cohorts engage with competing and at times conflicting discourses of gender and sexual identity. They consider the way in which these generations of women differentially navigate increased sexualization in the media. But they go beyond simply describing the lived experience of women. Rather, they interrogate the way in which women's narratives reproduce or challenge existing power dynamics in society. Theirs is an analysis that crosses the borders of social science disciplines—most notably, politics, economics, psychology, and sociology—to illuminate the navigation of sex, identity, and pleasure with sensitivity to cultural and political context.

Two features of the volume are particularly noteworthy for embodying the critical vision of the series. First, the research takes an empirical approach that is sensitive to history through its consideration of two distinct generation-cohorts of women. The significance of generation-cohort remains underappreciated in social science research, apart from life course perspectives on human development and the sociology of aging (e.g., Elder & Shanahan, 2006). In the volume that inspired and inaugurated this series, *The Story of Sexual Identity*, Bert Cohler and I argued that a new interdisciplinary sexual science cannot neglect the significance of generation-cohort in both individual and collective construction of gender and sexual identity, for the politics of identity is not static but constantly in motion (Hammack & Cohler, 2009). Women and sexual minorities are particularly attuned to the experience of subordination; we inhabit a cultural context in which male and heterosexual privilege continue to dominate social and political structures in most nations, even as challenges to sexism and heterosexism have resulted in some significant legal and social changes. But our experience of gender, sexual desire, and injustice is intimately shaped by the discourse of the world in which we first became aware of our subordination. A woman coming of age in the 1980s has a different relationship with the discourse of gender and sexuality than a woman coming of age in the early 2000s, for discourses and representations have shifted, even as the experience of subordinate status endures. Evans and Riley are able to directly interrogate the historical contingency of the lived experience of gender and sexuality by employing a multi-cohort design. Their findings are invaluable, for they reveal the way in which generational identity shapes women's understandings of themselves and their social and political surround.

The second key feature of the book that I want to highlight is its rigorous use of qualitative methods grounded in an analysis of discourse at the level of both the person and of society. Evans and Riley provide a blueprint for the social scientist interested in linking societal discourses of gender and sexuality, embodied in artifacts such as media representation, to personal narratives of sense-making and self-understanding. This approach embodies another element of the new sexual science Cohler and I envisioned in that 2009 volume—the idea of *narrative engagement* (Hammack & Cohler, 2009). We suggested that sexual identity develops through a process in which individuals navigate and negotiate master narratives of sexual minority identity and that these master narratives are apparent in discourse that is publicly available (e.g., in film, literature, journalistic accounts, etc.). This theoretical perspective on identity development is not unique to sexual identity development, however (e.g., Hammack, 2011). The centrality of narrative in identity development is likely as universal as language itself is, for stories represent a universal form of human communication (e.g., Hogan, 2003). Stories about gender and sexuality shape our experience of self and identity, constructing states of relative privilege and subordination as we navigate the discursive waters of language and politics throughout our lives. The methods Evans and Riley employ give life to central theoretical ideas in the social sciences about sex, gender, and power (e.g., Foucault, 1978). Through the narratives of women, they reveal the power of context to shape sexual subjectivity.

Technologies of Sexiness is the first volume in the series since the death of the co-founder of the series, Bertram J. Cohler. Bert was extremely excited about this volume and would have been delighted to see it in print and to use it in his legendary seminar on Sexual Identity, Life Course, and Life Story at the University of Chicago. Bert was an extraordinary mentor, colleague, and close friend, and his vision for the series endures in this and future volumes.

Phillip L. Hammack
Santa Cruz, CA
April 2014

REFERENCES

Elder & Shanahan, M.J., G. H. (2006). The life course and human development. In W. Damon & R.M. Lerner (Eds.), *Handbook of child psychology: Vol. 1, Theoretical models of human development* (6th ed., pp. 665–715). Hoboken, NJ: Wiley.

Foucault, M. (1978). *The history of sexuality, Vol. 1: An introduction*. New York: Pantheon.

Hammack, P. L. (2011). *Narrative and the politics of identity: The cultural psychology of Israeli and Palestinian youth*. New York: Oxford University Press.

Hammack, P. L., & Cohler, B. J. (2009). Narrative engagement and sexual identity: An interdisciplinary approach to the study of sexual lives. In P. L. Hammack & B. J. Cohler (Eds.), *The story of sexual identity: Narrative perspectives on the gay and lesbian life course* (pp. 3–22). New York: Oxford University Press.

Hogan, P. C. (2003). *The mind and its stories: Narrative universals and human emotion*. New York: Cambridge University Press.

"Sexy" consumer texts address the twenty-first-century woman as an individualistic pursuer of erotic pleasure. This new sexual subjectivity celebrates an explicit, "up for it" female sexuality that is active, confident, and independent—a far cry from the passivity of traditional Western representations of female sexuality. Twenty-first-century Western female sexuality is also consumer-oriented, and a proliferation of sexual products directed at women has opened up new spaces from which women can express their sexuality and experience themselves as active sexual subjects. In this book we explore how women are negotiating the call to be sexy, sassy, and confident.

The foundations of the book are located in the spaces where neoliberalism, postfeminism, and consumerism fuse together to create a normative expectation to consume oneself into new sexual subjectivities. These new sexual subjectivities offer a different articulation of feminine identity, opening up spaces for women to speak of new sexual desires, and to present themselves as having fulfilled much of the ambition of second wave feminism for an acceptance and celebration of active and engaged female sexuality (see, for example, Greer 1970). But critics argue that the potentials in these new discourses of female sexuality are limited because they are attached to greater self-surveillance and self-discipline, while being ridden with contradictions that both mask structural inequalities and rehearse older notions of gendered expectations. In this book we contribute to these debates by asking two questions: How are women are making sense of themselves and others in this context? What are the consequences for them when they take up these forms of sense-making? To address these questions we offer an analysis of a series of discussions we had with two groups of women who had very different responses to the rise of new sexual subjectivities and women's take-up of consumer-oriented agentic sexiness.

In Chapter 1 we lay the foundations of our analysis by showing some of the relations between neoliberalism, consumerism, and postfeminism and how they have become key ways of understanding subjectivity in the early part of the twenty-first century. In Chapter 2 we look more closely at the problems of doing feminist research when women's sexual identity takes place in the social context of a high-profile public discussion of sexualization. The general noise about sexualization within public discourse has meant that we have seen moral panics and a frenzied hype concerning the risks that sexualization poses for young women and the possibility that consumer culture has merely repackaged traditional forms of female oppression. Our aim in Chapter 2 is to show how a change of perspective might allow us to think within these debates in more productive ways, by highlighting where the similarities are in how the "pop and policy" discussions and debates are articulated.

Our analysis of the "sexualization" debates also shows how this research area is reworking the core principles of feminist research, where issues of agency function at the epicenter of feminist thought (McNay, 2000). Theorizing female identity within the realms of self-determinism and agency is a political imperative for feminist research. If women are to overcome a range of limiting and oppressive social constructs, then they have to be understood as having some "free will" to escape the restrictive binds that hold femininity in place as an underprivileged gendered category. And yet, because of a neoliberal discourse of "choice" and "agency," which interpellates the individual as freely able to choose her identity through the practice of consumption no matter how constrained she might actually be (Gill, 2007a), feminists have remained critical of the sexualization of culture and of what is seen as a dubious claim to empowerment. Feminist research therefore has to negotiate a difficult political space in relation to new sexual subjectivities (Duits and van Zoonen, 2007; Gill, 2007a).

The positioning of women's agency has been further confounded by methodological choices that significantly shape how women's agency is figured. As we suggest in Chapter 3, we see research on the "sexualization" of culture (and more recently—in a move to emphasize the multiplicity of women's experiences—on "new sexual cultures") as having remained largely within either media analysis or first-person accounts of changing attitudes toward sexuality. The impact of these methodological positions to understanding the "sexualization" of culture has led to either deterministic media analyses that imply a top-down theory of power—reflecting the political ideology of the analyst and saying little about what might happen to this power when it reaches its audience—or first-person accounts of changing attitudes toward sex that risk ignoring the cultural context that may structure women's apparent choices. Arguing that these debates and methodological issues orienting around the term "sexualization" have produced a "doubled stagnation" within sexualization studies (Chapter 2), we avoid getting stuck in these stagnations by outlining new ways of conceptualizing a (hetero) sexual femininity located in the terms set out by postfeminism, neoliberalism, and consumerism.

As we move toward our theoretical framework, our aim in this book is to complicate accounts that detail how women are feeling or being sexy. We do not want to locate the "problem" of sexualization back into the bodies of women, pathologizing either their engagement in, or rejection of, new sexual subjectivities. We want to move away from simplistic notions of how people engage with the media and the way the media are understood to "influence" their psychological well-being. To do so, we put forward a framework for thinking within sexualization and doing research with/on women's sense-making set against a broader context of the sociopolitical that makes sayable what they think and feel. We term this theoretical framework "technologies of sexiness" (Chapter 3).

In what follows, we use this framework to explore how women are negotiating new forms of female consumer-oriented "sexy" identities by analyzing the co-productive relationship between the cultural, the material, and the subjective. To do so, we locate new female sexualities within our understandings of postfeminism, neoliberalism, and consumerism. The social landscape that these terms help us capture can be conceptualized as a response to accelerated social change and the uncertainties associated with globalization, deregulation, and de-industrialization. Women's increased entry into education, newfound wage-earning capacity in the workplace, and access to developments in contraception have deemed women new citizens in an increasingly global mediated world. Accepted wisdom assumes that women are now able to "have it all"—a high-flying career, equal pay, delayed motherhood, and independence—without the trouble of discrimination and inequality. Alongside these shifts, free market politics have forced a push toward competitive consumerism on a global scale and have provoked a feminization of labor through increasing dependence on the service sector (Harris, 2004; Harvey, 2005; Walkerdine, 2003). These shifts have had a dramatic effect on the kinds of selves people in postindustrial societies can be.

More than this, however, we are interested in the ways in which cultural discourses around sexuality are taken up and made to feel our own—of how the logic at the intersection of postfeminism, neoliberalism, and consumerism comes to be activated. To do so, we analyze how discourses of postfeminism, neoliberalism, and consumerism were personalized and deeply felt in the discussions we had with women about sexiness. In our analysis chapters, we respond to the need in sexualization studies to combine analysis of the cultural and media discourses with regard to how they have shaped identity by asking important questions of these cultural shifts: How are women making sense of themselves in the context of new sexual subjectivities? What inclusions and exclusions are engendered by the creation of a social discourse in which women's empowerment is enabled through consumerism? How do women come to enact agency within and through the discourses of neoliberalism and postfeminism? And what might sexualized consumer-oriented cultures mean for female identity in the twenty-first century?

To address these questions we analyze the discourses drawn on by two cohorts of women (aged 25–35 and 45–55). We offer extracts from a series of individual interviews to help frame and provide evidence for our arguments in our opening chapters that contextualize and theorize new sexual subjectivities. And in our analysis chapters (4 and 5), we draw on data collected in cooperative inquiry-inspired focus groups to provide an in-depth empirical analysis of how two groups of very differently positioned women celebrate, reject, and otherwise negotiate new sexual subjectivities. In doing so, we draw on a form of analysis that cycles between macro and micro processes, with the aim of engaging with how societal discourses come to be felt so personal by the women we spoke to.

The book aims to develop creative and dynamic approaches through multi-modal and polyphonic analytics, informed by a methodology that engages both cultural analysis and first-person accounts of women's changing relationships with sexual subjectivity. Drawing on a series of key theoretical concepts to help us understand women's negotiations of sexiness, we develop our insights into various "technologies of the self" through analyses of space, nostalgia, and claims to authentic sexiness. We apply these analytics to the data to open up new ways of thinking through cultures of sexiness. We theorize the doubled nature of sexualization discourses and analyze both the cultural conditions of possibility that have enabled new forms of female sexual identity and the discursive and emotional processes involved in how women take up, negotiate, and make these discourses their own. We conclude by arguing that women embody, rework, and resist dominant discourses of neoliberalism, postfeminism, and consumerism in ways that rupture passive modes of femininity. Through such ruptures we suggest that women are able to produce themselves as good people and good consumers—becoming "ethical subjects of the self" (Foucault, 1988). Yet power was refigured in ways that excluded certain identities along the trajectory of gender, age, class, ethnicity, and sexuality. Throughout the book, theoretical and methodological contributions to the literature are made, and we conclude with a challenge for future feminist methodology. But perhaps the most important contribution comes from the data—the opportunity to understand how women are making sense of sex, identity, and consumer culture and technologies of sexiness in the twenty-first century.

Technologies of Sexiness

Sex, Identity, and Consumer Culture

Jane was very nervous about attending her first pole-dancing class. She was worried about what other people would think of her body. But once she got there she found the experience fun. It felt empowering—until she noticed another woman scrutinizing her cellulite.

Sasha felt uncomfortable passing the adult-only store a few streets away from her house—it just wasn't the same as the High Street sex store she shopped in.

Loretta couldn't believe her eyes when her 11-year-old daughter's part in the school show involved a grinding dance with the other girls in her class that imitated a hip-hop video currently in the charts. Her daughter looked like a lap dancer.

"Sexiness" has become a consumer good. It is packaged to the female consumer through discourses of "choice," "autonomy," and "liberation," creating a new female sexual subjectivity that celebrates female sexual agency and empowerment through consumption.

No longer valued for its passivity, contemporary femininity is now more likely to be articulated in terms of being "active, recreational, material, independent, [and] consumerist" (Evans, 1993, p. 41). Mainstream media presents a figure of youthful femininity who is empowered through her sexual identity and her consumption of "sexy" goods, so that sex has become a stylish "source of physical pleasure, a means of creating identity, a form of body work, self-expression, [and] a quest for individual fulfillment" (Attwood, 2006, p. 86).

Terms such as "raunch" culture, the "sexualization of culture," and "porno-chic"[1] have entered public discourse as ways of making sense of these new representations of "up for it" femininity that articulate a fashionable, sexually savvy,

---

1. "Raunch" culture and "porno-chic" are terms synonymous with the work of Levy (2005) and McNair (1996), respectively, while "sexualization" is often associated with the various policy initiatives around particular sexual forms of address in the media and in consumer culture. These

and active woman who engages with the proliferation of consumer opportunities as part of her identity practices. These opportunities include burlesque and
pole-dancing classes; ownership of sex toys; porno-chic fashion styles such as
G-strings and porn-star T-shirts; magazines that publish images of "empowered,"
sexually assertive models; the publication of sex/porn manuals, erotic memoirs,
mainstream "mommy" porn; porn made by female directors and sold by female
sex shop owners; and the proliferation of web-based texts, DVDs, and television
programs that bring commodified sex directly into the private sphere.

But does an increase in sexual products aimed at women democratize desire?
Or do sexualized products reproduce objectification? The development of new
discourses of empowered female and sexual agency has occurred concurrently
with a mainstreaming of sexual explicitness for women so that a defining aspect
of contemporary culture, predominantly within postindustrial societies, has been
a dramatic re-sexualization of women's bodies in the media and a mainstreaming
of pornography in public space and corporate culture. Questions are therefore
raised about the effects of this culture on women's lives when, for example, alcohol advertisements make jokes about young women preferring sex-toy rabbits to
"real" rabbits, girls are reported to be kissing each other in nightclubs for heterosexual male titillation, and women participate in pubic hair removal and genital
modification that emulate porn styles.

These questions demonstrate the complexity of understanding sex, identity,
and consumer culture, which is further complicated by debates on what it is that
we're debating. For example, while governments in the United States, the United
Kingdom, Australia, and elsewhere have commissioned reports detailing the
"problem" of sexualization, some feminist academic analyses have questioned the
very existence of the "sexualization of culture." And while the media appears to be
a key source of production in terms of images of sexualization, it is also the site in
which we see panics about the effects of sexualization on girls and young women,
as well as calls for more regulation.

In this book we explore ways in which we can make sense of the apparent
sexualization of culture and the way in which new sexual subjectivities are both
enabled by a particular cultural context, and taken up and made to feel deeply
personal. We ask: How has sexuality seemingly come to occupy such a central
place in contemporary female identity? How are women responding to sexualization? Are they using it to make sense of themselves and others? And if so, what

---

terms reflect some of the debates that we outline in this book, with Levy taking a more critical perspective, while McNair's rhetoric can be described as more celebratory. "Sexualization"
appears to be used as a way of describing a context that is itself very difficult to describe, given
that it can be applied to multiple contexts, it is often used as an umbrella term (see, for example,
APA, 2008, and Papadopoulos, 2010), but others have critiqued its use because it masks the
multiplicity of context and experience. We perceive these terms as still open to debate and contestation, and while the book remains critical of their ontology, we show a preference for the
term "sexualization" as a discourse of contemporary culture that structures the way we can think
about sexiness. Further discussion of the term "sexualization" occurs in Chapter 2.

are the consequences of this for what they can say, think, and do in relation to themselves and other women?

To address these questions, we begin by mapping the cultural conditions that we feel have enabled sexualization to become such an issue for contemporary Western female identity. We argue that three interconnected concepts—neoliberal subjectivity, consumer society, and a postfeminist sentiment—form the backdrop, or the technologies of subjectivity, that make possible new forms of feminine sexual subjectivities. In the following sections we examine this backdrop in detail to show how these concepts have become gendered in ways that have enabled new sexualization discourses. We dedicate this chapter to these concepts because they set the scene for the rest of the book and are central to making sense of gender relations in the twenty-first century.

I SHOP, THEREFORE I AM: NEOLIBERALISM, CONSUMERISM, AND POSTFEMINISM

[C]itizenship is to be manifested through the free exercise of personal choice among a variety of marketed options.

ROSE, *1999, p. 230*

During 1979–1980 two election results occurred that ultimately changed how people at the beginning of the twenty-first century would come to understand themselves. These were the elections of Ronald Reagan in 1980 as president of the United States and Margaret Thatcher in 1979 as prime minister of the United Kingdom. These elections arguably ushered in a new global political and economic landscape known as "neoliberalism" (Hall, 2011).

Appropriating biological theories of self-adjusting systems, neoliberalism is a form of governance that argues that market forces, rather than state intervention, should be allowed to drive the economy. The logic that neoliberalism applies to economic freedom is also passed on to its citizens, who are encouraged to think of themselves as autonomous individuals responsible for their own welfare: a standpoint that requires them to engage in self-surveillance in order to implement necessary acts of transformation so that they may develop the skills required to remain economically viable in changing economic contexts.

Neoliberalism was developed as a response to economic recession and the failure of some significant large-scale government interventions in economic and social life (Kelly, 2006). For the Republican Reagan regime, the recession of the 1970s called for a new way of organizing economic relations. With the help of Paul Volcker (chairman of the Federal Reserve Bank and instigator of the "Volcker shock" of 1979, which brought inflation down, to the detriment of employment levels), Reagan was able to pick apart the New Deal, America's reliance on Keynesian economics, and the policy of high employment above that of monetary growth. A process of political deindustrialization, deregulation, and globalization then began. For example, factory work was outsourced to the new developing economies, rendering redundant a large proportion of the US workforce, while the industries that remained were deregulated to ensure competitiveness in the market and were bolstered through tax cuts for big business.

In a series of similar moves, the Conservative Thatcher government of the 1980s and early 1990s implemented policies that aimed to remove people's dependence on the state. For example, trade unions were disempowered as workers became reimagined as "companies of one"; the dual processes of privatization and marketization celebrated competitiveness and economic success over and above public provision, allowing for a proliferation of companies that offered the same service (Read, 2009); and home ownership was promoted with the "right-to-buy" policy, allowing people to buy their state housing. Such shifts in property ownership made the home an important showcase of capitalist testament of self-worth, seen, for example, in contemporary reality television (*How Clean Is Your House*, BBC, UK; *Property Ladder*, Channel 4, UK; *Location, Location, Location*, Channel 4, UK) and the rise of home DIY and renovation that was also supported by new generations of television programs (*60 Minute Makeover*, ITV, UK; *The Home Show*, Channel 4, UK; *Double Your House for Half the Money*, Channel 4, UK).

While Reagan and Thatcher were able to push the neoliberal agenda onto a global scale in the 1980s, Michel Foucault historically traces the origins of the political discourse of neoliberalism to before the Thatcher-Reagan era, with the ordoliberals in Germany in the 1920s and 1930s. These ideas were then developed in the form of the neoliberalism of the Chicago school of economics and the work of Milton Friedman, which were then implemented in the free market policies in the 1973 military coup in Chile. Within this economic "liberalism," Foucault claimed, was a technology of governance whose aim was to always demonstrate that the state was too involved in the lives of its people. The logic of neoliberalism always proposes that state intervention could be rolled back, and the government's responsibility for the state could be replaced with an emphasis on and belief in the rationality of the market. To create this rational market, neoliberal politics presuppose the production of competition between private and public institutions to secure economic success, and the installing in people of a responsibility for the economy through their adoption of a form of competitive individualism, in which citizens are expected to understand themselves as individuals who are responsible for their own welfare and economic participation.

For Foucault, the creation of neoliberal individualized self-regulating subjects was the result of a new form of governance concerned with not only managing and measuring the population—a biopower—but also enabling the population to manage themselves—a biopolitics (Foucault, 2008). By placing the responsibility of the economy with the population, the state was thus able to "govern without governing" (Read, 2009, p. 29). This form of governance is a process of collapsing the social into the economic, so that a range of personal and interpersonal human action and experience become practiced and lived within the language of economy.

The policies put in place by both Reaganism and Thatcherism drastically altered the social, economic, and political landscape in the United States and the United

Kingdom. As the largest global political powers, they exported these ideas, with the United States, for example, driving a steady globalization and sale of their economic power abroad—most notably in the Middle East and East Asia. Combined with the escalating anti-communist ethic of the 1970s and 1980s[2] and the fall of the Berlin wall in 1989, there was a seeming disappearance of a feasible alternative to free-market capitalism; neoliberalism was set in place as a major and ostensibly inevitable global, economic, and political movement.

That neoliberalism is an adaptive ideology has enabled its rapid growth; it has been able to shape itself to the political, social, and cultural values of different countries and contexts, so that neoliberal ideology is constructed in different ways, depending on the history and situation in which it is applied. For example, see Hall and Soskice (2001) for an account of "varieties of capitalism," such as those between the flexible workforce in the United Kingdom and the stable workforce in Germany and Scandinavian countries, and Ong (2006) in relation to neoliberalism in Southeast Asia.

Thus, even though the Reagan and Thatcher administrations ended in the late 1980s and early 1990s, neoliberal political ideology continued to progress (Hall, 2011). For example, in the 1990s the United Kingdom elected a "New Labour" Party, which employed a political language of "modernization" that combined Right and Left political rhetoric to construct the role of the state as that of enabling social mobility, equal opportunity, and empowerment. Its aim was to help its citizens become subjects who could manage the risk of living in a rapidly changing postindustrial society by being flexible, autonomous workers within a market-driven economy (Fairclough, 2000; Harris, 2004; Kelly, 2006). The current UK government, a coalition between the Conservatives and the Liberal Democrats, has also maintained the neoliberal project. For example, it justified its dramatic reduction in state funding for universities through the rhetoric of market forces, self-management, and self-enterprise.

Neoliberal rhetoric saturates the contemporary social and cultural landscape in Britain through a range of what Foucault would call "apparatus of governmentality." These apparatus reproduce neoliberal sense-making across a range of institutions that come to speak on behalf of the subject, creating "a plethora of indirect mechanisms that can translate the goals of political, social, and economic authorities into the choices and commitments of individuals" (Rose, 1996, p. 165).

For example, the self-regulating entrepreneurial subject is often reiterated in print and broadcast media discourses. In television programs, such as *The Apprentice*, candidates articulate a "self as project" understanding of themselves by describing themselves as "a grafter" or "a rough diamond" and employ a competitive individualism enabled through the language of the economy: "I've never failed at anything," "you can't perfect on perfection," "there's no I in team but there's an I in winner," "I invest in relationships," or "Alan Sugar should invest in me" (for

---

2. These anti-communist sentiments are still evident today, for example, in the *Daily Mail*'s 2013 press coverage of Ralph Miliband, which declared that the political theorist "hated Britain" on account of having been a Marxist.

further discussion of reality television and neoliberal subjectivity see, for example, McRobbie, 2004; Ouellette and Hay, 2008; Ringrose and Walkerdine, 2008; Skeggs and Wood, 2004). A parallel can also be drawn here to George W. Bush's 2004 re-election remark: "I earned political capital in [this] campaign and now I intend to spend it" (cited in Brown, 2006).

Marketization saturates so much of how we narrate ourselves. We talk for example about "payoffs" in relationships and a "fair exchange" in friendships, and consider our position in the "marketplace" of Internet dating (see, for example, Illouz, 2007). Gill (2010) calls such forms of sense-making "intimate entrepreneurship," where, for example, women's magazines construct sexual intimacy as a well-managed and profitable meritocracy, where the amount of work that goes into preparing for sex brings intimacy in line with repertories of finance, employment, and marketing. In the same way that "nobody 'went off the rails' before the advent of railways and nobody was 'on the same wavelength' before radio was invented" (Richards, 2002, p. 10), neoliberal economies have created a context in which people now understand themselves *through* the language of the economy—we have become, as Foucault (2008) suggests, "homo-economicus."

The power of neoliberal "governance through self-governance" is not just in the plethora of institutions that indirectly translate its goals, but also in how it is able to take a hold on subjective experience, giving it a very personal dimension. Because neoliberalism requires subjects to devise and implement their own practices of improvement (e.g., going to night school, going to the gym, watching what one eats), the experience of taking up neoliberal sense-making feels authentic and self-driven (and not a form of top-down governance). In short, the experience of neoliberalism feels like a process of freedom.

Within this "freedom" the neoliberal subject is offered a range of new identifications: the hard-working taxpayer, the upwardly mobile working-class family, the strong career-driven woman (Morley and Chen, 1996; Walkerdine, Lucey, and Melody, 2001), and more recently, as we explore in this book, the female sexual entrepreneur, who works on herself and body to maintain an "up for it" sexual agentic identity (Evans and Riley, 2013; Harvey and Gill, 2011). And so a range of subject positions are created, where people are able to draw on a series of discourses about the self in order to create the self. These subject positions hail us in some way, so that through various processes of internalization we take them up and make them our own. We use these subject positions to create our sense of our actual and ideal selves, and conversely the subject positions that form our shadow selves that must be rejected and abjected. Taking up the various articulations of neoliberal subjectivity may thus feel "choiceful," but they reiterate neoliberal constructions of ideal subjectivity, so that neoliberal subjectivity becomes a taken-for-granted understanding, acting as a form of logocentrism that contains people's ability to imagine anything other for themselves "to the point where it has become incorporated into the common-sense way many of us interpret, live in, and understand the world" (Harvey, 2007, p. 3; for an empirical example, also see Riley, Thompson, and Griffin, 2010).

A significant apparatus for these neoliberal identity-effects are the "psy-disciplines" (e.g., Parker, 1999; Rose, 1996, 1999). Psy-disciplines include those institutions and sets of beliefs that are built on an understanding of the self as a psychological entity, ranging from the distinct set of ideas within the discipline of psychology itself to the chat shows and advice columns that permeate our social worlds with the rhetoric of psychology (such as talk of attitudes, personality, anxieties, or repression) or which rehearse the narrative of becoming psychologically better people (see, for example, Illouz, 2007 and 2008). Psychological concepts make sense in the context of a neoliberal project because they allow us to define ourselves in individualistic, self-governing ways. From the language of psychology, the social context in which a person lives is reduced to the immediate context of interpersonal relations, locating any personal, social, or health problems, and their attendant solutions, within the individual.

For example, the normalization of psychological talk within the context of neoliberalism means that we are now much more likely to understand unemployment as a personal lack of motivation, rather than an outcome of poor employment opportunities. Similarly, we might make sense of employers' excessive demands in terms of their flawed personalities, rather than considering them as engaged in the exploitation of other people (Walkerdine, Lucey, and Melody, 2001). Psychological discourses are now so pervasive that it's hard to conceptualize a way of thinking without them—to recognize that everyday notions such as repression and the unconscious can be traced back only recently to Freud in the early twentieth century, or that Shakespeare, for example, with all his eloquence on the emotionality of the human race, would not have used the concept of "repressed anger" to describe the feelings that his characters were experiencing.

Neoliberalism and the psy-complex enable an emotionalizing and internalizing of regulation, in which new forms of surveillance draw on the emotional and "private" world of the individual. Neoliberal subjectivity is thus inherently contradictory; one must understand oneself as making free choices, while choosing only "appropriate" choices. Freedom thus becomes compulsory, in that we are expected and obliged to present ourselves as "choice biographers," creating ourselves in the likeness of our choosing as if our choices are made without limits or constraints. In this apparatus of governmentality, the focus on individual responsibility makes even more visible those who make "bad" choices (Brown, 2006; Skeggs, 2005). Locating failures in economic autonomy, and more generally in self-regulation, at an individual and psychological level both constrains the possibility of collectivist discourses (Walkerdine, 2003) and legitimates the stigmatization of new "folk devils"—teenage mothers, people on welfare, publicly drunk young women—who must be submitted to increased surveillance by the population at large to encourage them to better self-regulate (Blackman and Walkerdine, 2000; Cohen, 2002; Hall et al., 1979; Mackiewcz, 2013). Thus, those who are socially disadvantaged through structures of class, race, ethnicity, and so on, are held individually accountable and are blamed for their position (Harris, 2004). As Stainton-Rogers (2011) argues, neoliberalism is "an ideology that has adopted the language of commerce—markets, efficiency, consumer choice—to shift risk from those in power (governments and multinationals) on to less power-ful individuals and communities... [creating] a 'blame the victim' culture, where the poor, the obese, the dispossessed and the pathetic losers, the homeless and the stateless are held responsible for their misfortunes, shifting responsibility away from those who otherwise might be held to account" (p. 77).

So while neoliberal subjectivity offers a way for people to think of themselves as good citizens and productive people through a process of self-regulation that enables economic autonomy, it is based on an ideology that people, like the mar-ket, can be free, autonomous, and independent from state control/support, which critics argue renders invisible forms of structural inequality, discipline, and sur-veillance. Furthermore, in loading the risk onto individuals, the expectation that one is individually accountable and responsible for one's fate and must therefore continuously survey and work on oneself creates incredible pressure. For exam-ple, "binge drinking," understood in the rhetoric of neoliberalism as an individual problem, may in fact be better conceptualized as a temporary escape from the pressure of neoliberal governance (Measham and Brain, 2005).

In a book about sexual identities we have, so far, not discussed sex as much as might be expected, but we argue, when thinking about contemporary sexual sub-jectivities, we first need to have an understanding of neoliberal forms of gover-nance. This is because the apparatus of neoliberal governmentality disperses the power of neoliberal politics throughout personal, social, and institutional levels, and at every level sexual identities are implicated. An ideal form of subjectivity emerges from these apparatus: a subject who is choiceful, autonomous, risk man-aging, and responsible for oneself, and is reiterated in such a pervasive way that it dominates our sense-making (perhaps to the extent that it becomes hard to imagine another way of thinking about subjectivity). As we will argue further, this choiceful autonomous subject structures forms of thinking about new sexual subjectivities, as does the context of compulsory freedom, so that within neoliberal sense-making women are expected to consider their engagement with sexual cultures as acts of free choice. These choices are therefore not just in relation to maintaining economic autonomy, but also about identity and consumption practices—since "appropri-ate" forms of consumption offer a route for the subject to meet neoliberal ideals of self-management and enterprise. So it is to consumption we now turn.

The Consumer Society

> the subjectivity that can consume oneself into being, the subject for which happiness is apparently possible
>
> WALKERDINE AND RINGROSE, 2006, p. 44

Consumerism takes on a special role in neoliberal bio-politics. As Foucault's the-ory of power suggests, governmentality is enabled by the reduction of the power of the sovereign and toward the individualization of the population; people come to think of themselves, any problems they experience, and their attendant solutions at an individual or interpersonal level. To manage the freedom of this "individualized crowd," neoliberalism places emphasis on the various consumer practices that allow people to create themselves as authentic individuals, and to do so in ways that are productive toward the state, market, and economy.

The tying in of individualism and citizenship to consumption (such as the right-to-buy policy of the Thatcher era) initiated a seismic shift in the relationship between consumerism and identity. The early neoliberal policies of detraditionalization, modernization, social mobility, privatization, and marketization encouraged people to let go of traditional anchors of identity (such as class, gender, ethnicity, parental occupation, or geographical region) in favor of more "liquid" identities based on individual market choices and consumer lifestyles (Bauman, 2000; Beck and Beck-Gernscheim, 2001; Giddens, 1990, 1991). As Bauman (2000) suggests, in the move from heavy capitalism toward "light" and value-obsessed capitalism that defines this erosion of traditional anchors, what one can make of the self, as an individual, has become paramount. Older structures have melted away, making way for new identities that are in the process of being re-formed. This context suggests freedom and choice, in which the subject should "*become what one is*" (Bauman, 2001, p. 144). However, the privileging of these constructs in liquid modernity also implies never-ending self-transformation: liquid modernity says to the subject that "'you are no more free when the end has been reached; you are not yourself when you have become somebody.' The state of unfinishedness, incompleteness and underdetermination is full of risk and anxiety" (p. 62). Consumption has been promoted as a means by which individuals could exercise the autonomy and freedom of neoliberal subjectivity and develop their own "choiceful biography," creating a life narrative articulated through the possession of goods (Harris, 2004).

Our consumer practices are thus a tool for constructing the self. Within neoliberal discourses of self-development, consumption became a tool for mobilizing the consumer into a particular state of productive market-orientation in which the citizen was encouraged to consume himself or herself into being (Miller and Rose, 1997; Rose, 1999). In relation to sexual identity, for example, a plethora of sexual consumer products have been developed with the female consumer in mind. New generation vibrators, for instance, hold within them the possibility of autonomously created pleasure and the ability to transform the user, who becomes what she wants to be—empowered, agentic, and sexy.

But there is inherent contradiction in the expectation for people to use mass-produced products in the production of their individual biographies. For example, Riley and Cahill (2005) described how young women drew on notions of the self as a project to use body art practices as tools for constructing an original self. However, their identity management was threatened by a context in which body art's fashionableness undermined this sense of individuality. Similarly, when Fiske (1989) asked his students to describe their clothing "choices," jeans were described as markers of individualism ("freedom to be myself"), despite jeans being the most common item of clothing among this cohort. In a neoliberal consumer society, our material possessions are therefore taken to represent something of our true, authentic, and individual selves, and are used as tools (or technologies of self; see Chapter 2) to consume ourselves into being, a kind of mass-produced freedom of expression. The folding in of neoliberal subjectivity with consumerism thus enables certain freedoms, but these freedoms are primarily exercised through consumption, either of goods or of less tangible resources, such as gym memberships and other entertainment and leisure practices.

Neoliberalism and consumerism have affected not only the subject's relationship to the self, but also the subject's relationship to the state. Changes in how we conceptualize identity, citizenship, and consumption have rewritten and depoliticized citizenship, so that citizenship is made sense of, not through a discourse of rights, but of consumption (Harris, 2004; Riley, Morey, and Griffin, 2010). For example, Cronin (2000) notes that concepts once associated with citizenship, such as individual freedoms and rights, are now coupled with consumerism, making consumption "one of the few tangible and mundane experiences of freedom which feels personally significant to modern subjects" (Cronin, 2000, p. 3).

Consumption is thus the process in which we produce ourselves and experience freedom. It is also where we are encouraged to find solutions to any difficulties we have in self-actualization, because in shifting our understanding of what were once considered social problems to the realm of the individual, neoliberalism presents individual consumption practices as the site for solutions to any problems we might experience. For example, Brown (2006) cites a range of consumer-oriented solutions to what might be considered collective problems that include the sale of bottled water to overcome pollution of water systems and the growth of anti-depressant pharmaceutical companies to quell the meaningless of a life dedicated to the acquisition of wealth. She concludes, "the conversion of socially, economically and politically produced problems into consumer items depoliticizes what has been historically produced and it especially depoliticizes capitalism itself" (Brown, 2006, p. 704). In relation to sexuality, Tiefer (2006) offers a similar critique of Viagra: an individual, consumption-based solution to sexual problems that abstains the user from considering the wider interpersonal, relational, and social context in which solutions to sexual problems may be sought (see newviewcampaign.com for a range of attempts at offering alternative sense-making to neoliberal informed discourses of sexuality).

Consumerism and neoliberalism thus reiterate shared concepts of ideal subjectivity in which consumption has become an ethic and care of self, a way of expressing the authentic self so that "good" consumption becomes conflated with being a "good" person. Discourses of neoliberalism and consumption thus rehearse the same sense-making, although we identify one notable difference: while neoliberal subjectivity is constructed through discourses of choice, autonomy, and risk (extoling in its citizens the need to manage risk through self-surveillance and transformation so as not to rely on state support in uncertain times), discourses around consumerism minimize the notion of risk, emphasizing, along with choice and autonomy, notions of freedom and pleasure—as in the concept of "retail therapy," which draws on psychological discourse to construct consumerism as a pleasurable "fix" to life's little difficulties.

This is not to say that there is no risk in consumerism. Fulfilling neoliberal citizenship requires the subject to constantly work on and improve the self. This need to continuously transform the self underscores the logic of neoliberal consumerism, as we have to understand ourselves as already inadequate in order to improve: what Bauman (2000) refers to as both a compulsion and an addiction, a state where in "the consumer race the finishing line always moves faster than the fastest of runners" (p. 72). This cycle of failure is made more salient because one must have the freedom to consume (within the logic of neoliberalism), but one must also consume "appropriately" and avoid the visibility of those who make "bad" choices (the obese, publically drunk, the person with no style, etc.). And because consumption is intimately bound up in the self, those who get their consumption choices "wrong" risk having to also construct themselves as "wrong." Such pressure to engage in appropriate consumption, for example, can be seen in the rise of show-home furniture stores, ensuring that the interior of a shopper's home is in line with current concepts of appropriate, fashionable, successful consumption.

Because neoliberalism ultimately supports a successful economic citizen, "bad" consumption choices are constructed as those that limit the subject's ability to participate in the economy. This is evident, for example, in drug use, where users who engage "recreationally" are deemed different from those who are defined as "addicts," with the difference being in the divisions between "good" and "bad" consumption (Riley, Thompson, and Griffin, 2010). "Bad" consumption choices are also constructed in relation to social categories. Class, ethnicity, and other social categories structure people's consumption opportunities, choices, and taste cultures; yet the individualism-choice framework of neoliberal consumerism masks these structural differences.

Ringrose and Walkerdine (2008), for example, identify a form of symbolic violence in the plethora of television programs that examine "real" women's clothing choices (e.g., *What Not to Wear*). In these programs, female viewers are encouraged to scrutinize and judge other women's appearance in accordance with middle-class norms (see also Ouellette and Hay, 2008). Similarly, Skeggs (2005) has identified the working class "hen night" (bachelorette party) as a site of extreme class hatred that allows class divisions to be redrawn in a context where class is no longer seen to count. Attesting to this, our own interviewees often distanced themselves from the hen night, identifying it as "skanky" (Eve, aged 25), "not a good look" (Clair, aged 28), "not my thing" (Ellie, aged 23), and simply unimaginative (Sue, aged 49). A new rhetoric of class hatred is thus evident; for example, terms such as "white trash" and "chav" have allowed consumer "choices" to become equated with social worth, with "bad" consumption symbolically held up as the root of abject working-class identity (Hayward and Yar, 2006; Tyler, 2008; Skeggs, 2005).

As the examples above show, the dynamics between neoliberalism and consumerism have shifted the meanings of class from the masculine figure of the manual worker and trade unionist to a much more feminine and consumer-oriented notion of class (Tyler, 2008; Ringrose and Walkerdine, 2008). Given the recent historical dominance of neoliberal consumer discourses in society and women's relatively new status as subjects in their own right (largely through the gains of the feminist movement), it is perhaps unsurprising that neoliberal discourses have become highly feminized (Gill, 2008a). But one outcome of women becoming the subjects par excellence of neoliberal consumption is that they also carry the burden of the obligation to be free (Rose, 1999).

For example, in Gonick's (2006) analyses, the seemingly contradictory discourses of Girl Power (e.g., "having it all") and Reviving Ophelia (e.g. "girl-in-crisis") are shown to create a femininity that is bound by the need to always be consuming. For Gonick, both Girl Power and Ophelia are located within white middle-class discourses—they represent those subjects who have the economic and social capital to count as "good" consumer citizens, who are extolled to work on themselves either through individualistic psy-therapy discourses to remedy the girl-in-crisis or through consumption practices that allow girls to make sense of themselves through "girls can do anything" rhetoric. For Gonick (2006), what seem like contradictory discourses of femininity ("having it all" or "girl-in-crisis") function together to produce femininity as a slippery subject position, so that the middle-class girl is always cycling between the two, and where the required response is always the consumption of products. Thus, always needing to be worked on, the female middle-class, economically active, neoliberal consumer is always at risk of failing, so that neoliberal femininity becomes an ongoing process, which women and girls may never complete.

The other to Gonick's (2006) middle-class discourses of Girl Power and Ophelia is the working-class girl who is left out of this cycle of appropriate neoliberal consumerism. Harris's (2004) notion of the "At Risk" girl, for example, demonstrates the consequences of being unable to engage in the same forms of consumption as the successful neoliberal girl. Whereas the Ophelia subject position requires the appropriate response of, for example, therapy or drug and alcohol rehabilitation, the At Risk girl, unable to pay for such costly support, might end up in jail. As Ringrose (2013) notes in her analysis of "mean girls," such a discourse was publicly witnessed in the 2011 London riots, where young women involved in the riots were imagined in the media as unfeminine, violent, and aggressive, with personal psychological problems that had led them to take part in the looting. These girls were understood as abhorrent criminals, in contrast to the more general normalization of pathological middle-class mean girls, whose "indirect" aggression is understood as part of the natural development of femininity (Ringrose, 2006, 2013).

What we have described above is a context where consumption is constituted within neoliberal sense-making as a tool for creating authentic selves, so that we are expected to consume ourselves into being as part of our own "self as project." Here, neoliberal subjectivity is constructed not just as an economic citizen but as a "consumer citizen" where people are compelled to participate in the world of goods in order to count as members of society (Miller and Rose, 1997; Rose, 1999). These markers of identity are read by others, and in a context where neoliberalism emphasizes freedom of choice, the individual is held responsible for her own consumption, and any "inappropriate" choices are deemed worthy of contempt. Consumer-oriented identities thus apparently erase older categories of identity, despite the fact that social categories, such as class and race, continue to structure many people's life chances (Walkerdine, Lucey, and Melody, 2001; Walkerdine, 2003).

As we suggest above, neoliberal consumption is also gendered. Women's opportunities for economic activity, education, wage-earning capacity, and delayed motherhood have intersected historically with the uptake of neoliberal politics and the importance of consumerism in defining ourselves, making women the subjects of neoliberal consumerism par excellence (Harris, 2004; McRobbie, 2009). Within this cultural context, women are encouraged to work on their bodies and identities through consumerism and within the discourses of empowerment, liberation, and autonomy. The constant transformation required by this kind of consumerism means that femininity is constituted as a site of self-surveillance and discipline.

Women's identity projects have always been positioned through discourses of consumerism and self-transformation. For example, historically Westernized accounts of the heterosexual family unit position the man as breadwinner and the woman as responsible for stocking the home with consumer goods (with food, cleaning products, etc.). Women's beauty regimes have also been historically constructed through narratives of self-transformation into heterosexual desirableness. These older constructs of consumerism and self-transformation are easily harnessed to neoliberal and consumer discourses. In the following section we show how the particular historical intersections of neoliberalism and consumerism, combined with a point of change in gender relations through feminist activism, have produced a contemporary context identified as "postfeminist." This term pulls together the backdrop of this book, and is the ground on which we move forward to consider sexiness and sexualization more specifically.

Postfeminist Sentiment

Postfeminist sentiment[3] is a form of sense-making that incorporates neoliberal constructs of subjectivity and the centrality of consumerism in individual biographies to articulate a particular form of contemporary femininity (McRobbie, 2009). Gill (2007c), for example, identifies several features of the postfeminist sentiment, including an association of femininity with bodily property, so that

---

3. Within feminist debates the term "postfeminism" has become a difficult concept. The term has been used to denote a theoretical perspective, a movement of third wave "do me" feminists, an antifeminist backlash against women, a sentiment of contemporary culture, and an era (Genz and Brabon 2009; Gill 2007c, 2008a; Gillis and Munford 2004; McRobbie 2009; Negra 2009; Scott 2005; see also Chapter 2). In this book, we are interested in the intersections, re-appropriations and blendings of the ideologies of consumer culture, neoliberalism, and feminist politics and, in exploring these, we employ the term "postfeminist sentiment."

femininity is something that women do in attempting to meet social bodily norms (e.g., hair removal) rather than something that they are. These practices are constituted through discourses of individualism, autonomy, liberation, and choice, so that women are understood as wanting to look beautiful or sexy for themselves, not for men—a form of sense-making that Gill describes as a shift from sexual objectification to sexual subjectification (Evans et al., 2010a; Gill, 2007), but one that requires the female subject to engage with ever-increasing amounts of self-monitoring and self-discipline in order to perform consumer oriented sexy femininities (Gill, 2007b, 2007c).

The inscription of femininity as a bodily property has made the body a marker of successful femininity. Consumer practices and products oriented around beauty have increased exponentially, requiring time, effort, money, and skill. New forms of sexual subjectivity and beauty work encourage normative beauty regimes of bodily scrutiny and work that now, in neoliberal and consumerist frameworks, all can engage with equally. This sense-making is both reproduced and enabled in media fascinations with the bodies of celebrity women and the rise of celebrity culture.

In celebrity culture, women's bodies are a key source of power and identity, but nevertheless they always fall short of perfection (Gill, 2007c). The magazine industry, of course, has thrived on this contradiction—in the same week, across the surplus of women's weeklies, female celebrities may be deemed too fat or too thin, or are scrutinized and critiqued for having fake tan lines, "visible panty lines," "muffintops," a piece of chewing gum in the mouth, deodorant marks, or evidence that they might sweat. All aspects of women's lives and bodies are circled and zoomed in on—often literally—and are intricately discussed (see Gill, 2007b; McRobbie, 2009).

As Gill (2007c) notes the "ordinary" woman isn't immune from this intense focus on her body. A plethora of makeover shows address her. Makeover shows such as *How to Look Good Naked* (Channel 4, UK) and *What Not to Wear* (TLC, US; BBC, UK), for example, center attention on the ordinary woman who has "let herself go"; through expert advice on how to reclaim or participate in middle-class feminine aesthetics, the female participant is overwritten with a discourse of confidence that enables her, as "empowered" and "liberated," to either engage in a naked photo shoot or a public catwalk in her underwear/bikini (depending on the season).

Other programs focus on the woman who is "over the top." In the BBC3's *Snog, Marry, Avoid?* for example, the program's expert sci-fi beauty surveillance computer "POD" (Personal Overhaul Device) evaluates the hyper-feminine body of the participant. Over-confidence is regulated as male members of the public rate the participant's appearance. A "make-under" is then administered and male approval is again sought to deem the transformation a success. Meanwhile, shows such as *10 Years Younger* (Channel 4, UK) and *Extreme Makeover* (ABC, US) focus on the need for transformation through cosmetic surgery of the woman who is deemed to look too old or simply too ugly to function in today's society. These programs reiterate a postfeminist sentiment of women's bodies as the source and focus of uncertainty through which the body needs to be constantly remade.

Within postfeminism the body is thus a source of continuous uncertainty, forever in need of work to facilitate self-transformation (after all, fashionable wardrobes will go out of fashion, requiring the make-over subject to update as well as maintain her newly acquired culturally approved performance of femininity). Yet, underscoring the inscription of femininity as a bodily property is a discourse of empowerment, in which the body is also constructed as the site for women's empowerment, gendered identity, and confidence. For example, the 2006 Pretty Polly hosiery campaign, *Stairway to Heaven*, depicted model Anna Torkarska on the first rung of a ladder leading to the sky, with the reader positioned beneath her, permitting a view of her fishnet tights and blue underwear. This advertisement reproduces an image that, on the surface, appears to be inviting the male gaze. However, as with much postfeminist advertising, the woman is positioned as the subject of her own objectification, posed as confident with her own sexuality and ascending her own "stairway to heaven." This is more complex than the female body directly selling a product through the discourse of sex. Instead, discourses of empowerment and liberation imply that the woman pictured is presenting herself as an object through autonomy and "choice."

Gill (2003) argues that we can interpret such media representations as a shift from sexual objectification to subjectification. The shift from sexual objectification to sexual subjectification draws on the neoliberal discourses of autonomy, choice, and pleasures in consumption to permit a cultural discourse in which women are constructed as no longer constrained by social inequality and thus able to choose to enjoy their sexuality in the form of their choosing—including molding themselves into images of the woman-as-sexual-object. The postfeminist subject is addressed as media-savvy and knowing; thus, women are represented as participating in practices typically understood as objectifying, but it is done with a knowing wink—a reassurance that because women can now "have it all," they are no longer tied to a humorless feminist critique and are able to laugh at the ironic and seemingly retro-sexist contemporary media landscape in which they find themselves (Evans et al., 2010a; Gill, 2007; McRobbie, 2009).

The Alpen company's (2009/2010) *We Know You Know How Good It Is* advertising campaign performs exactly this function in its use of irony. This advertisement featured five women exercising on a floating pontoon in leotards. The Alpen voiceover informs the viewer that "[w]e know you know Alpen is deliciously healthy. So five girls doing aerobics overlooking a lake whilst eating bowls of Alpen isn't going to convince you any more...and besides it's sexist." At the point of feminist lexicon, the camera switches to reveal five men exercising on the bank of the lake. One of the men knowingly winks directly at the camera as the voiceover states, "That's better." Alpen's subsequent tag, "We know you know," thus comes to mean both that Alpen knows that we know their cereal is good for us, and that we know that the advertisement is "just for fun." The advertisement complements its audience on their media savviness. It suddenly becomes futile or indeed petty to critique this advertisement on the basis of sexism or objectification, as the critique has been incorporated—and then shown not to count.

The use of irony in the postfeminist address above provides the final core concept of the postfeminist sentiment that we want to discuss, which is that postfeminism simultaneously takes into account and neutralizes feminist critique. To do this, the postfeminist sentiment re-appropriates feminist discourses of individualism and autonomy by coupling them with consumer-oriented neoliberal subjectivities, so that the postfeminist figure is represented as a savvy, sexy, knowing woman who uses consumer products to produce these subjective experiences. Simultaneously, the postfeminist sentiment refutes feminism itself as a spent force, relegated to history and a time of structural inequality when women were not able to make claim to the kinds of consumer citizenship to which they are currently entitled (McRobbie, 2009; Reay, 2010). Thus, within postfeminism, feminism is both accounted for and repudiated, a move that works to silence feminist critique because its logic and nod to postmodernist irony means that the postfeminist woman is, "despite her freedom, called upon to be silent, to withhold critique in order to count as a modern sophisticated girl" (McRobbie, 2009, p. 17).

Postfeminist sentiment can therefore be understood as a fusion between neoliberal subjectivity and a feminist politics reimagined through the logic of consumerism. Postfeminism, neoliberalism, and consumerism are three interconnected aspects of contemporary culture, or technologies of subjectivity, against which we make sense of new female sexual subjectivities. In this chapter we have shown how the development of a neoliberal biopolitics has reorganized the social world into market terms; how it formed an ideal subject who is a responsible, risk managing, autonomous, self-made entrepreneurial self; and how citizenship is now made sense of though one's economic and consumer activities, so that people are expected to use consumer products and practices as technologies that produce themselves as ethical subjects. We have also explored the gendered nature of neoliberal consumer-oriented subjectivity, in which women's newfound status in education, employment, and delayed motherhood has been harnessed to the notion of the neoliberal consumer citizen; and we have considered how women's position as ideal neoliberal citizens has folded into a postfeminist sentiment that has a number of reoccurring features, including the notion of femininity as a bodily practice, a shift from sexual objectification to sexual subjectification, a focus on self-regulation, surveillance and improvement, and a simultaneous drawing on and refuting of feminism (Gill, 2007; McRobbie, 2009). The conceptual mapping in which we've engaged in this chapter has been in the service of showing how a range of diverse and divergent practices and apparatus associated with political, social, cultural, economic, and historical space has created the conditions of possibility in which women can articulate contemporary forms of sexiness. These concepts form the heart of what we believe are most important in understanding sexiness in the current cultural context. It is within this matrix of neoliberalism, consumerism, and postfeminism that this book is located.

2

Doubled Stagnations

Mapping Debates

A discourse of choice, in short, is central to neoliberal culture generally… Is it any wonder, then, that such ideas dominate women's accounts?

GILL, *2007, p. 76*

[W]hat does feminism gain—politically and analytically—by immediately countering any girl's or woman's appeal to autonomy by pointing out her false consciousness and putting her under all the constraints of patriarchy and capitalism?

DUITS AND VAN ZOONEN, *2007, p. 168*

The quotes above reflect some of the questions being asked about sexualization that have informed debates on how we can make sense of women's sexual identities given that, as we argued in Chapter 1, discourses within neoliberalism and postfeminism have tied together feminist ideas of sexual autonomy and liberation with consumer-oriented forms of governance.

Such attempts to theorize the interactions between sex, identity, and consumer culture have produced, we argue, a "doubled stagnation"—sticking points, for example, between a feminist desire to both give voice to women's experience and to challenge what seem to be new forms of oppression dressed up in the wolf's clothing of "empowerment." We call this a "stagnation" because our reading of the ways that sexualization is discussed reproduce a set of emotive, polarized debates that create a context in which these debates become reiterated rehearsals of themselves. Furthermore, the breadth of practices and products encompassed in the umbrella term "sexualization of culture" means that debates rarely focus on an issue or specific context, but link a range of factors together as part of the same phenomenon—Bratz dolls and burlesque dancing, for example, despite differences in their medium, audiences, and histories. The way that discussions of sexualization often split off in often vastly different directions reduces our ability to explore complexities in context and limits the creation of overarching frameworks from which to make sense of women's sexual identity. We are left with a sense of a doubled stagnation—of analytical sideways oscillations that reproduce and rehearse somewhat tired, but still emotive, arguments, seemingly unable to develop forward momentum.

To tease out such concerns further, we turn to the ways that the cultural phenomenon of "sexualization" has been discussed, identifying the underlying discourses of "sexualization" that have enabled, limited, and constrained the way in which sexualization has come to be seen as a significant public concern and scholarly debate. The term "sexualization" is complex, difficult and ambiguous. It is a term that makes sense in relation to Derridian erasure;[1] the word is insufficient in relation to the range of complex media and artifacts that it is used to describe; and in being used to include such a broad range of cultural products, it appears to mean very little when looked at closely. It is nevertheless part of a wider global, cultural, and social discourse, and arguably therefore still useful as a way of defining or describing a certain set of ideas attached to the bodies of young girls and women in the twenty-first century. Thinking about "sexualization" thus allows us to explore the culture of media and artifacts relating to sexiness, creating a framework for us to examine points of (to use Patti Lather's term [2007]) "stuckness" and stagnation.

For us, the "doubled stagnation" occurs in a series of debates that take place at various points and at multiple levels. But in this chapter we focus on two spaces. First, in a public discourse of concern taking place in policy, social commentaries, and public debate, and, second, in feminist academic debates examining the implications for women's agency within postfeminism. Sticking points in debates around sexualization are not limited to these spaces, and these spaces are not mutually exclusive. We choose to focus on these two sites because this is where we hear the most noise, in the sense of repetitive framings of sexualization that work to structure the boundaries of debate, creating further iterations.

In Berlant's analysis of political speech, such as George W. Bush's claim that he wanted to "go over the heads of the filter and speak directly to the people" (2011, pp. 223–224) (and the subsequent series of similar requests by other politicians to remove "the filter"), she suggests that what the "filter" does is to separate or mediate out noise from communication and that what these politicians seemed to want to give "the people" was the noise. Berlant (2011) defines this noise in a similar way to Foucault's notion of an incitement to discourse, calling it a "noisy affectivity" and a moral feedback loop that appears both repetitive and emotive.

A similar kind of "noise," we suggest, also seems to be evident in the debates around sexualization that we explore in this chapter. Like Foucault's notion of "apparatus," this noise seems to be multilayered, coming from innumerable points that connect the discursive and the non-discursive (Foucault, 1977; see also Chapter 1). And like a moral panic, the noise around sexualization seems

---

1. Derrida's notion of erasure refers to the written practice of crossing out concepts. The word is still legible, because it needs to be used. However, because it only exists as a trace and a play of differences between signs, it also needs to be crossed out. We make reference here to sexualization being under erasure because we have to use this word, but recognize its limitations.

to tap into social anxieties around particular groups of people (namely, women and children) who are at the same time understood as both vulnerable and dangerous (Egan and Hawkes, 2010; Cohen, 2002; Blackman and Walkerdine, 2000).

Debates around sexualization also seem to map into what Illouz (2007) has called an "emotional field." Illouz uses this concept to explain the way that people are incited to tell stories of themselves through, for example, discourses of therapy and self-help that orient toward a normalization of their own suffering (e.g., buying a self-help book means recognizing yourself as someone in need of help). She describes this "emotional field" as "a sphere of social life in which the state, academia, different segments of cultural industries, [and] groups of professionals accredited by the state and the university... intersect to create a domain of action and discourse with its own rules, objects, and boundaries" (p. 63). But where Illouz identifies a "narrative of suffering" in relation to how we make sense of emotion, we argue that within the discourses of sexualization, we see a "narrative of concern."

We want to suggest that within the noise of sexualization, it becomes difficult to say anything useful without also becoming involved in the noise. Part of the problem with this noise is that it traps us within its own logic, so that we can often get drawn into the anger, disgust, pleasure, or concern that surrounds sexualization discourses. This book is not a call for us to think more rationally about sexualization, or to do away with the researchers' emotions. To try to position ourselves outside or above the noise would suggest that we are somehow able to remove ourselves from the cultures in which we are embedded (Haraway, 1991). But we do think that the call on behalf of sexualization discourses to "emote" can be part of the object of our analysis, and that it is useful to consider who the objects and subjects of our concern might be, and to explore why they trigger such concern in us.

We also think that "stuck" places can be the site of research, and can create positive spaces to think through some of the difficulties of the research field. Like Lather's (2007) metaphor of "getting lost" as a fertile ground for thinking about research after the poststructuralist critique of final truths and universal knowledge, we want to think about getting stuck in doubled stagnations as a way of recognizing those sticking points and a way of thinking about what it is that produces that sticking.

Underlying this chapter, we ask: How should we make sense of "the sexualization of culture," both as a public discourse and as a researchable and scholarly topic? In what follows, we attempt to map why the idea of a "sexualization of culture" has been so difficult for feminist analysts to deal with, causing a fierce amount of debate and contention in both public and academic spheres. To map these debates in the following sections, we discuss how sexualization is represented in popular culture, social commentaries, and concerns around the sexualization of girls. We also attempt to explore the historical antecedents to contemporary academic debates on sexualization. We conclude by turning to more contemporary debates within sexualization, identifying how academic debates around sexualization have been concerned with pleasure, agency, and empowerment. The sheer complexity and depth of the discourse of "sexualization" highlight why coming to terms with sexualization is so difficult for those involved in these debates. Our aim in attempting to map some of these issues is to begin developing, in this chapter and the next, a more theoretically sophisticated perspective that might allow research to better work within this doubled stagnation, and to begin addressing sexualization in a way that allows us to speak without having to address or position ourselves within either celebratory or critical approaches, or to remain stuck in the noise without recognizing the potential of this noise for new, different ways of thinking.

OF PUBLIC CONCERN

'...like what you tend to read in magazines or you know your television programs or about you um it there seems to be so much about people's body image...' (Sue, aged 49); 'I have heard about young girls ten twelve wearing t-shirts with that on...' (Lilia, aged 52) '...and I think with the whole sex thing, because its always on the media, you know, there's always people commenting...' (Eve, aged 25); 'I mean I read something the other day that, I don't know where I read that about um...' (Clair, aged 28); 'I mean I have heard things, I mean obviously, I mean it's a fairly well known...' (Cara, aged 47).

The topic of sexualization has been of increasing concern in Western countries. This concern around sexualization has been mapped elsewhere (e.g., Attwood, 2009a; Gill, 2012a; Ringrose, 2013; Smith, 2010), but it is worth rehearsing here, to the extent that it locates the kind of talk that we heard from our participants in the individual interview extracts above.

One space in which the noise about sexualization has been taking place is in the wealth of government, policy, and institutional reports on the "impact" of this sexualization—which usually are oriented toward young people, especially young girls. In the United States, for example, the American Psychological Association's (APA) 2007 *Task Force on the Sexualization of Girls* identified the psychological "damage" that could be caused by sexualizing products. The focus of the Task Force was on young girls, with the report understanding the term "sexualization" as something that "occurs" to young girls. Thus the APA states that: "sexualization occurs when

- a person's value comes only from his or her sexual appeal or behavior, to the exclusion of other characteristics;
- a person is held to a standard that equates physical attractiveness (narrowly defined) with being sexy;
- a person is sexually objectified—that is, made into a thing for others' sexual use, rather than seen as a person with the capacity for independent action and decision making; and/or
- sexuality is inappropriately imposed upon a person"
(APA, 2007, p. 1).

The report states that it "describe(s) the potential mechanisms by which the sexualization of girls occurs and the known and likely effects of the sexualization of girls: on girls themselves, on others with whom girls have interpersonal relationships (boys, men, adult women), and on U.S. societal institutions" (APA, 2007, p. 4). The APA's framing of the debate in terms of constructing the effects of sexualization as already being known allowed it to make certain truth claims and to identify a range of stakeholders who were also at risk of this occurrence, including the institutional risks that were implicated in the (non-agentic) application of sexualization on the bodies of girls.

Meanwhile, in the United Kingdom, British governments have produced several different reports on sexualization. Before their defeat in the 2010 general election, the ruling New Labour Party commissioned *The Sexualization of Young People Review*; as with the APA report, *The Sexualization of Young People Review* was written from a psychological perspective, with the aim of summarizing and collating previous research. The report was produced on behalf of the Home Office by psychologist Linda Papadopoulos, and suggested a range of recommendations, including better sex education and media literacy across the whole curriculum; regulation of broadcasting (especially music videos and computer games); an increase in interdisciplinary research; and more support and guidance for parents.

In addition, other British government reports included Bryon's (2008) *Safer Children in a Digital World* and Buckingham et al. (2010) *Sexualized Goods Aimed at Children*, the latter being commissioned by the Scottish Parliament's Equal Opportunities Committee, and notable for its inclusion of children's voices (see Bragg and Buckingham, 2009, for a discussion of their more "child-centered" policy approach). Most recently, the newly elected coalition government in the United Kingdom commissioned and released *Letting Children Be Children* (Bailey 2011), a report led by the chief executive of the Christian-based Mothers' Union, which aimed to address parental concerns of the sexualization of children within consumer culture. Responses from the government regarding this report included that of Prime Minister David Cameron, who articulated a need for "social responsibility, not state control" (Curtis, 2011), thus reproducing a neoliberal ideology against state intervention, and also launched "Parent Portal"—a website for parents to register their complaints about sexualized media (a news story deemed significant enough to appear on the front page of the *Telegraph* newspaper on Christmas Day 2011).

Elsewhere, the Australia Institute has published a report entitled *Corporate Paedophilia: Sexualization of Children in Australia* (Rush and La Nauze 2006), which led to the *Sexualization of Children in the Contemporary Media* (2008) report published by the Senate Standing Committee on Environment, Communications and the Arts. Both Australian reports have formed the basis of changes to advertising regulations and media directed to children (for further review of reports and regulations in Australia, Canada, Norway, and South Africa, see Statham, Mooney, and Phoenix, 2011).

Recommendations within these government reports address sexualization in two ways. First, reports often make the suggestion that sexualized media require further regulation; and second, reports often call for more "self-esteem," media literacy, and better parental regulation by individual members of society, in ways that echo earlier discussion of Gonick's white middle-class "girl-in-crisis" (see Chapter 1). The first recommendation highlights a tension at the center of policy around sexualization. The call to regulate the media through heightened censorship is also a regulation of the market, an anathema within neoliberal ideology (see Chapter 1). These calls for censorship are thus at apparent odds with neoliberal sense-making, although they are tied into a history of media regulation around sexuality (which we discuss in more depth later in this chapter). In contrast, the second recommendation often takes the form of the need for heightened self-governance by individuals that is very much located within the logic of neoliberalism (again, see Chapter 1). What appears to allow these iterative recommendations to fit together so well, despite their contradictions within the neoliberal rhetoric espoused by these respective governments, is the notion that the person addressed by this mediascape is at risk, vulnerable, or already damaged by sexualization, and thus is someone who is always already positioned as failing in their ability to take up ideal forms of neoliberal subjectivity.

The ways that government reports manage this contradiction in their response to sexualization are also evident in the everyday sense-making of their citizens. In our individual interviews we identified an embodiment of what we would call the figure of the "liberal parent": a parent who was responsible enough to incite his or her child to discourse about the sexualization of culture, so that a notion of "speaking sex" was used to regulate the child. We can see this in the extract below, for example, where Kacy describes her parenting style.

> I mean I don't I I, I'm quite free with sex and provided that they are making the choices for themselves, and they're being intelligent about contraception and sexually transmitted disease I think it's fine. Again, I don't want my fourteen-year-old to have sex, but chances are he will, you know, he might grow up early, and I I mean as a parent I want to equip him with that knowledge. I don't want him to feel that it's wrong, I don't want any, so you know, when I say healthy I think if you're, if you grew up, for example, in a um household where sex is not talked about and you don't have a, you know if for whatever reason it seems a bit taboo, and then your first full on images of sex are what you would see online, on a pornography site or whatever at your mates house. And it depends on what you see, I mean some of it can be quite animalistic and quite violent, and, you know, and very fake, very staged and, you know it must be quite confusing if that's the only thing you see, you don't see how it's supposed to be. And I think that can be quite confusing. (Kacy, aged 45, part-time teacher)

In the above extract, we identify parallels between how an individual parent talks about young people's sexuality and the British prime minster's response to sexualization in his call for "social responsibility, not state control." "As a parent" and a figure of authority, Kacy constructs the role of the parent as enabling children to make choices "for themselves." But these "self-made" choices must also comply with the governance of sexuality—they must support the governmental shift toward responsibilization of the individual regarding contraception and sexually transmitted disease, so that the "choices" of the child fold into the choices of the parent. Thus, as the responsible parent, it was Kacy's duty to enable her son to make these regulated choices—"I want to equip him with that knowledge," so that, in line with the apparatus of media, government, parental advice, and so on, we have a form of parenting that does not orient to state regulation of the media as the ultimate solution (although the media are problematized in her discussion of pornography) but toward an individualized solution of self-regulation "through the promotion of subjectivities...[so that the] autonomous responsible family stands as the emblem of a new mode of government of the soul" (Rose, 1999, p. 213).

Governmentality can thus be seen at the heart of neoliberal policy regarding the management of those considered vulnerable to sexualization. The policy discourse produced by governments and institutions, and subjectivized by people, has at least served to highlight the international importance of the concept of sexualization. However, several concerns have been raised about the focus, scope, and political implications of such reports. In political terms, the production of these reports has been of benefit to these governments, allowing them to claim that issues of gender are no longer just the concern of feminists (Barker and Duschinsky, 2012). For example, the current British government's adoption of the cause of sexualization arguably says more about the capacity for the Right's rearticulation of left-wing and feminist concerns (such as women's limited role in society) and the ability of this rearticulation to further limit women and girls' capacity for self-determination (for example, through censorship and/or patriarchal concern for girls' sexuality).

Whether this is a politically motivated move by various governments and institutions seems particularly pertinent when questioning how necessary it is to produce so many reports that are similar in their recommendations for more media regulation and individual self-governance (Duschinsky and Barker, 2013). Others have noted the lack of attention to more complex and nuanced views of sexualization (see, for example, Attwood et al., 2012). Instead, taking place within largely top-down and simplistic views of "media influence," such reports tend toward a view of women as the victims of media output and focus on the damaging effects that cultural products have on young girls. This view of women as the psychologized vessels of media influence misses the complex relationships that people have with the media with which they engage. And as Duits and van Zoonen (2011) suggest, there is no better way to reinforce the neoliberal values attached to the bodies of young girls than through reliance on largely psychological understandings of women's identities that propose individualistic "effects," against a wealth of research that suggests that girls' engagement with media is far more negotiated and fractured (see, for example, Jackson, Vares and Gill, 2012; Renold and Ringrose, 2008, 2011).

Older women rarely appear as the subjects of such concerns in these reports. So that, from our perspective, these reports also reproduce other problematic cultural constructions of women, such as absenting notions of older women as having sexual identities (or even feminine identities, given the folding in of sexual and feminine identities within consumer culture).

Meanwhile, in social commentaries and popular books on sexualization, work seems to be divided between those parental advice literatures that focus on young girls (e.g., Durham, 2009; Lamb and Brown, 2006; Levin and Kilbourne, 2009; Oppliger, 2008) and the more investigative journalist pieces and social commentaries on young women and contemporary culture (e.g., Levy, 2005; Walter, 2010) that tend to address the concerned (middle-class) parent and the disenfranchised feminist. Of the latter, Ariel Levy's (2005) *Female Chauvinist Pigs* has arguably been among the most widely read and critically acclaimed, with such culturally significant impact as to have introduced the term "raunch" culture into everyday language.

In *Female Chauvinist Pigs*, Levy (2005) takes issue with a series of cultural spaces that she identifies as part of an increasing "raunch" culture. These spaces include the television shows *Girls Gone Wild* and *Sex and the City*, the Playboy Bunny brand, female celebrity porn actresses, sexualized music videos, and female pole-dancing classes. But the central figures of her book are the "female chauvinist pigs"—a phrase she uses to constitute women who have been successful in male-dominated industries by appropriating male characteristics and who do not use their success to further the feminist movement (sometimes also referred to as "loophole" women, because they are understood as an exception to the rule). Such a performance of typically masculine traits, for Levy, gives the impression that it is femininity itself that prevents women from reaching the top spots in society. Combined with those women who contribute at one level or another to "raunch" culture—including third wave or "lipstick" feminists, who are also female chauvinist pigs on account of their collusion with sexism— a range of women are framed as aiding and abetting the general denigration of other women and helping to tie women even closer to a culture in which "genuine" success is secondary to sexual attractiveness. Thus "raunch" culture is set against a backdrop of women who have failed to follow through on the feminist gains of the previous generation.

While Levy's interviews with young women on, for example, the psychic fallout of kissing each other for *Girls Gone Wild* stand as testimony to the importance of exploring women's experience of participating in "raunch" culture, our issue with commentaries such as Levy's, and others like it, is how these texts appear to present a general disappointment with the ways that young women conduct themselves in today's culture. Such work, for us, pays too much attention to aggressively revealing and demeaning the "negative" ways in which young women are engaging with sexualization—a critique of young women that seems to double back on itself and reproduce the same limitations it claims of contemporary feminine sexual identities. (Also see Chapter 3, where we discuss how this form of aggressive disappointment is also evident in academic feminist analysis of sexualization.)

By identifying particular women as either doing a bad job at being womanly toward each other or doing a bad job of being feminist, such accounts seem to be prescriptive about what it means to be a woman or to be a feminist, while reinvigorating the same judgmental culture that makes a spectacle of women's bodies (Evans and Riley, 2013). Without enough attention to the social, political, and economic contexts that have allowed the existence of "raunch" culture or the entry of women into male domains of work, it is impossible not to blame women and make them responsible for their own oppression. Moreover, many of these accounts seem to appeal to a conservative sentiment in which women's bodies become the key source of concern and contention, and tap into a benevolent middle-class sexism in which young women need to be protected from themselves. The popularity of social commentaries such as *Female Chauvinist Pigs* is thus situated in a wider body of work that provides further "evidence" on the damaging effects of "pornification" (see, for example, Paul's [2006] *Pornified: How Pornography Is Damaging Our Lives, Our Relationships, and Our Families,* and Dines's [2011] *Pornland: How Porn Has Hijacked Our Sexuality*), which seems to reflect a broader paternalism and a need to control the psychology of women. Thus it is not just the female chauvinist pigs who become the target of the critique, but all those weak femininities that lose out to them, thus setting up femininity as a binary of "bitch" versus "vulnerable."

In exploring other women's roles in, and responses to, sexualization, the work of Levy and others usefully captures a discourse within and about feminism concerning the construction of fractions between "second wave" and "third wave" accounts of sexualization. In particular, Levy captures something of the framed tension between the "third wave's" apparent postmodern play with the terms of sexual objectification, and the "second wave's" disappointment in the way this objectification has been taken up. If discourses of these debates can be said to have material effect, such debates become particularly evident in the public discourse in the time leading up to the 2011 "SlutWalks."

In 2011 a Toronto police officer made the suggestion in a lecture to students that women should dress less provocatively in order to protect themselves from sexual violence. The suggestion that appearance could provoke rape produced a series of international demonstrations and protests that took place, first in Toronto, and then in several major cities around the world. For many, the events provided the opportunity to re-claim the term "slut" from its negative associations, and served as a challenge to the blame culture around violence against women. For most of the women involved in the SlutWalks, there was a clear discourse of empowerment surrounding the event and its international reverberations. For example, many saw the events as representing a revival of feminist politics that mirrored the "riot grrrl" movement of the late 1980s and early 1990s (Filar, 2011), in which women were "demanding both the right to pleasure and the right to safety" (Schwyzer, 2011). However, a significant amount of the press coverage of the event was critical of the ability to reclaim the word "slut," given its historical resonance with "good" girl/"bad" girl dichotomies, and the idea that the women involved in the SlutWalks could make claims to empowerment. According to some, the SlutWalks were an example of the way that younger women had misinterpreted what is needed from feminist activism, and that such a reinvigoration of feminist activism needed to be something more worthy than the right to be called a "slut" (see, for example, Dines and Murphy, 2011).

The SlutWalks were also an opportunity for journalists to reproduce the police officer's position. In the *Daily Mail* newspaper, for example, journalist and commentator Melanie Phillips put forward the argument that "if you walk across a motorway and get knocked down by a car, or if you leave your house unlocked and it is burgled, no one would say you 'deserve' to be killed or burgled. But a reasonable person would surely say that it was reckless to cross the motorway or leave your house unlocked. In other words, you must take some responsibility for what happened to you" (Phillips, 2011). Calling into the piece the figure of Pankhurst, who, it is suggested, would be disappointed by the SlutWalks, Phillips claims that the SlutWalks demonstrate that feminism is irrelevant to these young women, who are mistaken in calling themselves feminist.

Phillips's argument reflects a regressive sentiment concerning women's active and public expression of their sexuality, and we argue that comments such as these also draw on a discourse of responsibility that is underpinned by neoliberal rhetoric. At the same time, however, those celebrating the SlutWalks do so through postfeminist discourses of empowerment and agentic sexuality. Our sense of the media discourses surrounding the SlutWalks is thus one of the impossibility of taking up either a "celebratory" or "critical" position without at the same time drawing on postfeminist discourses with which this book attempts to critically engage. So, regardless of whether they are voiced by a SlutWalk supporter or detractor, responses to the SlutWalks ultimately refer back to a postfeminist discourse of empowerment, autonomy, and accountability and a series of discourses that make it impossible to say anything that doesn't end up remaining within and reiterating postfeminist sentiment. (Also see Ringrose and Renold, 2012, for an in-depth discussion of the SlutWalks' cultural impact on debates around gender equality.)

Drawing together our brief mapping of how sexualization has been publicly debated, we note that, along with a developing consumer culture of sexiness, we have witnessed an increasing public concern and general noise about sexualization. In the public spaces where sexualization has been evident, we note how sexualization is framed within a narrative of concern, enabling forms of regulation and governance compatible with neoliberal ideology. We have suggested that popular books on the subject locate the problem of sexualization as something that women do to others or have done to them; and we have implied that even the recent invigoration of feminist action in the context of sexualization has the capacity to be rearticulated within the framework of autonomy, empowerment, and responsibility for the self, creating an inability to comment within these public debates without also being drawn into the logic of postfeminism, neoliberalism, and consumerism.

The capacity of neoliberal and postfeminist frameworks to reposition themselves and so fold back any debates on sexualization within their own logic has created a cyclical and self-fulfilling presence of media discourse, marking out sexualization as a distracting and disorienting context in which to think about contemporary gender relations. It has limited the ways that debates can move forward, incapacitating new ways of thinking, in part because it often fails to account for the complex places that sexualization comes from historically; it does not question the ontological validity of what "sexualization" means; and it does not recognize (or else denies) the way in which contemporary articulations of feminism echo older feminist activity (given that commentators are quick to deny a feminist identity to younger women). To address these absences, we use the following section to show the ways that contemporary discourses of sexiness are part of a larger history, which has come to define how we understand "sexualization" and the forms that debates around this topic can take. In doing so, we reveal a further set of doubled stagnations that enable and limit how sexualization can be spoken about today.

LEGACIES OF FEMINISM?

One space where debates about "sexualization" have had a significant influence in framing the ways we can understand sexualization is in the feminist movement. In this section we focus on how debates on sexualization have intersected with a particular branch of white Western feminism that has been concerned with the cultural limitations imposed on female sexuality. In taking this focus we acknowledge Hemmings's critique (2005) of rehearsing popular narratives of the feminist movement, where a "dominant story is secured through our publishing and teaching practices *despite the fact* that we know it obscures the complexities we cherish" (p. 117). And we acknowledge that these shortcomings are partly going to be reproduced here, as we do reproduce the debates about a dominant story; however, we do so in order to demonstrate how they have framed the debates about sexualization and how they limit the ways we can understand sexualization differently.

Debates in the area of sexuality within the strand of feminism that we focus on often have aimed to identify an authentic and positive sexual identity for women to embody. These aims can largely be traced back to the feminist movement's ties to the socialist and Marxist "counterculture," in the 1960s and 1970s, but also to the feminist movement's major shift away from concepts of "free love" and "liberation," and toward more critical voices concerning the representation of women, which largely took place in the 1980s (see Segal, 1994). The debates in the 1980s arguably divided feminist perspectives on sexuality like no other (Segal and McIntosh, 1992)—their contentious nature evident in the terms now used to refer to them: the "sex wars" or "porn wars." To help document where our contemporary public and academic discourses and debates around sexualization come from, we will explore those debates in the following text.

The most publicly recognizable and well-disseminated feminist standpoint is often identified as the anti-pornography stance associated with 1980s radical feminists such as McKinnon and Dworkin. Feminists from this perspective argued that pornographic texts reproduce unequal power relations in society: not only a negative and demeaning representation of women, but quite literally driving men toward rape and violence against women (captured, for example, in the classic maxim that "if pornography is the theory, then rape is the practice" (Morgan, 1980)). Given pornography's ability to drive men to such practices, the anti-pornography perspective suggests that such texts necessarily and unremittingly require censorship and legal regulation. Echoes of this perspective still resonate today, for example in the assumption that the sexualization of children can be eradicated by regulated controls on the media, including Internet controls, or "porn filters," that Internet service providers made the default setting in 2013, following lobbying by members of Parliament and newspapers in the United Kingdom, and which turn out to be blocking sex education and charity (NSPCC, Childline) websites.

Although arguably coming from a different set of concerns, the behaviorist "text and effects" model that was scientifically popular in the 1980s helped support the feminist anti-pornography perspective. This model of media influence implies a direct correlation between what people see and do, usually focusing on the ability of the media to cause psychological harm to the viewer (see Barker and Petley, 1997, for a thorough critique). The "text and effects" model relied on behaviorist logic that watching pornography increased men's feelings of violence or contempt toward women (this model is supported by scientific research, but ignores the fact that within the institution of scientific publishing, findings that support the null hypothesis are rarely published); it also fit with 1980s morally conservative Western politics, being defiantly heteronormative in its assumption that all men desire sexual intercourse with women. This anti-pornography stance thus drew together those holding radical feminist, behaviorist-scientific, and conservative morality positions to produce a paradigmatic stronghold.

While not attracting the same amount of media attention or cultural influence, feminist discontents with the anti-pornography position did develop a counterpoint to this perspective. Arguments from this "anti-censorship" or "pro-sex" perspective included, for example, challenging the idea that legislation will solve gender asymmetry in pornographic representation. Instead, the pro-sex feminist movement claimed that it would be more beneficial to women if feminism challenged the inequalities of a socially organized gender hierarchy, therefore changing sexual representation rather than attempting to censor sexual imagery.

Pro-sex feminists also critiqued the anti-porn perspective for ignoring the variety of responses to pornographic images, including pleasure for some women (see the collection in Vance, 1984, for a more detailed exploration of these arguments). Moreover, the pro-sex perspective questioned the very terms of the debate; it was less about celebrating pornography than about providing a more nuanced perspective. Identifying with the pro-sex perspective, and echoing our own current concern with mapping the doubled stagnations around sexualization, Segal (1998) has suggested that the anti-porn/pro-sex divide was a "maddeningly deadlocked debate where my side...has the least titillating lines...because it has to argue the unexciting case of 'sweet reason': to insist on complexity, and reject any single analysis or unitary viewpoint" (p. 44).

The anti-pornography/pro-sex divide in the feminist movement may now seem largely redundant to contemporary debates around sexuality. One reason for its lack of relevance for contemporary feminisms has been an increasing awareness of the cultural differences of pornographic production and consumption. In demonstrating how pornography has been practiced differently, the development of cross-cultural histories of pornography has highlighted the Anglo-centricity of the "porn wars" debate, and the need to loosen the grip of this particular feminist story. For example, Paasonen (2009) discusses the Finnish context, where feminist politics has been less heavily influenced by the topic of pornography and the anti-porn/pro-sex debate—a position that has allowed Finnish porn studies the ability to "refuse" the dualistic legacy of the porn wars (p. 599).

Equally, the porn war debates seem less relevant when more recent approaches to pornography have offered increasingly interdisciplinary and critical perspectives that recognize pornography as a media text now embedded and ingrained in our popular culture (Attwood, 2002; Williams, 2004). Cultural and socio-historic approaches can be seen, for example, in groundbreaking texts such as Linda Williams's *Hard Core* (1989). Less concerned with the psychological effects of pornography, Williams's analysis of sexually explicit materials attempted to treat these texts as important representations and iconographies, emphasizing the historical context in which these cinematic and filmic texts are produced and the performance of the sexual acts on the screen. Meanwhile, contributions such as *The Secret Museum* (Kendrick, 1987) have mapped the construction of pornographies throughout history, showing that defining and regulating pornography have always been in the hands of the powerful. Other accounts have also addressed contemporary representations of pornographic material, as the Internet and other media communications become more globally, culturally, and financially significant in the production and consumption of pornography (Attwood, 2010; McNair, 1996, 2002).

A key site of these shifting discourses and approaches has been in the development and visibility of both women's and gay men's pornographies. This growing market has produced the need to recognize the multiplicity of these representations, their users, and the meanings that these users give to their engagement with the pornographic text. While "mainstream" pornography still appears to reproduce limited representations (despite both sides of the feminist porn wars attempting to challenge this very representation, albeit from different perspectives), the visibility and multiplicity of texts that no longer addressed only the heterosexual male have opened up room for marginal and oppressed groups in society to represent their sexualities—even while these texts themselves may not always be progressive (see Sonnet, 1999).

These new forms of analysis and the general "pornographication" or "porno-chic" aesthetic landscape (McNair, 2002) continue to position pornography as an important site for feminist studies of sexual identities and representations. But, the legacy of the porn wars debates appears to continue to structure feminist thinking and action around contemporary sexualization. A clear dichotomy between celebratory or critical analyses has emerged (Gill, 2011) to the extent that we seem stuck in a series of polarized positions and are now living with the range of consequences of this polarization. For example, while we have critiqued the range of contemporary public concerns about sexualization above, we also argue that sexualization requires critique. We believe it is necessary to speak back to a culture that frames sexiness in consumer terms and treats it as a concept differently available to women based on race, class, sexuality, and narrow forms of embodiment. But articulating such critique creates "uncomfortable alliances," paralleling the folding in of radical anti-pornography feminist concerns with those of right-wing Christian perspectives of the porn wars, and opening up the assumption that all feminist concerns can be addressed by the call to censorship (Segal and McIntosh, 1992; Church Gibson, 1993; Vance, 1984).

The porn wars and their legacy for feminist engagement with issues concerning sexualization is also partly re-enacted when feminist discussion about sexualization reaches the mainstream. More nuanced perspectives on sexualization are often silenced, regularly deemed "unsellable" within the public discourse or incompatible with policy recommendations. For example, academic views that reach the mainstream are often simplified and resignified in ways that regrettably reproduce a focus on young women's sexuality as a concern for all (see Ringrose, 2013). Meanwhile, having something to say about sexualization in the public domain from a feminist perspective calls to the minds of many a particular figure of feminism (the imagined angry, banner-waving feminist), or else is met with disappointment when refusing to wholly take up either a celebratory or critical perspective (an experience we have had, in everyday social interactions, at academic conferences, and in discussions with people writing for the press). A significant outcome is that these polarizations appear to stop and/or limit a range of thinking and action. The porn wars and resulting fractions among a range of feminisms still seem to structure many of the ways we can make sense of contemporary articulations of female sexuality as it is defined through consumer culture, so that the above concerns about pornography are rearticulated in different ways in the growing body of "sexualization" studies, which we will discuss further.

But there are also a number of differences between the porn wars and the current framing of academic feminist debates on sexualization in their orientation toward different sets of polarizations. The polarizations within contemporary debates seem to concern at least three interrelated questions: How much should we celebrate an apparent democratization of desire when social inequalities are still evident? To what extent can we talk about women doing sexiness "for themselves"? And how we are to speak of women's pleasures and talk of empowerment in the context of neoliberalism? We briefly hint toward each of these polarizations in the following discussion, before unpacking the last and most useful of these questions for the arguments we want to put forward in this book, suggesting that what ties these concerns together is the need for a more sophisticated concept of agency.

The democratization of desire thesis suggests that sexualization appears as part of a more general move toward a progressive sexual politics. For example, scholars like Plummer (1995), Weeks (1998) and McNair (1996, 2002) suggest that sexual citizenship has been opened up through a culture increasingly at ease with hearing the stories of different sexual practices, identities, and fantasies, permitting rights for those previously outside mainstream culture and allowing them to become intelligible. McNair (2002, p. 87), for example, argues that the sexualization of culture "presents to the public gaze opinions and sexualities rarely, if ever, granted visibility in mainstream culture before." The opening up of new discourses leads Weeks (1998) to suggest that new forms of sexual citizenships are in the process of fruition. While not yet "utopian," he implies that the detraditionalization of the family and the democratization of sexuality are providing new possibilities in the everyday politics of our lives. In terms of women's engagement with sexual consumption, Juffer's (1998) analysis of pornography in the home suggests that women have moved beyond the feminist porn wars of the 1980s through a domestication and democratisation of the market for sexual goods for women. This "moving beyond" has, for Juffer (1998) mobilized women and opened up space for new definitions of sexual agency and pleasure. Similarly, McNair (2009, pp. 55–73) suggested that potentially progressive politics could be built on the back of a pornographication of the mainstream, if only the critical paradigm in academia would release itself from its conservative, "return of the repressed" standpoint. Combined, such analyses suggest that democratization has, or can, create a more sexually tolerant and inclusive society, and a new multiplicity to feminine articulations of sexiness.

However, others have criticized the democratization thesis, suggesting that while there may be a progressive nature within sexualization, it is not truly democratic when so few people are able to take up a position within its discourses. A significant critique of sexualization, then, is that the discourses of sexual intelligibility through autonomous consumer choices are individualistic and mask the cultural, classed, sexualized, racialized, and embodied aspects of contemporary sexiness ideals that marginalize those who are not white, slim, middle class, and heterosexual (Craig, 2002; Evans et al., 2010a; Gill, 2009, 2011; Orbach, 2009; Ringrose and Walkerdine, 2008; Skeggs, 1997; Tate, 200; Tyler, 2008; Walkerdine, Lucey, and Melody, 2001).

We would support this critique of sexualization, agreeing that the consumer culture of sexiness may be said to speak largely to a normatively homogeneous woman. But we also need to be able to theorize for greater complexity, since consumer culture itself does not discriminate; it "neither loves nor hates social differences" (Brown, 2003, p. 9). Research on intersectionality within sexualization, for example, has identified that although young, white, heterosexual, slim women are less likely to be excluded, and cultural texts addressing this consumer might be more "mainstream," there are alternative discourses within sexualized culture that address different women in different ways. For instance, research has documented how black girls and women negotiate black sexual subjectivities presented in hip-hop, ragga, and R & B, within both lyrical content and the visual media forms of music videos (Skeggs, 1993; Weekes, 2004). Different discourses also address women in terms of class. Storr's (2003) research with Ann Summers

Party Planners examines the ways that women negotiate the potentially stigmatizing gendered and sexualized connotations of working-class femininity through reproducing notions of "respectability" around underwear. (See Attwood, 2005, and Smith, 2007, for similar examples in relation to online female sex shops.)

The consumer culture of sexiness thus opens up possibilities for new sexual subjectivities that the democratization of desire thesis celebrates, but it does so mostly in limited ways—by either marginalizing those who are not white, slim, middle class, and heterosexual or by interpellating women who are defined by their otherness through contracts of race, class, sexuality, and other markers of social inequality within discourses of sexiness that mask their differences. For example, women's fashion magazines like *Grazia, Vogue,* and *Marie Claire* mask intersectional and historical differences among women by reproducing the same style, format, and address to female consumers in non-Western countries as their counterparts do in the United States and United Kingdom (McRobbie, 2009). In advertising, L'Oreal's campaign for their skin-whitening cream, White Perfect, features models from Central and East Asia, but otherwise maintains the style of their advertising campaigns, including the tagline "because you're worth it" (see Lazar, 2011, for similar examples). Sexualization might not then be democratizing in the utopian sense, since this democratisation ("everyone can consume") is mostly homogenizing.

Alongside debates on how much we should celebrate an apparent democratization of desire when social inequalities are still evident has run alongside a set of debates on understanding how sexualized culture repositions the male gaze under the rubric of "doing it for yourself." For example, Gill's (2007b, p. 258) claim that women are "endowed with agency on condition that it is used to construct oneself as a subject closely resembling the heterosexual male fantasy" can be set in comparison to Attwood's (2009b, p. xxii) argument that "we need to move beyond the simple assumption that sexualization is in the interests of boys and men." As a highly visual culture, contemporary sexualized texts often present women in ways that have been typically understood as objectifying. However, the sexualization of culture has complicated notions of the male gaze. In a culture where women now increasingly gaze at both other women and at themselves, the male gaze, it seems, has sometimes been removed altogether (Evans and Riley, 2013; Mackiewicz, 2013; McRobbie, 2009; see also our example in Chapter 3). In terms of reinstating women as the objects of sex, therefore, sexualized culture may be considered a cultural space for resisting objectification, and of concern for both reproducing the male gaze and producing a narcissistic neoliberal self-policing gaze in relation to women's apparently "freely chosen look" (Gill, 2007b; McRobbie, 2009, p. 66; Storr, 2003; see also Chapter 1).

Thus the final debate that sets current concerns about sexualization apart form older feminist concerns is that contemporary "up for it" female sexual subjectivities appear to be framed within notions of autoeroticism, rights to pleasure, and "for themselves" rhetoric. The problem with such notions is the way that these new mantras of contemporary femininity appear to impose individualized neoliberal discourses that regulate the subject through an internalization of regimes of disciplinary power. As we outlined in our opening chapter, neoliberal discourses of choice and freedom have been tied to notions of empowerment and liberation so as to produce the "injunction to render one's life knowable and meaningful through a narrative of free choice and autonomy—however constrained one might actually be" (Gill, 2007b, p. 260). Gill (2007b, p. 260) provides us with the example of Brazilian waxes that have been rebranded through a "pleasing yourself" discourse, implying that the practice of genital hair removal is a personal choice rather than a culturally defined notion of beauty and sexiness; a "discourse of choice, in short, is central to neoliberal culture generally.... Is it any wonder, then, that such ideas dominate women's accounts?" (Gill, 2007, p. 76).

And here we come to what we see as the heart of contemporary contestations of sexiness: How do we make sense of women describing their participation in consumer-oriented subjectivities as choiceful and pleasurable when their discursive context offers few ways of making sense of this engagement other than through a discourse of choice?[2] This is a question about agency. And we cycle down to this question as it is one that addresses the tensions within both women's experiences and social analyses of female inequality, and is therefore one of the significant methodological issues of feminist academic research.

Women's identities within sexualization are often framed in terms of what to do with women's accounts of the pleasures of sexiness within consumer culture. How are we to speak of women's pleasures and talk of empowerment in the context of neoliberalism that requires women to understand their practices through discourses of choice, pleasure, and empowerment? But also, "what does feminism gain—politically and analytically—by immediately countering any girl's or woman's appeal to autonomy by pointing out her false consciousness and putting her under all the constrains of patriarchy and capitalism?" (Duits and van Zoonen, 2007, p. 168). At the extreme ends of these debates, women who engage with the sexualization of culture are positioned as either cultural dupes (as a form of false consciousness) or as agentically engaged in their own liberation (for further discussion of these debates, see Evans et al., 2010a). The discourse of "choice" through new femininities that value an agentic sexuality has, therefore, troubled feminist scholars, as well as creating contradictory positions (see the collection in Gill and Scharff, 2011, for example).

To map the debates about agency within contemporary constructs of sexualization, we want to unpack some of the significant contributions that have taken place in recent reflections on women's capacity for self-determination and agency within feminism. We focus first on a debate in the journal *Sex Roles*, which allows us to explore the construct of "empowerment" within postfeminist, neoliberal, and consumer discourses and the stuck places this discourse of "empowerment" produces for feminist analysis. We then unpack further the exchange between Duits and van Zoonen (2006, 2007) and Gill (2007) on the issue of agency that we have pointed toward earlier, and with which we opened this chapter.

---

2. See, for example, our discussion of the logocentric nature of neoliberal rhetoric in Chapter 1.

TEASING OUT PLEASURE, EMPOWERMENT, AND AGENCY

Feminism has always had to negotiate a difficult space in understandings women's participation in culture. To engage politically in feminist work, it appears necessary to critique a culture that binds women to a gender category that is still structured through the oppression of women: an oppression multiplied by the structural oppressions of race, class, sexuality, and embodiment. This has been compounded by the matrix of neoliberalism, postfeminism, and consumerism that we have already documented, where "choice" has become a marketable commodity (Bauman, 2000). To acknowledge women's "choice" within such a culture thus appears not only naïve, but can be understood as an affirmation of the neoliberal imperative toward autonomy in support of individual self-governance (Gill, 2007). But at the same time, and to overcome the oppressions that women face, feminism needs a notion of choice and autonomy. Without one, the work of feminism becomes an empty critique; that "choice" is always "false" is not enough if we are to understand the aim of feminism to be an orientation to the world that wants to improve women's lived conditions, since this requires in the first instance that we understand people as having the capacity to choose and resist the conditions in which they are living.

A simple solution to this stuckness might be to suggest that there is a middle ground between culturally defined choice and genuine authentic choice. But such a position calls into play the problematic nature of naming what is culturally defined and what is genuine. Moreover, when arguing from both sides, feminism still seems trapped further in the doubled stagnations that we have been mapping. In this occurrence of the doubled stagnation, we are referring to a state of having nothing useful to say, where we always end up playing devil's advocate or sitting on the fence, relying, as the middle ground argument does, simply on positions relative to what the opposing argument is: if one person wants to celebrate, then we respond with critique, and vice versa.

One further concern (to which we return in our conclusions in this book) is that, while a critique of sexualization is necessary, the act of locating sexiness as a problem that needs resolving increases the likelihood of academic discussion missing its own "blind spots." These blind spots include the difficulties of recognizing pleasure, since the moment you go into critique you position the pleasure as false consciousness, which undercuts what is genuinely felt as pleasurable (even while this experience is structured by social discourses). The blind spots also include the homogenization of the critique, where the attention paid toward the limitations of a sexiness defined as white, middle class, heterosexual, and so on, fails to identify people who are not only located outside dominant notions, but also actively resist them. These resistances might not be revolutionary or progressive—for example, young women's celebration of the term "slut" does have its limitations (see Ringrose and Renold, 2012), and as we suggest in Chapter 5, feminist resistance can be more conservative than progressive. But by locating sexiness as something that is problematic, the academic discussion also remains within the broader public discourse where sex, sexual relationships, and sexiness is also a problem, and thus easily lifted into a framework where we need to better govern ourselves and respond to this governance by addressing our psychological issues (e.g., through the consumption of goods, thus evoking psy-disciplines and consumption as the mode to self-transformation).

We believe that what these problems in making sense of sexualization come down to are issues concerning pleasure, empowerment, and agency, and the relationship between these concepts. To reach something different means understanding in more depth the terms of the debates we mention above. In analyzing this social landscape, feminist theorists have to engage with the complex and contradictory nature of discourses around contemporary active female sexuality—for example, that it can be experienced as pleasurable and liberating, and yet reproduces an image that appears objectifying. For our purposes, two sets of debates are useful for us to delineate before mapping out our own theoretical framework for engaging with these concepts: the exchange between Lamb and Peterson (and others) in *Sex Roles*; and the disagreements between Duits and van Zoonen and Gill in the *European Journal of Women's Studies*. Both sets of discussions provide an outline of which issues are stagnated by current debates within feminist literatures, and provide us with the basis for how we can begin to move forward within this stagnation.

In Lamb's (2010a) paper, she seeks to reassess the feminist image of a version of femininity that is active, self-motivated, and desiring (e.g., Fine, 1988; Greer, 1970) in the context of a postfeminist sexualization of culture that we have been discussing. Lamb suggests that the context of sexualization creates an impossible space for such a utopian feminist image of sexual agency. Poignantly referring to this as a "hall of mirrors" (2010a, p. 302), Lamb highlights several limitations of previous concepts of healthy feminist-inspired female sexuality. These include, first, the creation of another cultural ideal (this time a feminist one of healthy sexuality) toward which all women are expected to strive; second, the implication that the search for "authentic" sexual desire appears to be too closely harnessed by a neoliberal rhetoric of individualism; and finally, that a double-bind is created when the healthy, self-determining, self-knowing feminist female sexuality is easily replicated in the sassy, hedonistic, postfeminist femininity propagated by consumer and media culture.

Of particular interest to our own concerns, Lamb (2010a) highlights the reification of the subject/object binary that these ideal feminist constructs of female sexuality appear to support, including the moral implication of "good" active sexual desire and "bad" passive sexual desire. As Lamb (2010a) points out, the binary of subject/object fails to account for the complexity of pleasure when self-objectifying practices can be subjectively experienced as sexually pleasurable. For example, becoming the object for another person's sexual desire or feeling sexually attractive to another person (even if through a process of objectification) can be experienced as sexually pleasurable (subjectification), even if it takes place in a patriarchal society that delimits what is understood as sexually attractive, and would constitute sexual passivity on behalf of the person being found to be sexually attractive.

In response, Peterson (2010) takes up Lamb's (2010a) discussion by attempting to better define "empowerment" as a multidimensional process. For us, Peterson's approach does problematically suggest that empowerment is a construct that is learned, developmental, and psychological (see Lamb's response, 2010b). And while Peterson herself highlights that definitions of empowerment are culturally and historically specific, what is missing from Peterson's approach is a consideration of those who lose out to this culturally and historically specific Western construct of sexual empowerment. However, what we find useful in Peterson's (2010) rejoinder is the emphasis on ambivalence. For Peterson (2010), empowerment is not "all-or-nothing." Rather, women experience "empowerment" through a complex array of meanings that are multidimensional, including feeling in control in situations that are also experienced and understood as disempowering.

Empowerment, from this exchange of positions, can be understood as a "both/and" construct that disrupts the subject/object binary (e.g., objectification can be understood subjectively as "empowering") and is multidimensional (e.g., the same situation can be experienced as both empowering and disempowering). Both of these perspectives on empowerment are useful for opening up a range of issues. And highlighting our general claim in this chapter that debates often become stagnated around iterative and unproductive positions, a joint paper by both authors reflects back on the process and practice of conducting this debate in academic publishing. In this work, they note that the framework of "point/counterpoint" had pushed them into taking up places within a debate that they themselves were not comfortable with and that, because of the point/counterpoint formula, lacked a more in-depth consideration of the spaces of overlap between their competing views (Lamb and Peterson, 2012).

And yet, in their co-authored paper, we read a slippage back into positing subject/object binaries, such as: "If a girl sees herself as a sexual object who must perform to get or keep a boy's attention, aren't the consequences likely to be different than if she sees herself as engaging in fun, playful experimentation?" (Lamb and Peterson, 2012, p. 6). Once again, we are left with a concept of "empowerment" that is either for the attention of boys (and therefore, we can assume, the consequences are bad) or part of youthful experimentation (and therefore good). The authors also spend time discussing the age at which feelings of sexual empowerment might be developmentally appropriate: an approach that we want to avoid, given that developmental perspectives on sexuality often normalizes individual development without recourse to the social structures (race, class, gender, and so on) and how these structure the social milieus that define what is seen as appropriate. And with others (e.g., Gavey, 2012; Gill, 2012b), we find the perspectives on empowerment presented by the authors interesting, but we would also like to see more of a critical perspective on what is actually taken by the term "empowerment," beyond the assumption that it exists as a psychological construct that can be observable and measurable in accordance with feminist criteria, and that implicates choice, pleasure, and autonomy.

There are several points at which we diverge from the approaches presented by both Lamb and Peterson. We understand concern with girls' "empowerment" as being part of the doubled stagnations that we are attempting to map, and thus view such concerns about whether or not girls are *really* empowered to be part of the ontology of sexualization. That is, we see these debates as themselves producing what we could call "sexualization"; it is the emotional grip of these concerns and "point/counterpoints" that create a space of incredible noise. "Empowerment" would be, for us, one of the significant sticking points within sexualization—one that we want to see as part of the emotional dimension, interiorization, and psychologizing of sexualization that comes to feel deeply personal, especially when combined with heavily loaded terms such as "empowerment" (see Chapter 5 for feminist-identified women's engagement with these issues).

"Empowerment" is not an analytic that we can use to make sense of women's understandings of sexiness; it is an object of analysis. It is, as Gavey (2012) suggests in her commentary on the *Sex Roles* debate, too "conceptually flabby" (p. 2) in the range of ways that it can be applied. Ideas of "empowerment" are too readily part of the same set of cultural constructs that we want to critically assess in our account that hopes to attend both to the governance of subjectivity within the matrix of neoliberalism, postfeminism, and consumerism, and to the subjective activation of this governance, without reliance on individualizing concepts. "Empowerment" doesn't have the political edge to get to the problem of how empowerment is felt deeply within conditions of possibility, nor framed by race, class, sexuality, and other social structures, within the frameworks of neoliberalism, postfeminism, and consumerism (Gavey, 2012). We make no claim in this book regarding whether or not the women we spoke to were "empowered" or not; and with Gavey (2012) and Gill (2012), we can identify little talk in our data where women proclaimed to have experienced "empowerment" through contemporary consumerism, even while feminist academics and advertisers alike seem so eager for this experience to be had.

The concern around whether the experience of empowerment can actually be described in feminist terms *as* empowerment underlies the stuck place between a position of accepting women's accounts, and thereby assuming agency, or, on the other hand, remaining critical of women's capacity for agency, and seemingly jettisoning feminist aims for female emancipation (see, for example, Benhabib et al., 1995; Davis, 1995; Gavey, 2005; McNay 2000). The recent and most revealing illustration of debates around agency in relation to sexualization can be seen in the exchange of positions between Duits and van Zoonen (2006, 2007) and Gill (2007a). These two accounts have been insightful and provocative in our own thinking. We therefore only briefly describe them here, before moving on to our own contribution in the following chapter.

Duits and van Zoonen (2006) argue that women's bodies have been stigmatized as dupable and problematic through a variety of institutional discourses, including those from schools, media, and academia, and that these regulatory discourses impede women's ability to sartorially or parodically represent their sexualities. Furthermore, this is set in contrast with men's clothing choices, which are often framed within freedom of speech discourses. As such, Duits and van Zoonen (2006) suggest, female research participants should be considered as "capable and responsible agents, who produce 'speech acts' with their choice of clothing" (p. 115), regardless of whether these choices involve covering one's head with a headscarf or displaying the body in porno-chic fashion. In response, Gill (2007a) argues that, while respecting the voices of women in research, feminist academics should critically engage with the cultural context in which women make these choices and should not assume that participants can behave as if apart from their cultural context. Developing her position, Gill (2007a) argues that such critical engagement need not understand the social structure as deterministic of identity construction; rather, a more nuanced analysis is needed that allows for some of the complexity of dynamics around choice, agency, and power.

Provocatively entitled "Who's Afraid of Female Agency?" Duits and van Zoonen's (2007) rejoinder, however, critiques Gill (2007a) on her claim that "porno-chic" fashion styles are "virtually hegemonic" (p. 71). They argue that such a claim ignores the variety of diverse responses of girls and women to consumer culture, highlighted in their paper by their comparison of porno-chic with headscarf fashions. Furthermore, Duits and van Zoonen contend that in Gill's self-reflexive account of her own fashion resistances and complicities, she indirectly grants herself the agency that she refuses other women.

In outlining some of the key debates on the sexualization of culture and its implications for female subjectivities, we have shown that the issue of agency appears to run through much of the literature. While there is a range of divergent views, none in our opinion satisfactorily theorizes women's engagement in the sexualization of culture in a way that engages with the complexity of choice and agency within the context of postfeminism, consumer culture, and disciplinary discourses of neoliberalism. As we have suggested throughout this chapter, a significant problem of understanding women's identities within this context emerges because of a series of doubled stagnations. These doubled stagnations include the noise that these discussions of sexualization produce, seemingly always spoken; that this noise calls on us to emote about sexualization; and the ways these debates oscillate between narratives of concern and the right for women's voices to be validated, against a backdrop of further stagnations in feminist thought such as the polarizations concerning sexual media and pornography. At each level we have shown how these stagnations are folded back into neoliberal sense-making, since this sense-making now "owns" the notion of autonomy in relation to women's sexuality—producing a stuck place in thinking around the sexualization of culture, with little sense of forward momentum. For us to create a space for working in stuck places, there is a need to outline a theoretical approach that may meet Gill's (2007a) call for a more nuanced concept of agency. We suggest that a better way of theorizing the complexities of the cultural, material, and subjective may be reached by engaging with the concept of a "technology of sexiness."

3

Technologies of Sexiness

[T]he task of the Single Girl is to embody heterosexuality through the disciplined use of makeup, clothing, exercise, and cosmetic surgery, linking femininity, consumer culture and heterosexuality.

RADNER, *1999, p. 15*

In the above quote, Radner is referring what she calls a "technology of sexiness"— a term derived from Foucault, and used first by Radner (1999), then Gill (2007b) and later by ourselves (Evans, Riley, and Shankar, 2010a) and Harvey and Gill (2011). These writers have used the term "technology of sexiness" to account for women's engagement with material and non-material practices in the pursuit of (hetero)sexy subjectivity. In this chapter, we explore this relatively underdeveloped concept to give a detailed theoretical account of how we may conceptualize "technologies of sexiness." We argue that doing so is one way in which we can move beyond the stagnated debates discussed in the previous chapter. The concept allows us to both identify the limitations of postfeminist consumer culture and to explore how discourses associated with this culture may hold within them the potential for unpredictable subversions, slippages and resistances. It also allows a theoretical space for critically analyzing the sense-making of individual women, while locating that sense-making within the broader technologies of subjectivity, thus avoiding making women the "problem" of sexualization. Finally, an account of technologies of sexiness, we suggest, provides an understanding of agency that doesn't overvalue the concept of agency or treat all agency as radical in its potential, but instead as something that is produced through the play and difference between different technologies of the self.

In this chapter we ask, how can we imagine this "technology of sexiness"? And how might it help us think through the complexities of women's engagement in sexualized culture in ways that allow us to value women's choices of participation, while also maintaining a critical standpoint toward the cultural context within which sexualized culture has emerged, offering new ways for women to make sense of their sexuality? To address these questions, we draw on Foucault's concept of technologies of the self and Butler's notion of performativity and identify three "doubled movements" in which women's agency appears to be simultaneously enabled and disenabled within sexualized culture.

TECHNOLOGIES OF THE SELF

Foucault's work on the formation of the self through discourse—understood broadly as sets of meaning through which we come to understand ourselves—included two key terms that we employ in this chapter to develop the concept of a technology of sexiness. These two terms are "technologies of subjectivity" and "technologies of the self."

Technologies of subjectivity refer to those broader ways of sense-making; whereas technologies of the self refer to the ways in which these technologies of subjectivity are applied and made personal. Technologies of subjectivity are the wider social discourses that shape the way we can understand the world: a body of meanings that opens up and closes down ways for us to understand ourselves. For example, the discourse of psychology opens up the subject positions for us to understand ourselves as "self-actualized," "motivated," or "emotionally intelligent." Feminism demanded that the social structure should permit women to become "empowered," "liberated," and "free"—as we have suggested in Chapter 1, these technologies of subjectivity produce a heady mix of successful individualism when amalgamated with those provided by neoliberalism and consumerism. Equally, we might think of the example of medical apparatus as one that creates a space for understanding illness.

However, simply having a set of apparatus through which we are able to shape subjectivity is not enough; we could, for example, choose to understand illness in relation to alternative therapy. These technologies must then be able to "hail" us so that we take up certain subject positions. Technologies of the self are practices that allow people to take up a subject position and make it their own because these technologies of subjectivity can be inhabited in some way. To borrow from Hook's (2007) example, the law of apartheid did not insist that white people embody racism in their interaction with black people. Rather, apartheid provided the discursive landscape through which to embody racism. In the framework we've been developing in this book so far, the sense-making provided by neoliberalism, consumerism, and postfeminism would constitute the technologies of subjectivity. But it is one thing to be a subject within a broader set of meanings that create a capacity for a subject position (e.g., the new sexual subject), and another to, for instance, buy and use a new generation vibrator—to make oneself that subject.

Technologies of the self thus constitute those moments when we work on ourselves to make ourselves. Technologies of the self are concerned with the betterment of the self, defined as "practices by which individuals seek to improve themselves and the aspirations that guide them" (Foucault, 1988, 1993; Rose, 1996, p. 95). Although Foucault died before he was able to deeply explicate this concept, we argue that his concept of technologies of the self offers potential to move within and against the agency debates when attempting to rethink contemporary femininities.

Foucault's theorizing developed throughout his life, so that there are contradictions and multiple ways of reading his work. The three volumes that make up *The History of Sexuality* (1976, 1987, 1990) are located toward/across the end of his work. Representing some of the changes in his thinking around issues of agency and subjectivity, this later work highlighted a theoretical move from the passive subject who was spoken by discourse to a more autonomous self.

Foucault's overture was largely concerned with understanding power as diluted and dispersed (as opposed to the top-down theories inherited from classical Marxism). But much of his earlier theorizing was concerned with how this power acted on subjects, for example, how power in the prison system was able to discipline subjects without the active threat of punishment, or how the discourses of mental health delimited some people as abnormal and mad. Recognizing that his theorizing needed to account for how this power worked through the subject led him to theorize in his later work a more agentic subject who could employ technologies of the self to actively construct his or her own identity. The more autonomous subject of Foucault's later theorizing was thus endowed with agency, where:

> technologies of the self [...] permit individuals to effect by their own means or with the help of others a certain number of operations on their own bodies and souls, thoughts, conduct, and way of being, so as to transform themselves in order to attain a certain state of happiness, purity, wisdom, perfection or immortality. (Foucault, 1988, p. 18)

Foucault often uses the terms "technologies" and "techniques" interchangeably, so that by "technologies" Foucault is not referring to technological developments (although these play a part), but instead to all those material and immaterial tools that can be used to construct the self. The concept of "technologies" therefore conceptualizes individuals as acting upon themselves in order to transform themselves. Applying this idea to contemporary femininities, we can argue for example, that many women follow a particular morning "regime," which while differing in the specifics for every woman, may include a recognizable pattern of washing, styling hair, putting on clothes, and perhaps applying makeup. Such processes allow women to "transform themselves" in the morning.

Technologies of the self (or ways of working on the self) are not produced in a vacuum, but are instead tied to the wider technologies of subjectivity (or ways of understanding the self in a particular sociohistorical moment). So while people may be conceptualized as agentic in terms of having the potential to "choose" among a variety of discourses and material practices, they are limited by what is discursively and materially available to them in their social milieu. Technologies of the self are thus "the way in which the subject constitutes himself [sic] in an active fashion, by the practices of the self, [but] these practices are nevertheless not something that the individual invents by himself" (Foucault, 1987, p. 122). From this perspective, a woman's morning routine of transformation—facilitated by the likes of, for example, indoor plumbing, contemporary cosmetics, hair dryers, straighteners, work-related clothing, and/or child care—involves sociohistorically contextualized processes that are products of recent history.

Technologies of self are thus located within wider discourses of subjectivity, so that new sexual subjectivities are produced not just through technologies of self (e.g., buying vibrators and so embodying contemporary femininity) but the wider technologies of subjectivity that inform it (e.g., those contexts informed by neoliberalism, consumerism, postfeminism). In the context of liquid modernity that Bauman (2000) describes, for example, in which identities are in need of constant reformulation when all traditional and fixed forms of life melt away, attention is drawn to the self creating itself, to a "compulsive and obligatory *self*-determination" (2001, p. 145), which is met by consumer culture as one of those ways that the individual may create a self. However, "good" identity projects within the context of such liquid modernity still matter, such that "people have convinced themselves that what matters is psychic self-improvement; getting in touch with their feelings eating health food, taking lessons in ballet dancing, immersing themselves in the wisdom of the East, jogging, learning how to 'relate'" (Lasch, 1979, p. 4, cited in Bauman, 2001, p. 150), and of course we would add employing those technologies of the self that allow for the creation of agentic, knowing, and sexually savvy femininity. Technologies of subjectivity thus form a "bricolage" that "invites and incites" people to take up a set of discourses about personhood that forms the sense-making behind certain aspirations, practices, and identities (Evans, Riley, and Shankar, 2010a; Harvey and Gill, 2011).

Foucault also explicitly linked technologies of the self to governmentality because the ways in which we work on ourselves often support and feed into the relationships between macro and micro power (Rose, 1996). In previous chapters we've noted how the rise of consumer culture has interacted with particular feminist discourses around equality and economic participation so that in contemporary Britain (and elsewhere) the subject of the neoliberal, appropriately consuming, economically active citizen is female (Harris, 2004; McRobbie, 2009). From this standpoint, a women's morning routine may also be located within economic and capitalist systems whereby she is required to engage in forms of transformation in order to be a good citizen-worker, part of which involves maintaining the appearance of the appropriately feminine woman; it may also require her to employ other women to do domestic and child-care work, so furthering the economic relations of domination, and highlighting how not all women can or do engage in these practices in the same way.

In working in the "space between" the feminist debates on sexualization, the concept of technologies of the self could thus usefully address the calls for a more nuanced theorization by opening up the relationships between the cultural, material and subjective in research on the sexualization of culture. Our suggestion would be that the technologies of subjectivity, represented by the earlier chapters of this book, form the backdrop against which women are making sense of their sexual selves. This would move beyond approaches where the media influences identity, or where individuals are free to play with media messages, to take account of the more interactive and dynamic ways in which culture, material conditions, and subjective experience shape and form each other.

In relation to agency and contemporary female (hetero)sexuality, we theorize a technologies of self in which one works upon oneself and one's body (as an expression of agency) to reproduce oneself through discourses of sexual liberation (as the available technologies of subjectivity provided through neoliberalism, consumerism, and postfeminism). So that if what we have outlined so far in the book constitutes some of the potential technologies of subjectivity within the discourses of the sexualization of culture, as well as the material effects and conditions that this culture has on possibilities for consumer products and practices, then technologies of the self should permit us a space to begin talking about women's subjectivities; of how this cultural context is taken up and subjectively engaged with in emotional and meaningful ways. But to do so, we argue that we need to further develop the notion of a technology of the self.

We want to add more depth to the concept of subjectivity we are drawing on. As we observed in our discussions with women, sexiness is not experienced as merely a potential discourse or subject position ready to be taken up. Sexiness entails a huge amount of insecurity, pleasure, desire, and pain; it can make women feel like they don't belong, and it can be a starting point for joining in, for being part of something; feelings of sexiness, while always taking place within a historical and cultural setting, often feel deeply personal, complex, ambivalent, and emotional. Embodying a subject position in relation to those technologies of subjectivity discussed so far often means more than applying technologies of the self to work on the self in the betterment of ourselves. To better understand how women take up, take part in, and make technologies of subjectivity their own, we have to revisit agency, this time through the work of Judith Butler.

PERFORMATIVE SEXINESS

Judith Butler has both drawn on Foucault and engaged with agency through the concept of performativity. Butler (1999, p. xiv) states that it is "difficult to say precisely what performativity is…because my own views on what 'performativity' might mean have changed over time." With this caveat in mind, and understanding Butler's work as open to multiple interpretations, we draw on the concept of performativity to inform our theorizing of agency within the sexualization of culture. While specifically addressing gender as central to subjectivity, we note how this concept can be used to provide a more doubled understanding of agency. If Foucault's account of subjectivity suggests that agency is enacted through the ability to self-reflexively adopt a discourse from the available discourses, Butler's work allows a deepening of this agency. In Butler's notion of performativity, there is an extended notion of agency with the ability for alterations of the available discourses, while these alternations always remain within power structures.

Butler contends that all gender is parody. Rather than there being an original femininity, the performance of gender identity imitates an "original" that is in fact historically and discursively constituted and, furthermore, unstable in this construction. To explicate this, Butler uses the example of drag. Drag as a performance of gender has received much criticism from feminists for appearing to take the form of a mocking of femininity by representing femininity largely in its aesthetic forms through the use of clothes and makeup (hooks, 1992; Raymond, 1980; Williamson, 1985). However, Butler (1999) suggests that drag provides a destabilization of gender in which our "usual cultural perceptions fail" (p. xxiv). Drag can therefore be considered the imitation of an imitation, a parody of parody. This "perpetual displacement," while not necessarily being transgressive (Butler, 1993, cites Dustin Hoffman's performance in *Tootsie* as an example where drag reinforces gender norms), does constitute a break from normative understandings of sex and gender. That is to say, drag does not escape from gender binaries, but does show gender binaries to be essentially unstable and socially constructed, with femininity containing the possibility to be parodied, imitated, or repeated through a stylization on the body.

Butler argues that the sustained and repeated acts of gender produce the illusion of a unified self through the process of simultaneously negotiating the power and resistances working within the subject. Her theorizing draws on Foucault's concept of the coproducing relationship between power and resistance, so that "[w]here there is power, there is resistance, and yet, or rather consequently, this resistance is never in a position of exteriority in relation to power" (Foucault, 1976, p. 95). It is this dialectical process of subjectivation, where power and resistance are a necessity to each other in constituting the subject, which forms the foundation of Butler's theorizing on the potential for agency. Subjectivation enables an understanding both of how subjects are brought into being through powerful discourses, and yet how these subjects can change their constitution.

Agency is therefore a central concern to Butler in her notion of performativity. Butler's subject is imbued within powerful discourses. Indeed, Butler's theory suggests there is no subject without subjectivation, and therefore to have an identity, to be a subject, and to be intelligible, is to be part of gender power structures. The law of gender is, however, shown by Butler to be essentially unstable and socially constructed, giving the impression of being "real" through imitation and parody, which is continuously repeated. The instability of this repetition of gender poses the potential to repeat that gender differently. Yet, equally, repeating differently depends on reference to and recognition within gender norms. For example, Butler argues that in the context of drag the preservation of the male/female binary is obligatory if the performative gender identity is to undermine the law. As such, dominant discourses are both necessarily rule-bound, and also the site of agency and the breaking of those rules. With the "compulsion to repeat," agency is enacted through "the possibility of a variation on that repetition" (Butler, 1999, p. 198), which must always be intelligible to be recognized as subversive.

Butler's theorizing thus allows us to examine the contradictions in contemporary (hetero)sexual femininities by understanding them as intelligible acts, based upon the repetitions and subversion of gender norms. Butler's work is useful in considering new femininities as reiterations of variable discourses of femininity, since it both advances the view of technologies of the self as methods of producing selves that are intelligible, and highlights the contradictory nature that the proposed sexual liberation posits in that subversion is only intelligible vis-à-vis the normative.

"Subversion" has become a loaded term in feminist scholarship. It can be taken to be a challenge to gender norms. Conversely, it can be thought of as slight changes in the discourses, depending on how they shift in line with the other discourses through which the subject is being constructed (for example, constructing oneself through the discourses of vegetarianism might shift the way one engages in sexual practices; see Potts and Parry 2010). The former interpretation, we feel, has the potential to discredit anything that is not seen as a "good" subversion. Furthermore, it can suggest that some people can escape ideology more than others: that some people have more agency. We read Butler as saying that all repetitions have the implication of destabilization, so that subversion can be subversion without challenging the gender order.[1] This is why, in this book, we have used "transgression" or "transgressive" as a "move beyond," where we believe there is a case for troubling the gender order, and "subversion" where there is a change in the way women are presenting themselves, regardless of its critical potential.

We argue that Butler's work can be used to inform the disparate arguments on the sexualization of culture. Drawing together ideas of technologies of self and subjectivity with performativity, we conceptualize agency as produced through more complex interactions than choosing one available discourse over another; rather, it is produced by both choosing and subverting these discourses, even if that subversion is limited by the necessity to cite the norm.

In relation to the sexualization of culture, we also note further layers of complexity, which we will discuss in detail. First, there is not one agentic female sexuality but multiple discourses of being "up for it," and second, these discourses intersect with factors that produce particular limitations on who can take these up. Such factors include structural identities derived from class, ethnicity, embodiment, and sexuality, and the role of the media in the cultural recuperation of alternative identities.

In noting the multiple forms of sexually agentic femininity, we recognize that cultural discourses are not monolithic and uniform. They are instead composed of varying discourses. These discourses shift in meaning, produce multiple readings, and are intertextual in their relationships with other discourses and in the production of new ones. In a culture in which women's spaces have multiplied away from the domestic space, the sites for female subjectivities have proliferated. For example, there are increasing multiple and complex discourses *within* the discourse of sexiness so that there is more than one way of being "up for it." Such multiplicity is identified by Attwood (2007a) in her study of the "alternative" porno-chic aesthetics of the Nerve and SuicideGirls mainly female online communities, who represent "smart smut" or subcultural pornographies. In these examples we can see how the rise of new discourses may open up, or unfold, into newer discourses, where

---

1. This reading is despite *Gender Trouble* (1999, p. 189) and *Bodies That Matter* (1993, p. 120), where Butler negates the term "subversion" to certain performances of gender.

their "persistence and proliferation...provide critical opportunities to expose the limits and regulatory aims of that domain of intelligibility" (Butler, 1999, p. 24).

However, the possibilities enabled by the multiplication of female sexuality discourses are reduced by the homogenization of the media, where representation is often limited to identities that conform to normative ideals of beauty. So, for example, a practice like burlesque is potentially transgressive, particularly in its celebration of differing embodiments from the beauty ideal. However, the potentially transgressive practice of burlesque is recuperated through its mainstreaming, where the media's icon for its resurgence, Dita von Teese, seamlessly reproduces normative beauty standards. Thus, recuperation further limits agency because it is only enabled by buying into, to some extent, transgressive identities that themselves are often popularized, in turn making reiterations somewhat redundant (for a similar argument in relation to female bodybuilding, see Martin and Gavey, 1996).

Thus, while female sexual identities may be performed in ways that subvert traditional discourses of femininity, this subversion is tempered in two ways: by the limitations imposed on who may participate in these practices, and by how they are read by others/the media. Below, we develop these arguments by using the example of "porn star" T-shirts. "Porn star" type T-shirts, as garments with sexually assertive slogans embossed on the front, may challenge traditional definitions of passive femininity, but they do so by drawing on already available discourses that construct the subject in potentially contradictory ways. These already available discourses permit active sexual identities on the understanding that women do this in a way that fits conventional notions of beauty and sexiness. Gill's (2003) account of the fashion for sexualized T-shirt logos ("hot chick," "porn star," "FCUK me"), for example, suggests that only some women, namely those who are young, slim, and heterosexual, are permitted within this fashion discourse. Furthermore, even if one wears a porn star T-shirt as a knowing, ironic, pastiche signifier, one still had to purchase the T-shirt, and thus this act is embedded in consumerist discourse. Similarly, problems arise in agentically performing reiterated identities where social structures impinge on readability. For example, embodiment may be implicated in readability where those embodiments that fit normative notions of beauty are less likely to be read as subversive. Thus, to draw on celebrity culture, if Beth Ditto, lead singer of The Gossip, wears such a T-shirt it may be understood as transgressing bodily norms around sexiness. Although Ditto's celebrity status and public knowledge of her private life would necessarily impinge on this reading, it is conceivable that more subversive inferences may be drawn about a larger woman wearing a porn-star T-shirt (albeit with the risk of humiliation and derision). A similar act by a celebrity such as Paris Hilton or Miley Cyrus is unlikely to be read as such. Slight changes in the repetitions of gender need to be intelligible, but presumably a shift has to be understood as beyond the gender norm that is being referred to. Otherwise it is read merely as another repetition. To return to drag, readability is essential to the gender-troubling nature of drag, in as much as "passing" as the opposite gender would do little to destabilize sex/gender binaries (Lloyd, 1999).

Issues of recuperation and readability can also be observed in the Madonna, Britney Spears, and Christina Aguilera kisses at the 2003 MTV Video Music Awards. These same-sex kisses, first between Madonna and Britney Spears, and then between Madonna and Christina Aguilera, were not read as expressions of same-sex desire by either the press or the public. Indeed, web-forum discussions deemed the kisses shared between these celebrities as "phoney" (Diamond, 2005). While perhaps expressing a "media-savviness," such assessments preclude any potential for the broadcast serving to question the boundaries between homosexuality and heterosexuality (Diamond, 2005). In an analogous line to our argument, such popular culture representations both serve to increase the visibility of same-sex sexual contact, and simultaneously have the effect of essentially depoliticizing same-sex sexuality or recuperating the heterosexual norm (Diamond, 2005; Thompson, 2006). In terms of readability, even if a self-reflexive critical consciousness was involved in the planning of the kiss, the heterosexual lives of the three celebrities within the public consciousness would have excluded this interpretation in exchange for comprehending it along the lines of a spectacle for the male gaze.

To reassess at this point, our theoretical framework of the self is one in which technologies of subjectivity provide certain subject positions that resonate with some women. By taking up a subject position, women then engage in technologies of the self so that they can articulate themselves into creating themselves as successful identities as defined by the technologies of subjectivity. These rearticulations enable agency but also recuperation. Performativity allows us to understand the doubling nature of sexiness as it is read in the cultural conscious.

This moves us beyond Foucault, but not enough. In Foucault we have an account of subjectivity as it is enabled through the interaction between technologies of subjectivity and the self-reflexive effectuation of those technologies of subjectivity, and Butler's notion of performativity allows us to bring this subjectification into the social sphere where gender is performed and read. What we are still missing is an account of the ways this subjectification is felt so personally. What we are not able to explain through this framework so far is why women are hailed in first place. This for us is significant, given the emotive and deeply impassioned way that our participants spoke about their various engagements with sexiness. To deepen our framework one step further, we will develop our account through drawing on the work of Althusser and his concept of "hailing," and we argue, along with Hook (2007), that if a hailing is to take place, power needs a psyche (or something like a psyche) for this hailing to work itself into the way we experience the world. We will then return to Butler to develop an understanding of that psyche.

To understand the mechanisms behind why people take up certain discourses of subjectivity—why they resonate with some women so that they employ technologies of self to transform themselves into these subject positions—we draw on Althusser's notion of interpellation. In different ways, both Althusser and Foucault distinguished between governance through domination and governance through consent, and conceptualized governance through consent as occurring in a process of interpellation—of being "hailed" by a form of sense-making.

One of the most famous (and debated) examples of interpellation is that of the hailing policeman (Althusser, 1971). When a policeman in a street shouts "hey you!" and you turn around, your actions represent you recognizing yourself as the subject of the policeman's attention—you respond to being hailed as a subject. Although this act happens on the street, and is therefore seemingly outside ideology (or at least outside the institutions where ideology is commonly thought to "happen," e.g., the education or judicial system), Althusser argued that it produces us as a subject in ideology—it is a recognition of ourselves, and a reproduction of us as a subject within systems of power. Self-recognition—or the function of "I"—is, for Althusser, an example of the most basic effect of ideology, because it is ideology creating this sense of ourselves as individual and distinct people (Althusser, 1971). As we have argued in Chapter 1, a new female sexual subject who is actively desiring and pleasure pursuing has emerged through the context of postfeminism, neoliberalism, and consumerism; and we can draw on Foucault and Althusser to argue that through a nexus of media, education, arts, psychology, and other heterogeneous elements, many women have been "hailed" by this new sexual subject position.

Thus, we work on ourselves to turn us into a particular self because we are hailed by that identity/subject position. Althusser gives us the mechanisms of interpellation, or how we recognize ourselves when we are located with technologies of subjectivity. But we are still left with the question of why we respond. How are we hailed by this relationship and interaction of power? Why do some discourses hail us differently from others? And how and why does this interpellation come to feel so deeply personal?

For this hailing to take place, there needs to be a psyche that is spoken to and responds in some way to the subject positions made available by certain technologies of subjectivity. To address these questions, we draw on Hook (2007) and return to his distinction between the concept of technologies of subjectivity and technologies of self. As we have already suggested, technologies of subjectivity are the wider sets of discourses that shape the way we can understand the world. However, it is only once we take these on as part of our own identities that these technologies of subjectivity come to "lend an unprecedented depth and dimension to subjectivity" (Hook, 2007, p. 31). How we are interpellated by technologies of subjectivity, "what it might mean to take on, to assume or personalize, such a subject position" (p. 31), is therefore the theoretical space of technologies of the self. As Hook (2007, p. 247) goes on to state, "[a] gap is thus opened between the general structure of given technologies of subjectivity and their individualized activation and/or rearrangement, between normative morality [technologies of subjectivity] and ethical individuality [technologies of the self]." Although Foucault himself was highly critical of psychology as a discipline, what we are dealing with in the work of Foucault is in fact a very psychological form of power that is internalized into the subject's ways of being through this personalization of the various technologies of subjectivity (Hook, 2007). We can only make sense of ourselves because of the very internalized, personal nature of power.

Butler, here, provides another critical link in developing the concept of a technology of sexiness. Butler's account brings with it a depth to the subjective and psychic processes that take place through this performance of gender, through incorporating this performance with psychoanalytic approaches to the subject. In Freudian terms, loss is experienced as a consequence of the denial of the parent of the opposite sex, and thus leads to identification with the same-sex parent, which in turn then leads to the child's internalization of the prohibition of incest, which results in heterosexuality. In the logic of Freudian subject formation, by denying our desire for the opposite-sex parent, we are able to identify with heterosexuality—a denial that is always repressed because it is taboo.

However, Butler's rereads Freudian concepts of subject formation in the context of a "symbolic," which is understood as a language-like structure where discourses operate to reproduce dominant notions of what it means to be a man or woman. In doing so, she is able to demonstrate the way in which the psyche is structured by power. Incorporating Lacanian interpretations of this process into this account, "woman" comes to signify "what is desired" and what reinforces or reflects male power, and so comes to represent gender power (or the phallus) but does not have it, whereas men have gender power, but having power means not being or personifying it. In the logic of this argument, a man dating a woman who perfectly reproduces notions of heterosexual beauty is in a state of having culturally constructed masculinized power—with the proviso that this woman (the representation of his power) may also be taken away from him. Gender identity thus becomes a state of constant displacement of either being but not having, or having but not being. Moreover, for Butler, the structure and formation of gender norms only works when the taboo of same-sex desire precedes that of the incest taboo. A compulsory heterosexuality is produced because in heteronormative contexts having power (or "bearing the phallus") necessitates the denial of same-sex desire that comes before the "original" taboo of incest.

To clarify and expand this argument further, we draw on McRobbie. McRobbie (2009) has reinterpreted the psychic formation of the heterosexual matrix in the postfeminist context to suggest that in contemporary society a new "luminosity" on women works to reproduce male power. McRobbie argues that in a context that has witnessed significant threats to masculine power and the phallogocentric order (e.g., economic independence, delayed motherhood), women must produce a form of femininity that is spectacular: a "postfeminist masquerade." In theorizing this postfeminist masquerade, McRobbie draws on Riviere's notion of the feminine masquerade, which suggested that for women in positions of power, bearing gender power was a real possibility. But this gender power would result in *having* and *coming to represent* power. As a result of the potential to trouble gender norms, this powerful woman was obliged to wear femininity as a mask. In doing so, she was able to demonstrate that she was still the object of desire (representing power), rather than a challenge to it. Butler (1999) asks of this formulation, as there is no natural essence of womanliness to begin with, what is the mask actually masking? Butler locates this mask as doing the work of heterosexual melancholy: that being the loss that cannot be articulated, because it is first tabooed and then repressed. For the heterosexual woman the powerful position becomes untenable, "for masculine identification would, within the presumed heterosexual matrix of desire, produce a desire for the female object" (Butler, 1999, p. 72) that must be both denied and incorporated into the self.

In the postfeminist context, it is not just same-sex desire that is repressed, but also a feminist discourse closely bound to concepts of a masculinized woman/feminist. In media and popular discourse, notions of lesbianism and "butchness" have become tied to notions of taking up gender power, so that women are required to deny any feminist discourse to "count" as women. Women are now made significant actors within economic relations of power; they have increased success in education, extend or deny motherhood through contraception, and can in principle share housework with their male partner. They cannot, in this context, claim that they are still oppressed, or that much of this suggested "freedom" has been channeled into forms of consumption: for example, in the way women's economic independence has come to mean a new pair of shoes or a handbag, repackaged as "empowerment" (for examples, see McRobbie, 2009; Gill, 2008b). Postfeminist sentiment means giving up feminism so that you don't challenge the gender order because it's deemed unnecessary. This means that everything comes under the individual/consumer umbrella, leaving women with few words to make sense of continued gender inequalities.

As a result of this loss, McRobbie locates contemporary femininities as in a state of illegible rage in which "young women are perhaps driven mad by the situation within which they now find themselves" (p. 105). As such, we have witnessed a normalization of disordered femininity. Unable to contest her social position through feminist discourses that would de-feminize her and challenge the gender order, the modern woman's melancholia is aggressively directed at the self and, we would argue, at other women (see our discussion of a postfeminist gaze later in this chapter and our discussion of a nostalgic feminism in Chapter 5). For example, such aggression can be witnessed in the public sphere in 2011 when 13-year-old Rebecca Black received media attention for her Internet-released pop song, "Friday." The song was dubbed "the worst pop song of all time," with its production being heavily auto-tuned, while the lyrics were described as "inane" (Sherwin, 2011). In an interview with ABC, Black claimed that responses to the song included, "I hope you cut yourself and I hope you get an eating disorder so you'll look pretty, and I hope you go cut and die." After being questioned by an ABC reporter as to her reaction to such comments, Black concluded that she initially felt these responses to her song were her own fault (another pertinent example that McRobbie draws on is the now deceased signer Amy Winehouse, whose self-directed aggression appeared spectacular in its mediated form).

Women are now told that they can "have it all," that they are not prohibited in their sexuality, and that sexiness is something that they can possess through the continuous purchase of consumer goods. But, as we discuss when we come to our analysis, this context never seems to cumulate into the actual experience of feeling sexy, so that women are left feeling that they could do more, or are saddened by the doubled binds of postfeminism and the shutting down of alternative ways of understanding. Drawing together our analysis so far, we suggest a nexus of loss: through prohibition of both same-sex desire and feminist discourse; of those who end up angered by the current limited roles for women, yet who often direct this anger at other women; and by means of a "future facing" loss that tells women to always keep "trying and buying."

However, despite the levels of aggression directed at women and by women, we are not as pessimistic, as McRobbie for example, about the subjective effects of postfeminist sentiment. In our analysis we read a doubling of performative sexiness in the context of postfeminism, and with it the possibilities for new "lines of flight" (Ringrose, 2013). It may be possible that such an illegible rage provides fertile ground for the re-engagement with forms of feminist activism and feminist criticism—even while the logic of some of these arguments remain limited and limiting (for example, Levy's [2005] account of "female chauvinist pigs," discussed in the previous chapter). And arguably within an economic downturn that is currently pervading the cultural context, we could hold out hope for a reinvigoration of feminist politics as women re-engage with more visible and heightened gendered oppressions.

We may be left with a set of discourses at the intersections of postfeminism, neoliberalism, and consumerism that take the form of "freedom," but which create limited forms of female sexual subjectivities (Bauman, 2000). But women are taking up these technologies of subjectivity and experiencing them in ways that shift these discourses. There are spaces for resistance. Many women continue to find feminist politics highly relevant, or experience the interpellation of the postfeminist masquerade as only one of many possible gendered performances. As we come to show in our empirical analysis, this complex play of psychic mechanisms is enacted in ways that provide something for women; these discourses permit spaces for women to think of themselves in ways that are powerful, even while the power of their positions isn't self-evident or is underscored by the limitations of this power. Below, we explore such doublings in which agency is complexly enabled and disabled, explicating our theoretical framework—"technology of sexiness"—before moving the discussion toward the methodological implications of "technologies of sexiness" in terms of shifting the "stuckness" in how women are framed within research on the sexualization of culture.

TECHNOLOGIES OF SEXINESS: A THEORETICAL FRAMEWORK

Women's participation in new sexual subjectivities can be located within a context of shifts in gender relations, including the rise of women in paid employment, postfeminist rhetoric, and a culture dominated by consumerism and neoliberal sensibilities. This context has produced a nexus of complex discourses from which women can perform gendered identities.

Women's participation in new sexual subjectivities has become a contentious area for feminist analysts. And as discussed in Chapter 2, we see these debates as orienting around the issue of agency, reflecting a long-standing tension in feminist research concerning how we value women's "voice," which is further complicated through the neoliberal imperative to make sense of oneself through a discourse of choice and autonomy. Since valuing women's choices and reported pleasures in participating in sexualized culture has become more contentious for feminist analysts, we have thus been left with few ways to theorize the complexities and understand women's engagement in these new subjectivities.

Our contribution to these debates is to suggest analyzing the complex contradictions of postfeminism in popular culture through the analytic of technologies of sexiness. Through this account, we have suggested that the current context can be identified as part of a blurring between subjectivity and consumer and media culture, since "the world we understand is also the world we make [the] binary division between means and metaphor misses something crucially important: that means and metaphor are dynamically interacting with each other" (Hayles, 2006, p. 163). Such an inextricable relationship can be seen in the rise in popularity of pole-dancing classes.

Pole dancing has shifted from an activity typically associated with the sex industry to all female exercise classes. Here, full embodiment in sexualized culture is contextualized as an expression of empowerment (Holland and Attwood, 2009; Whitehead and Kurz, 2009). Furthermore, since pole-dancing classes often take place in women-only spaces, the male gaze historically associated with pole dancing is absent. Pole-dancing classes thus produce a consumer practice that is constituted as liberating, and yet is tied into a culturally historical context that constitutes pole dancing as sexist and objectifying. The meaning associated with those female sexual identities produced through this form of consumerism is thus inherently contradictory, highlighting the dual nature of consumer culture discourses. Pole-dancing classes have, for example, an ambivalent relationship to the male gaze, given that its history locates it as a practice performed for the sexual pleasures of men and the commodification of the female body, but it is just as often practiced today in the cultural location of women-only spaces. Pole-dancing classes bind women to concepts of sexiness that are not of their own making; and yet they are notable for providing pleasurable sites for female comradeship (Holland and Attwood, 2009).

In the previous discussion we argued that Foucault's concept of technologies of the self, combined with Butler's notion of performativity and a psychosocial concept of the way cultural discourses take hold and come to feel deeply personal, provides a useful way of exploring the double nature of women's engagement with new sexual subjectivities. We have argued that women can use the technologies available to them to reproduce, but also subversively parody, gender norms, even if they must refer to these norms for their parody to be readable. The recent rise in the sex blog and book memoirs provides a pertinent example (see Attwood, 2009c). Belle de Jour, whose blog detailed Brooke Magnanti's life as a high-class prostitute, reproduces many accounts that are intelligible within wider discourses of prostitution, the chick-lit genre, and the production of femininity through the use of makeup and clothing. The account appeared to parody all these things.

Indeed, the self-presentation of the author openly drew on these available discourses, for example, in defining another woman as not "the do-me bravado of, er, me and people like me, nor the giggle-cuteness gosh-I'm-so-inept-Love-Me! of Bridget Jones" (de Jour, March 29, 2007). Evidence that this narrative was further troubling to common-sense notions of female sexual passivity can be witnessed in the disbelief that the press and public showed toward Belle de Jour's sex (prior to her revealing her "true" identity). Many argued that the anonymous author had a masculine perspective and must be male.[2]

Performances, such as those in the Belle de Jour blog, of more active, confident and autoerotic contemporary feminine sexualities may be subversive, but they draw on normative discourses in order to do so. The performativity thesis is therefore useful in identifying how articulations of contemporary feminine sexuality, while appearing different from earlier motifs of femininity, are constructed within the available discourses, in that re-workings are only permissible within the "law" or available sense-making of gender. However, we additionally suggest that these new femininities are taking place in an unprecedented proliferation of popular discourses on women's sexuality where there are multiple ways of enacting sexiness, which simultaneously are reproduced along the inclusions and exclusions of class, ethnicity, embodiment, and sexuality, implicating both issues of recuperation and readability. These doubled movements in which agency is complexly enabled and disabled draw more nuanced concepts of how women are negotiating and being negotiated through sexualization discourses.

Technologies of sexiness, in this account, are therefore doubled. On the one hand, the sexualization of culture calls on women to construct themselves through the powerful discourses of postfeminism and neoliberalism that reproduce regulatory and disciplinary regimes of power; on the other hand, it harbors potential where women struggle to find a way of articulating an active sexual identity through negotiating aspects of power and pleasure (Foucault, 1987). This blurring of consumer culture into subjectivity may therefore be "on the threshold of new and important re-locations for cultural practice" (Braidotti, 1996, p. 2).

As we have argued, these technologies of sexiness constitute a shift in the normative expectation for women to feel and look sexy. Foucault allows us to understand how these wider cultural discourses and technologies of subjectivity filter down to the individual's self-reflexive identity work. Disciplinary power therefore involves an interiorization of this power (Foucault, 1980), but these ideas were under-theorized by Foucault. Some researchers have responded by arguing for a psychoanalytic-informed Foucauldian analysis of power in which the psyche is shaped by power (Butler, 1997; de Lauretis, 1989; Hook, 2007). Such theorizing accounts for both the processes of subjectification and the deeply personal significance of power's internalization that

2. Other authors have caused scepticism in regard to their sex. Most famously, *The Story of O*, published in 1954 under the pen name Pauline Reage, was deemed too explicit to have been written by a woman. In 1994 Dominique Aury announced herself as the author. See Attwood (2009c) for similar examples.

makes socially constructed ideals feel like they flow from individual convictions and unique personal choices (Gill, 2007). We will develop further the effect of power's subjectification by briefly exploring how postfeminism comes to be enacted within the way women make sense of being looked at.

Throughout our individual interviews with women, a strong sentiment of judgmental gazes was discussed. Although the male gaze continued to be important in these interviews, this male gaze was foregrounded by the "postfeminist" gaze, which was made sense of in terms of allowing women to judge how well (or not) they were performing embodied femininity. This gaze was constructed as problematic and unaccountable, which we make sense of in terms of understanding it as a transvestite gaze produced through a postfeminist sensibility that both draws on and rejects feminist political discourse. For example, in Dawn's extract below, we suggest that what is being discussed constitutes powerful gaze between women, that we consider postfeminist.

> this is gonna sound awful but I'd feel more comfortable [laughs] taking all my clothes off in front of a boyfriend or or a man you know than I would in front of even even close friends I suppose well maybe not close friends but a group of friends and even worse a group of strange women. Um and I guess that's again because I think I would look at other women and compare myself and therefore and I know that other women do do it. And that would make me feel uncomfortable. And more uncomfortable than say, er, don't know going to the beach or something. Oh that's not really a good example because then of course other women do look at you and you're aware of that and you do look at other women. Um but well I suppose or or if I was gonna have sex with somebody and, you know, and I took my clothes off I wouldn't feel uncomfortable. And I wouldn't necessarily feel I was being judged in that same kind of way that a woman might judge me. That sounds a bit strange [laughs]. (Dawn, aged 31, teacher)

In the above, Dawn articulates a preference for the male gaze, one traditionally considered oppressive for women (Mulvey, 1975), because she understands it as less judgmental than the female gaze. She describes this preference even in the most supportive of female relationships ("close friends"), although she softened this assessment to "friends," before strengthening it again ("even worse, strange women"), since presumably the potential for support in female friendships was removed altogether among women who are strangers. Feminist discourses of sisterhood outside interpersonal relationships were thus absented, although perhaps evoked in the problematizing of the postfeminist gaze (described by various participants as strange, awful, horrible, or ridiculous) so that feminism was called into account and simultaneously refuted (McRobbie, 2009; Reay, 2010). Dawn's talk thus describes the pervasiveness of the postfeminist gaze as she struggles to identify any woman who wouldn't judge her: unable to be confident even with close friends, or to imagine a situation where women would not judge her ("going to the beach or something. Oh that's not really a good example"). In Dawn's extract there was, however, a hint that "close friends" offered space outside this culture of regulation.

Dawn accounts for her understanding of the gaze in terms of her own behavior ("I would look at other women and compare myself and therefore and I know that other women do do it"). And while she does not explain how she knows that other women do it, the word "know" rather than, for example, "think" allows her to make a truth claim about other women's thinking. Yet Dawn also troubles this look. Dawn starts this extract by describing what she is about to say as "awful"—with her laugh afterward reinforcing the notion that her talk is problematic—and she finishes the extract by constructing her account as "strange." As already suggested, a reoccurring pattern in our data was the problematization of the postfeminist gaze, which orients toward an expectation that things should be different. If women's looks were being made sense of in terms of a normative direct competition between heterosexual women (for example, in the traditional sense of competition for a husband), then judgment to appraise the competition would not be "strange." Nor would it be "strange" if same-sex desire was being considered, given that looks are about appraising sexual attractiveness ("if I was gonna have sex with somebody"). We suggest that the break in logic makes sense if we consider this a transvestite gaze, an uncomfortable gaze because the looker is taking up a gaze from a position that she is not and because in doing so she evokes herself as a spectacle to be judged by other women.

In much of our discussions so far in this book, we have suggested that within postfeminism women are called upon to continuously scrutinize and work on their bodies in order to meet narrow definitions of femininity that orient around being white, middle class, and heterosexually attractive. But to do this women must be able to assess how un/successful they are through internalizing the male gaze and applying it to themselves ("how well am I doing") and to others ("how well am I doing in comparison to other women"). Thinking of sexualization from this perspective calls for a Foucauldian conceptualization of the relationship between historically constituted technologies of subjectivity and their attendant subject positions (identities or selves that these technologies permit), and their subjectivizations (or the individualized personification of these subjectivities). Moreover, we would argue that such an account of technologies of sexiness would be impossible without attempting to make sense of the deeply personal aspects of, for example, Dawn's accounts of the looks between women.

As an example, Dawn's account of female practices of looking is a very personal and emotional account, but one that would shape the social interactions between Dawn and other women. From female spectator theory we would argue that when women look and evaluate other women she may see difference ("she is doing it better than me, or worse than me") or see similarity and over-identify ("we are like each other") (Stacey, 1987, 1994). If seeing difference, the female spectator objectifies the other woman, viewing her through a transvestite form of male gaze. This transvestite male gaze is a judgmental look that may act as an uncomfortable disciplinary gaze in which the woman being looked at comes to understand herself as failing in her femininity. But this look is also uncomfortable for the woman doing the looking. This unease is not just because the looker must take up a trans-vestite gaze, but because, we theorize, this look reproduces the look from which she must also judge herself. Thus, even if a woman looks at another woman, and considers herself different and better, the very act of taking up such a postfeminist gaze reproduces a postfeminist gender order. The woman who looks (and any woman who looks back) becomes both spectator and spectacle—as much subject to the postfeminist gaze herself as the woman she looks at. Thus, we posit that women are hailed by postfeminist sentiment into a comparative and judgmental gaze where self-awareness and interiorization reproduce a matrix of looks that mimics the panoptic structure (Foucault, 1977).

As the preceding discussion demonstrates, by taking this complexity into account, the theory of a technology of sexiness is able to explicate both the pow-erful and pleasurable aspects of contemporary femininities that work to make their expression so contradictory. The technologies of sexiness framework sug-gests a more doubled reading of women's identities within the context of the sex-ualization of culture, whereby this doubling occurs at three levels. First, as we have noted above, while women may use technology in the production of sexual subjectivities, these technologies are already "out there," produced through con-sumer culture that has created a proliferation of materials that pre-package sexual knowledge. Constructing oneself as knowledgeable implicates a certain pleasure, where one may "attain a certain state of happiness, purity, wisdom, perfection or immortality" (Foucault, 1988, p. 18). Second, while the performativity of gender and sexuality opens up the possibility for different forms of repetition that enable parody, subversion, and pleasure, to be readable such parodies must draw on, and thus repeat, dominant discourses of female sexuality, including objectification. Third, the multiplication of porno-chic discourses opens up possibilities for radi-cal reworkings of female sexual subjectivities; however, these may be recuperated in the media to reproduce dominant discourses that objectify women and limit those who can participate in sexualized culture in relation to class, ethnicity, age, embodiment, and sexuality.

This theoretical framework aims to produce a more complex view of contem-porary femininities within the postfeminist sexualization of culture. We have argued that the multiple ways of understanding and producing identities within the context of sexualized culture have the potential to be taken up subversively, blurring the symbolic boundaries of gendered expectations. However, historical traces of (hetero)sex necessitates that any subversive act is likely to represent the male gaze ideal, causing issues in readability, which are further compounded by the recuperation of such identities by mass markets. And yet, given that there are multiple discourses of female sexuality, including more than one discourse of being "up for it," agency can be understood as a self-reflexive method of adopting, and potentially subverting, one discourse over another.

In theorizing technologies of sexiness, we suggest an approach to agency that would allow complex analyses of enacting agency within the limitations and pos-sibilities of gender identities and mediated subjectivities. In considering how women negotiate sexualized culture, we argue that academic work needs to engage with the intersecting, intertextual consumer discourses that work through the subject in producing the self. Here, these modes of being, where they are differently enabled by social structures, are important in mapping out the complexities. Similarly, and concurrently, spaces for contested meaning, in producing the potential for subverting identities, need to be highlighted where they are employed to further extend the discursive boundaries of femininity. In the next section we discuss how a technologies of sexiness framework might inform a methodology to understand different women's negotiations of sexiness in contemporary culture. The following chapters then apply this understanding.

AGE AND THE SUBJECTS OF SEXUALIZATION

The analysis of sexiness that we present in this book are formed form our discussions with women aged 23–35 and 45–57. These women reflect broadly and crudely two generations of women caught across various axes of distinction: mothers and daughters; the "baby boomers" and "gen-x"; the "feminist" and the "postfeminist" period; pre-Thatcher and Thatcher's children. And while these women could have been hailed in similar ways by postfeminist address, for these particular women their age differences facilitated in them very different responses to postfeminism, allowing us an exploration of how differently positioned women may engage and negotiate with new sexual subjectivities. The difference in age between these two groups of women therefore was advantageous to our research, but must we also account for theoretically taking a decentralized view of the subject—one who "becomes" rather than "is"—and then characterizing these women using the essentialist category of age?

To answer this question, we note that feminist academic work has increasingly turned to the figure of the young woman as the subject of research. With this subject being the addressee of government initiatives, feminized media output, and sexualized consumer culture, a new area in feminist "girl studies" research has been emerging. This area of research has produced a vast amount of valuable work (for example, Fine and McClelland, 2006; Gonick, 2003; Griffin, 1985; Harris, 2004; Ringrose, 2006, 2007, 2011, 2013; Walkerdine, Lucey, and Melody, 2001). But within it, a notable shift has occurred in the way that young women and girls are understood.

Where youth and femininity were once the sites of resistance and the reworking of cultural gendered discourses (McRobbie, 1994), more recent research has highlighted how the figure of youthful femininity is anti-feminist, vulnerable, and thus not a site of potential, but an object for feminist concerns. Thus, despite feminist researchers often critiquing the surveillance surrounding young girls and women, feminist research itself now also treats them as a site of concern. This was discussed earlier in relation to popular social commentaries such as Levy's *Female Chauvinist Pigs*, where we sense feelings of disappointment from certain feminist perspectives that young women are not making the most of a feminist legacy. Similarly, where Walter (1999) once hailed the "new feminism" as one that could combine discourses of femininity with those of feminism, her recent discussions of the possibilities of feminist dialogue are deemed severely limited in a context where young women are encouraged to be "living dolls" (Walter, 2010). We also see this in academic discussion. For example, in *The Aftermath of Feminism*, McRobbie (2009) begins her theoretical tour-de-force by suggesting that where once she had adopted a perspective that highlighted young women's resistant strategies and "ordinary" ways of coping with masculinist cultural spaces (see, for example, McRobbie, 1994, 1999), her view had significantly altered.

We recognize that such a pessimistic shift is connected to a recent cultural context, which, while offering a vision of sexual liberation serviced with a range of consumer products, has acted as a disciplinary force, requiring women to always be "up for it" and to participate in a form of sexual objectification under the rubric of choice and autonomy. In this shift we can see a re-articulation of progressive concepts of anti-racism, feminism, and the gay rights movement to a sellable and marketable product. But to enact our doubled movement, we feel it necessary to complicate this persistent figure of the "young woman," and ask: why her? We would suggest that the hidden "other"—the figure of the older woman—has remained implicit in thinking around sexiness. By bringing both subjects to bear on the further development and application of our theory we suggest a view that recognizes the age-related differences in how femininities are read in the culture of sexiness—of how these predispositions of age could be seen as at least unpredictable in their outcomes. The (mis)representations of age offer the potential for interesting research that compares the subjectivizations of younger and older women within and through the discourses of neoliberalism, consumerism, and postfeminism.

Moreover, we would suggest that the turn to the "paranoid" reading of the young woman's relationship with cultural discourses is compounded by a tendency within sexualization studies to engage in either cultural analysis or first-person accounts of changing attitudes toward sexuality. Neither approach, we argue, exclusively manages to capture the complexities of the relationship between the cultural and subjective. For example, one area of feminist research that has explored the figure of the young woman is in analyses of postfeminist television series and films such as *Ally McBeal*, *Bridget Jones*, and *Sex and the City*. These cultural texts have received a large amount of attention in feminist media analysis (e.g., Arthurs, 2003; Dow, 2002; Gill and Herdieckerhoff, 2006; Maddison and Storr, 2004; McKenna, 2002; McRobbie, 2004; Moseley and Read, 2002; Ouellette, 2002). Such studies have usefully analyzed the dominant significations in these media texts, showing how cultural discourses and media output have a cyclical relationship. However, the figure of the "young woman" in these analyses is delimited to the interpretations and underlying ideological assumptions of those academics that produce such research.

Relying on such hallmarks of postfeminist media production fails to question their relevance today and risks these texts unequivocally "standing in for" the figure of the young woman. There is the risk of determinism in the analysis of media texts. The persistent feminist analysis of *Ally McBeal*, *Bridget Jones*, and *Sex and the City* seems to make these cultural texts unduly hegemonic representations of contemporary femininity. These analyses engender the possibility of ignoring or excluding the sheer multiplicity of texts that bring contemporary women into being and silence the documentation of how these texts may "miss their mark" (Butler, 1997, p. 87). The focus on analyzing media culture overlooks "the difficult but crucial questions about how socially constructed, mass-mediated ideals of beauty are internalized and made our own" (Gill, 2007b, p. 260). Moreover, there is evidence to suggest that some of these representations are changing. For example, Attwood's (2009c) analysis of the sex blog memoir phenomenon identifies a shift in these performances of femininity in which the passive, anxious, and insecure postfeminist woman encapsulated by mid-1990s representation has been replaced by a version of femininity that is "much more playful and assured" (p. 16).

The cultural determinism engendered by the use of media to represent young women clearly has ontological risks. To return to McRobbie's (2009) recent polemic on the current state of feminism, for example, we would argue that McRobbie too easily positions power as overwhelming. Concepts such as the fashion and beauty-complex and consumer culture are personified, positioning a powerful doer behind the deed and ignoring the multiple and dispersible nature of power (Butler, 1993). For example, McRobbie's (2009, p. 9) claim that the "government and its willing helpers, the fashion-and-beauty complex, take young women by the hand" is a clear personification of power.

Moreover, these abstract powers are often figured as more agentic than young women themselves. The intensity of power granted to the fashion-and-beauty complex in McRobbie's most recent writing has meant that, for her, it is now obligatory for "flat chested" young women to undergo breast argumentation (McRobbie, 2008, p. 242). Given "the authoritative voice of consumer culture" (McRobbie, 2009, p. 62) it is unsurprising that McRobbie only ever positions young women as "feminist-influenced." The overwhelming emphasis on power in such accounts works to deny a feminist identity to the figure of the "young woman," so that there is no space where young women can hold on to a feminist identity within McRobbie's framework—reproducing the very same issues and concerns that McRobbie is attempting to critique. As Duits and van Zoonen (2009) have suggested, "One cannot help, when reading a well grounded feminist critique on neoliberalism, or a sincere concern about the effects of media and marketing, to think of mothers who always are critical, shocked, or disappointed by the choices of their daughters, and whose problems seem to be driven by the hidden question 'why aren't you more like me?'" (2009, p. 113). To present this argument differently, Adrienne, who was in her mid-twenties in 2009, read *The Aftermath of Feminism* with a sense that McRobbie had constructed a figure of young women that often could not be recognized within her own lived experience. While theoretically very useful, the postfeminist masquerade of highly stylized femininity seems to be a fiction maintained in films such as *The Devil Wears Prada*. Meanwhile, the actual lived complexities of the archetypes of the "phallic girl," "well-educated working girl," or "global girl" seemed to be missed in an analysis that, for us, is too located in media discourse.

As highlighted by Duits and van Zoonen's observation above, the cultural determinism in feminist analysis that often works to deny young women a feminist identity appears bounded up in another ontological problem. In feminist textbooks, we hear of the white middle-class "mistake" of second-wave feminism. Focusing on the perils of the white middle-class woman, the "concept of the housewife in effect facilitated a certain model of feminist inquiry, [which was] at the same time inattentive to the partial and exclusive nature of this couplet" (McRobbie, 2009, p. 13). Research is now more attentive to young women's class, ethnic, and sexual identifications (for example, see the collection in Harris, 2008). But in making the young woman the assumed subject of feminist analysis of postfeminist media and sexualized culture, feminist scholarship risks failing to account for how age-related femininities engage with the discourses of postfeminism, neoliberalism, and consumerism.

Every mention of the "young" woman has in its absence the "old" woman. Age takes on an often-unacknowledged presence in debates about postfeminism— even while many of the now "classic" postfeminist texts deal with representations of women who are indeed "older" than the feminist researchers' imagined figure of concern (Samantha in *Sex and the City*, for example). Some have attempted to redress the balance and have challenged this absence. A handful of studies have explored, for example, women's experiences of the aging body (Paulson and Willig, 2008; Tunaley, Walsh, and Nicolson, 1999) and the use of beauty practices to resist aging (Ballard, Elston, and Gabe, 2005; Biggs, 1997). In relation to discourses of sexualization, however, there appears to be silence. Where the older woman does appear, research often discusses her in relation to media representation, through the cultural discourses of disgust and humour used to represent the sexually active older women or the companionship and romaticization of the older couple (Coupland, 2000; Williams, Ylanne, and Wadleigh, 2007). We also see age covered in debates on the notion of "third-wave feminism," where the focus becomes one of the younger woman's dismissal of her "mother's paradigm," and vice versa—a discussion that, as we suggest in Chapter 2, is unproductive. One exception is Vares (2009). In Vares's (2009) research, older men and women negotiated the representation of the "sexy oldie" in the film *The Mother* by challenging the gendered double standard of aging while simultaneously positioning the film as "unwatchable" (see also Vares et al., 2007, in relation to male partner's Viagra use). However, Vares (2009) suggests that in the absence of a substantive field of research, her own research findings produce a corpus of unanswerable questions. Given the relative silence about older women's sexuality it is therefore difficult to "see with" the older women because she is so rarely seen at all.

To address the question of how to posit a decentralized view of women informed by a backdrop of "poststructuralist" theory, and to then group women based on the essential category of age, we argue that there is a need in feminist theory to accept difference where "generation is measured not chronologically but discursively" (Braidotti, 1994, p. 175). In academic research, there has been an over-determination of how the discourses of postfeminism, neoliberalism, and consumerism affect younger women. However, older women also have to negotiate their lives within these cultural discourses. Moreover, younger women's engagement in leisure and consumption does not always necessitate unthinking or unimaginative uptake of gendered assumptions, and neither do they necessarily reject feminist identity or ideology (Duits and van Zoonen, 2006; Harris, 2008). Our discussions on the age-related subjectivities of the women we spoke to are, at the very most, a speculative attempt to capture the discursive generational influences (but not determinants) of female sexual subjectivity that has thus far remained implicit in debates on postfeminism.

To summarize our argument so far, we began our opening chapter by identifying what we understand as the technologies of subjectivity that have created particular forms of femininity in relation to sexiness in the early twenty-first century. These technologies of subjectivity include a neoliberal imperative to work on the self through forms of consumerism. The new expectation to consume oneself into being has intersected with the development of a postfeminist sentiment, in which women have been granted new rights through the feminist movement, but are expected to use these rights in ways that orient toward heightened forms of self-surveillance, self-monitoring, and self-discipline. Meanwhile, feminist discourse is refuted, as in this moment it has become taken for granted that women have gained equal rights with men, and in many cases are deemed to be surpassing men in education, employment, and in forms of subjectivity defined by a regime of individualism, autonomous rationality, and self-directed entrepreneurialship (Ringrose, 2013). Along with others, we have suggested that this context could be defined by a postfeminist sentiment—one which is stratified through structures of class, race, and gender to reinforce structures of oppression and to create a new privileged form of female sexual subjectivity that is presented as choosing, agentic, hedonistic, sassy, and self-confident, so long as it is done so in appropriately feminine ways that do not challenge masculine dominance and power.

This more subtle recuperation of middle-class, white, masculine power has come together at a particular historical moment, set against the backdrop of neoliberalism, consumerism, and postfeminism. How we make sense of this context is thus still in the making. We have suggested that current sense-making is defined by a double stagnation. A noise concerning sexualization has drowned out more complex ways of understanding the intersections of neoliberalism, consumerism, and postfeminism, so that sexualization discourses call on us to emote, but without any sense of forward momentum. As we argued in Chapter 2, we are left with a sense of rehearsing sentiments of binaries, policies, or debates: we hear repetitions in ideologically driven policy reports and mediated and embodied concern about the sexualization of children; echoes of the porn wars in feminist academic work; and we see debates about the level to which women can claim to be empowered—so that feminist debates seemingly oscillate between concerns over how to value women's voice while remaining critical to the contexts in which women's empowerment is being claimed. At the level of trying to make sense of this context, difficulties arise in being heard differently from the noise when there is such a wide dispersal of apparatus discussing female sexuality in the twenty-first century.

In this book we have argued that the emotions that come with talking about the sexualization of culture can also become the object of our analysis. This is because talking about the sexualization provides people with a space to construct themselves as good people and citizens. Sexualization becomes a technology of the self, allowing people to create by their own means a certain number of acts on themselves that enable them to take up new sexual subject positions (Foucault, 1988, p. 18). We have attempted to develop this account, showing how Foucault's notion of a technology of the self might be developed by gender researchers to make sense of both the broader cultural contexts that have enabled a sexualization of culture, and the subjective embodiment of these feelings of sexiness. We have tried to develop this concept against recent feminist theorizing, incorporating a Butlerian account of how discourses work through reiteration, readability, and recuperation, and by attaching power to the psyche. We have also drawn on McRobbie (2009) to explicate the deeply personal way that these discourses of power act upon the subject.

In the remainder of this book we employ the technologies of sexiness framework in our empirical work to permit more nuanced analyses that attend to the complexities of the cultural, material, and subjective. The "technologies of sexiness" framework suggests to us a combination of cultural analysis and first-person accounts, given the inextricable relationship between the cultural, the material, and the subjective. In applying this framework we also seek to avoid positioning other women as problematic (either in terms of their choices or their agency to make choices), while also drawing attention to the regimes of power operating within neoliberal and postfeminist rhetoric. And we attempt to complicate issues around age, making both younger and older women subjects of our discussion. Meanwhile, we take a methodological cue from Foucault and others[3] by making use of a range of conceptual tools to make sense of specific technologies of sexiness (for example, space, emotion, nostalgia). It is the theoretical accounts that we have outlined here that guide us in the following chapters, where we blend theory with cultural analysis, while attempting to make sense of the way in which women understand sexiness today.

---

3. Foucault claimed: "I would like my books to be a kind of tool box which others can rummage through to find the tools they can use however they wish" (Foucault, 1974, pp. 523–524, cited in O'Farrell, 2005, p. 50). Other accounts of methodological pluralism are captured in notions of crystallization (Richardson, 2000), rhizomes (Jackson, 2003; Lather, 2007; Pierre, 1997), and bricolage (Kincheloe, 2001, 2005).

4

Pursuing Pleasure

Don't be misled: The imperative to "Enjoy!" is omnipresent, but pleasure and happiness are almost entirely absent.

Power, 2010, p. 57

This chapter examines the discourses drawn on by our younger group of women, who, because of their identification with new sexual subjectivities, we've called the "pleasure pursuers." The group consisted of Fay, Laura, Amy, and Zoë, who were aged between 25 and 31. They were recruited opportunistically, as a group of women who met regularly as part of a recurrent "Girly Night" and whose age meant that they were part of a generation who had grown up in a discursive space after the second wave of feminism. When approached, these women showed an interest in taking part in the research. All identified as heterosexual, all were white, and at the time, all were in a relationship. The group could be described as broadly middle class in relation to education/career, although the group came from a range of social backgrounds and lived across different areas of a large city in South West England. Only Laura was married and had a child.

For our research purposes, the group met three times to participate in action-research informed focus groups. The group's meetings drew on cooperative inquiry, a small group action-research method in which group members are encouraged to explore their experiences through individual reflection, group discussions, and individual and group activities set during and between the meetings. Participants were also encouraged to take a lead in identifying the issues that were most important to them, so that the group members took on a more active and participatory role in setting and defining the parameters of interaction (Reason and Riley, 2008).

Although not recruited for any special knowledge of sexual consumption, it became clear during the period of data collection that all four of these women regularly engaged with a range of sexual commodities. These consumption practices were often normalized by the women throughout their meetings. For example, they often assumed that all women owned vibrators or had viewed pornography. Such claims were not treated as extraordinary. Instead, consuming sexuality was seen as an everyday aspect of "women" as a whole. This sense-making seemed to articulate the pleasure-pursuing characteristic of the postfeminist sexual subjectivities we discussed in Chapter 1, thus suggesting the title of the group.

In what follows, we narrate these women's discussion by demonstrating how they employed technologies of sexiness in their project of becoming "good" new sexual subjects (see Chapter 1 for a discussion of the emergence of new sexual subjectivities). To do so, the chapter takes the form of three parts. First, we explore how, in constructing themselves as sexually discerning consumers, with appropriate tastes and knowledge, our participants were able to use their consumption practices as evidence of their "authentic" performance of new sexual subjecthood. They also positioned *all* women as sexual consumers, although some as more successful than others in using consumption to create an authentic sexual identity. Within this sense-making, our participants therefore had to engage in significant discursive work to ward off any notion that they were failed consumers. This form of discursive work meant that they could construct their own identities as unique and authentic. The discursive strategies they employed included the ability to demonstrate expertise in consumer practices and to be unfazed by the extreme. Such strategies became important markers of identity. Through the presentation of their sexual assertiveness and knowingness, these women were able to take up the new sexual subject position: that of an actively desiring, pleasure-pursuing woman, confident in her own sexuality and discerning in her consumption of a range of sexual products.

For our participants, taking up this new sexual subject position involved responding to the call of those technologies of subjectivity that constitute sexiness in contemporary society, including the need to be all-consuming and constantly self-transformative. Pleasure, for these women, became a pursuit and a privilege for those who could demonstrate their knowingness correctly. Despite this process, which allowed them to extend notions of femininity and sexuality, rejecting female sexual passivity in favor of a celebration of sexual agency and daring, this new sexual subjectivity was performed in contrast to a few significant "others." The women were able to imagine "other" women, and to exclude them from the pursuit of pleasure, deeming them either unable or unwilling to take part in appropriate sexual consumerism and develop appropriate, authentic identities in the same way. Taking up new sexual subjectivities thus involved articulating inclusions and exclusions through a process of "othering[1]" other women.

Part one of this chapter thus details the performance of this new sexual subjectivity, allowing us to develop the work on new sexual subjectivities explored through media analyses (e.g., Harvey and Gill, 2011) by examining the collective sense-making of young women who are actively engaged in producing themselves through these subject positions. In part two, we develop this work further through an analysis of how our participants made sense of and engaged with the

---

1. We use this term in both its psychoanalytic sense (e.g., the way the other comes to define the self as well as creating the potential for intersubjectivity, producing us as both potential subjects and objects for the other; see Benjamin 1997) and as a discursive act (e.g., through positioning a group of people as different [and usually inferior], see Said 1978; Hall 1997).

female-oriented sex shop. As part of the dominant shift in the visibility and accessibility of sexual consumer goods, the female-oriented sex shop was identified by the pleasure pursuers as an important space to perform new sexual subjecthood, and we explore further the functions of privilege and exclusion in relation to new sexual subjectivity, consumer culture, and physical space through the concept of postfeminist heterotopia.

In part three, we apply a deconstructive turn against ourselves, showing the reversal and moment of contradiction in the data to provide a different view of these new sexual subjects. The pleasure pursuers' constructs of pleasure appeared in their talk through always achieving something "new" and of being the best sexual subject possible through various forms of consumption. Having identified the pursuit of pleasure and a pattern of "othering" other women, in our third section we read for something different in the women's sense-making. The third section of our analysis explores our participants' appreciation of other women's bodies and identities through the celebration of the successful "ordinary" woman-turned-celebrity. But our analysis identifies the duality of pleasure and power within the discourses of the new sexual subject–in an ironic twist, the admiration for these celebrity women and their ability to perform a highly feminine, classy look worked to "other" our participants, highlighting their disappointments in the face of apparent postfeminist perfection. These three movements in our narrative and interpretation of the pleasure pursuers' sense-making serve to explore how technologies of sexiness were both appropriated and reworked by the pleasure pursuers in their construction and performance of the new sexual subject.

PART 1: THE NEW SEXUAL SUBJECT: TASTE, KNOWLEDGE, AUTHENTICITY

The pleasure pursuers constructed their own identities through accounts of taste, knowledge, and authenticity. Below we consider these accounts, drawing on our framework of a technology of sexiness to examine how the somewhat doubled discursive and material tools available to these women were employed in their performance as "new sexual subjects." The new sexual subject was enabled in two ways. First, these women performed sexually assertive femininities through positioning themselves as informed, knowing consumers and individualistic pleasure pursuers. This talk constructed our participants as sexual connoisseurs, demonstrated by their ability to play with sexual mores by pushing the boundaries of socially acceptable attitudes, seeking the "shock of the new" through what was deemed sexually extreme and grotesque.

The second way these women did new sexual subjecthood was in relation to other women: other sexual subjects who threatened the pleasure pursuers' claim to authenticity were disabled through categorization and exclusion. In this context, sexual consumption became a matter of the "right" kinds of taste, and a position of privilege for the knowledgeable.

The Sexual Connoisseur

As part of the process of the focus groups, the women were given a £5 gift voucher for the British female-oriented sex shop Ann Summers (see below for a more detailed discussion on Ann Summers), which acted as a pre-meeting activity. During the subsequent focus group meeting, the members of the group took turns to discuss what they had bought, which included a tasting session of Laura's purchase of "Edible Love Dust." The discussions took on the form of a review of the products, and much of the participants' talk was dedicated to giving advice, making suggestions, and sharing their opinions of a range of sexual commodities. These discussions worked to construct the participants as knowledgeable sexual consumers who were able to assess the quality of various market products. We first present an extract from this focus group, where Amy and Zoe discuss the "cock rings" they had both bought, which neither of them "rated."

Extract 1

AMY Yeah, so I was a bit disappointed [with the purchase] really. 'Cause it's not really like a proper cock ring. 'Cause I wanted the actual cock rings, but they didn't have any in the shop. It was more like a little vibrating thing on a jelly band

FAY See, jelly bands

AMY Which are still fun, but sometimes you just want a proper cock ring

LAURA I've never tried cock rings, if I'm honest

AMY I bought one in Amsterdam and it broke. But I was a bit disappointed really

FAY Was it was it like that one [points at Ann Summers catalogue]

AMY No

FAY 'Cause I think that one looks really fabulous

AMY The one I had before was like the two leather rings on the thing. And this one was just like the little jelly thing. Which I don't rate. And, to be honest, I don't think it's very hygienic. 'Cause it's just like, it just looks just looks dirty. And it's covered in fluff 'cause it fell under my bed

[Laughing]

AMY And I only had like eight minutes worth of vibration left, 'cause I thought, "Ah, save it for another time as well"

FAY But I think that's why you need to get the disposable ones as well, almost. It's like, you can't really clean

AMY If I had like a proper nice plastic or nice leather one, you could use, you know. But this one's like a bit cheap. I don't rate it. I'm sure it'd be better if you were on your own...

In the extract above, the women's talk takes the form of a review of the style, aesthetic, and quality of the current market for cock rings. The talk clearly positions most of the women as "experts"—for example, Amy's claims that the product she'd purchased was not in fact a "proper" cock ring and that the "actual" *real* cock ring she had desired was not available in the store. Such talk worked to demonstrate the speakers as knowledgeable enough about such products that they were able to evaluate them and, in Amy's example, demonstrate a pursuit of the authentic product.

The product's failure was identified as due to its "jelly" material, and knowledge of why this material was deemed lacking was assumed—as Fay states, "See, jelly bands," without the need for further elaboration. Continuing in the manner of a review, the utility of the product in terms of hygiene and battery time were added to the "cons," whereas the potential for autoeroticism and disposability of jelly cock rings were its highlights. Although clearly discussed in a humorous way, there appeared to be nothing out of the ordinary in assessing a product through this style of review. Being in the position to "judge" and rate the product, the women therefore constructed themselves as knowing sexual consumers.

Furthermore, we get a sense of the expectations and obligations associated with taking up the new sexual subject position. Laura's statement that she had "never tried cock rings" is followed by a confessional phrase of "if I'm honest," suggesting that this lack of sexual experience is problematic. Being a new sexual subject means being experienced and Laura, it seems, is not. But her confession of "if I'm honest" also works as a discursive strategy to allow her to inoculate against the threat of not knowing, since it allows her to demonstrate that she understands her lack of knowledge as problematic. Meanwhile, her construction of not knowing about the *specific* product also allows her to imply that she is an expert in sexual consumption, just not in the topic under discussion. She may also have been able to offer this (relatively small) confession with less fear of reprisals than other women because Laura was often viewed within the group as being the most experienced, with Fay identifying Laura's exploits as "pioneering." In this context, the small gap in Laura's knowledge does not threaten her ability to claim authentic take-up of new sexual subjectivities.

Shock of the "New"?

Across our pleasure pursuers' data, we find our participants positioning themselves as well-informed, knowledgeable consumers. Consumption is clearly a practice for producing themselves into this subjectivity, so that we see these women taking up neoliberal sense-making of individual fulfillment through consumer culture as outlined in Chapter 1, where consumption in this framework is not just about material possessions but also about experiences. We suggest that we see further demonstrations of this process of self-production through consumption in our participants' talk when they seek out "new" experiences that they deem to surpass usual acceptable taste values.

These women regularly drew upon new media, new taste cultures, and the Internet as modern resources to explore the potentials of new experiences. In particular, things that were deemed to surpass usual acceptable tastes or to be part of alternative sexual practices were often constructed as being so wrong they were right. Not only did reference to "shocking" sexual practices constitute knowledge about them, they were also considered testament to how much one could "take." For example, in the extract below, the women began to discuss the Internet meme *Two Girls, One Cup*. This video became a popular cultural phenomenon late in the first decade of the 2000s. It depicted two naked women defecating into a cup, eating the feces, and then vomiting onto each other. Originally the trailer for a pornographic film, the video has since sparked spin-offs, the recording of reaction videos posted on YouTube, and has been referenced in popular television shows such as *The Inbetweeners* and *Family Guy*.

For the women in the focus group, *Two Girls, One Cup* was assumed to be inauthentic, permitting them to demonstrate a minor amount of shock, followed by a more frank discussion of what the representation of feces in the video might actually be.

Extract 2

AMY Aw, have you seen "Two girls, One cup"

ZOË *Yeah*

[Laughing and shocked noises]

AMY We've got a bet that it's either peanut butter or refried beans at the minute

     [

FAY I reckon it's toffee

     [

ZOE I'd say ice cream

FAY Yeah, toffee chocolate ice cream

AMY Nah, you couldn't put ice cream in your ass, wouldn't keep shape with the heat

FAY No, but it it doesn't really hold its shape though, does it

AMY It doesn't, it it hasn't got that milky melting though

FAY Ah, yeah

AMY We reckon refried beans at the moment

ADY What is this?

[Laughing, everyone starts talking at same time]

ZOË Don't watch it

AMY It's wrong, but it's *amazing*. 'Cause once you've watched it once, it makes you want to watch it again and again and again

[Laughing]

AMY And show it to like your friends

ZOË You do want to show it, to pass it on

FAY Yeah, you do want to show it. But it's wrong

In the extract above, the women call on their expert knowledge in various ways. Although briefly producing the reaction of shock, their discussion of *Two Girls, One Cup* was used to show that the women had previously discussed or thought about this representation of "scat" pornography in terms of its authenticity. There was no confusion over Amy's statement that she had "a bet" on what the substance that appeared as feces might have been—this claim instead inciting other similar hypotheses. Furthermore, this was followed by a negotiation of what the substance might be given the possibilities of physical anatomy and the feces' consistency in the video. The pleasure pursuers were thus able to demonstrate that they had enough knowledge of the video to know that the faeces "doesn't really hold its shape" nor did it have "that milky melting" texture of ice cream. What the discussion presented shows is a rather thoughtful and "knowledgeable" understanding of this popular cultural representation, and the ability to critique, analyze, and assess it on its ability to appear authentic. So while scat pornography was not legitimized as a sexual practice, their discussion of *Two Girls, One Cup* was used as a tool to demonstrate knowingness.

Part of why *Two Girls, One Cup* can be used to demonstrate knowingness is explained in the participants' responses to the focus group facilitator question "What is this?" which produced an explosion of excitable and pleasurable talk. In the talk immediately after this question, the participants do not narrate the events depicted in the video as might be expected (although this came later in the transcript). Instead, what seems the most important thing to tell the facilitator is that the clip's shocking nature means that you want to watch it "again and again and again." Watching this video was deemed so wrong it was right, a pleasure to be repeated, and so good it should be passed on to others. This talk thus constructs a pleasure in transgressing norms and in an ability to view extreme sexual practices, so long as this was for the purpose of knowing about these practices and not taking part in them.

The ability to watch "shocking" pornographic practices was further demonstrated by these women's ability to take it upon themselves to seek out these thrilling or shocking experiences. For example, in the extract below, the women discussed searching for the obscene and macabre. Searching and viewing sexually extreme moving images were discussed by the women in ways that worked to demonstrate how much they were prepared to see this as a marker of being a sexual connoisseur. The extract below starts with Amy talking about looking on the Internet with her friend.

Extract 3

AMY … we were, what was, we were researching something about big cocks, right, and we came to this website like sex with animals, and there was this woman there having sex with a fox

FAY *What*. That's just not right

AMY Dogs. Dogs is wrong, but then we got to the fox we were like, "Oh my god, that's really wrong"

FAY That's wildlife

AMY Yeah exactly. It was just horrible. But the more you look at it, the more you wanna look at it

LAURA I can't. I wouldn't look at it

ZOË That's for like, you're not turned on by it, you're just like "*Oh my god.* What is that?"

AMY Yeah like curiosity

LAURA But still I've got this kind of denial thing that's I, "No no," "Don't want to look," "Might look?"

[Laughing]

AMY But it's like, you might start looking for something that turns you on. And then you look. But then out of the corner of your eye, you see something that is horrible and wrong. And before you know it you're on, like, that kind of mission

[Laughing]

LAURA I do do this thing, 'cause like Pete will say, "Aw, you have to come and look at this," and I do this thing where I start off like this [hands over eyes] so you can sort of see a blurry image, and then I decide whether I can do any more

AMY But like it just snowballs out of control. You start off seeing one thing and you don't, you just really wanna see more because, you're like, it's gross

LAURA But it's just curiosity. I'm the same with like people who have jumped off buildings and like lost their heads and like horrible horrible car crashes. It's awful but like, I wanna, I wanna see like the person's head over there

[Laughing]

LAURA You know I wanna see the beheading. And it's awful. And you think it shouldn't be 'cause it's, but I I'm not the same with err. Maybe I should. Ok, send me a link with woman having sex with a fox

In the discussion above, the sexual "wrong" was again legitimized as "right" through its ability to provoke the reaction of shock, rather than through participation in the sexual practice being discussed. Indeed, a clear distinction between pleasure in the shock and pleasure in sexual arousal is made, as Zoë says "you're not turned on by it, you're just like '*Oh my god.* What is that?'"

In this extract, we see both Amy's reflection on the processes of searching out the sexually shocking, and Laura's articulation of the techniques she's developed in order to watch it. Amy's account of the process of searching out this material began within the realm of the non-sexual (a project that required "researching") and sexual (the act of looking for "something that turns you on"). However, both of these reasons for searching on the Internet are overridden as the shocking sexual practice actually proves far more exciting—presented as a "mission," the enjoyment of searching for shocking representations of sex is described as eventually "snowballing out of control." Moreover, Amy suggests a depth to her knowledge of the grotesque by implying familiarity beyond the example provided above—where Fay was shocked by the fox, Amy stated "Dogs. Dogs is wrong," suggesting both knowledge and experience of viewing representations of bestiality. The "mission" and this desire to see something "wrong" were therefore positioned as by-products of the sexually discerning consumers' Internet consumption, a naturalized process in which one leads to the other. And indeed, the notion that the search for the extreme on the Internet becomes "mission-like" can be seen as a common societal discourse. In the *Two Girls, One Cup* scene from *Family Guy*, the character Stewie watches the video in utter horror, before turning to Brian, stating; "Could you imagine if two dudes did that? Oh my god, that'd be even worse. I mean like would that, would that even exist? Like where would you even find that? Let's type it in and see what comes up."[2]

In extract 3, the discussion is not just on the motivations behind searching for sexually extreme material on the Internet, but also techniques for viewing this material. Laura's comment regarding watching bestiality, for example, positions her as someone who cannot and does not look at this kind of video—she says, "I can't. I wouldn't look at it"—even though "I can't" suggests that she has had some experience of looking from which to make this judgment. Yet despite her claims for refusing such viewing, Laura's next contribution to the discussion involves her outlining a technique she has developed precisely for watching such sexually "disgusting" images: images that her partner finds on the Internet and invites her over to see. Techniques, such as covering her eyes with her hands and opening her fingers to gradually release the image allow her to decide "whether I can do any more," construct viewing sexually extreme material as some kind of challenge—a measure of how much she can take. Laura thus positions herself as potentially outside these women's co-constructed privileged position of the knowledgeable new sexual subject (in a similar way to extract one), while positioning herself within a construct of the sexual connoisseur as one who seeks out exposure to the grotesque images as a marker of a knowingness that has to be worked at.

But it is not just the consumption of sexually extreme material that is part of Laura and her partner's relationship with the Internet. Rather, under the rubric of "curiosity" the desire to see these images is naturalized, so that it includes both the sexual and non-sexual voyeurism in terms of the car crash, the beheading, and the suicide, so that gradually death and sex in Laura's account became more similar (and, indeed, theoretically always have been; see, for example, Foucault, 1976, and Sontag's [2009] commentaries on Bataille and de Sade). Within this extract, Laura somewhat revises her position so that, although underscored with uncertainty and perhaps a little irony, she finally concedes that the ability to watch "the beheading" should equate to the ability to view bestiality, and she imagines herself agentically inviting this material into her life—"Ok, send me a link with woman having sex with a fox."

Our analysis on the construction of the new sexual subject suggests at least two insights into how technologies of sexiness are taken up in the performance of assertive contemporary femininities. First, what extracts 2 and 3 point toward is a desire to transgress, to speak out about what is deemed unacceptable, enacting the shift of the pornographic into the public domain (Foucault, 1976; Williams, 2004). For the pleasure pursuers, the idea of the "shock-mission" served as a site of pleasurable grotesque. Knowledge and consumption of scat pornography and

---

2. This statement also plays on Stewie's gay identity that the producers of *Family Guy* use to create jokes with doubled meaning.

bestiality—in the sense of seeking out and watching these videos—permitted them a discursive space to demonstrate their knowledge. What was particularly interesting, however, was the privileging of "gross-out" material as a marker of sexual knowledge, rather than the sexual experience—the obscene became a matter of sexual representation, not sexuality, so that the practice of these sexual acts was neither sanctioned nor constructed as sexually exciting.

As an aside, we note that such an observation may have implications for statistics that claim higher viewing figures of pornography among adolescents and young people (Carrol et al., 2008; Kanuga and Rosenfeld, 2004; Villani, 2001). While reported viewing figures have increased, the data we present above suggest that young peoples' consumption of Internet pornography may be due in part to the desire to shock/be shocked as much as indicators of contemporary sexual mores. So that while our data does act as testament to these women's level of desensitization toward sexual representation, it also adds support to the claim that "porn may be less concerned with images of sexual pleasure than with various attempts to expose the body" (Jones and Mowlabocus, 2009, p. 616).

However, we would also suggest that in viewing the practice of these sexual acts as part of being a sexual connoisseur, the women seemed to distance themselves from the people they were talking about viewing—the beheading, the bestiality, and the car crash are constructed as grotesque entertainment in need of authentication (Sontag, 2003). The pleasure pursuers' desire to demonstrate sexual knowingness in their talk seems to mitigate or absent the production of this material. Such talk, we feel, means that the emotional upset of having seen, for example, the beheading, gets wrapped up within the discourses of consumerism. The consumption of someone's death is enabled through those technologies of subjectivity that are being spoken through, including consumerism. And this consumer subjectivity represented through their talk of the macabre doesn't provide a more critical language for making sense of these images or a sense of empathy or recognition of the processes of production and consumption.

Our final insight around this sense-making is how sexual knowledge and experience can be taken up. As noted earlier, Laura was often viewed by the other women in the group as being the most sexually experienced. Yet, Laura is the one who positions herself in the above extracts as least experienced. Our suggestion is that Laura's cultural capital with regard to her being identified by the group as sexually experienced allows her to introduce notions of uncertainty into her sexual connoisseur discourse. We develop this suggestion below by exploring the role of the slag/drag binary in this talk.

The slag/drag binary has been used to show how women are placed in limited roles in relation to sexuality: within this binary, women are positioned as sexually expressive and therefore a "slag," or else understood a sexually unavailable and therefore "frigid," or a "drag." Arguably, women have very little room to occupy other subject positions beyond this binary, and the dividing line between these terms is slippery, so that women have to manage a "tightrope" between becoming a "slag" or a "drag" (Cowie and Lees, 1981).[3] Yet in discussions of contemporary articulations of the slag/drag binary, it has been suggested that some women, who hold particular forms of cultural capital, may be able to avoid or sidestep this binary. For example, in Storr's (2003) research at women's sex shop parties, the term "slag" was understood as an insult by those working class women who were demonstrating at the events and who were present as part of their employment, while the middle-class partygoers used this term to describe themselves and discuss their sexual history. Similarly in Ringrose and Barajas's (2011) virtual ethnography of Bebo sites, young working-class girls used the term "slut" when their heterosexuality and desirableness were supported through their relationship status as "not-single." For our pleasure pursuers, Laura's willingness to express her potential lack of knowledge or unwillingness to "get involved" could have risked her becoming "drag"-like because of the way this group of women privileged sexual knowingness. But it seemed that as she was in possession of the right amount of cultural capital, and so would not be positioned as being outside new sexual subjecthood because she was already deemed to embody it, Laura did not need to negotiate appropriate sexiness or work too hard at it. Just as Ringrose and Barajas's participants could play with the word "slut" once they had the cultural capital to do so, our participants could play with the "drag" position because their sexual exploits upheld their new sexual subjectivity. Such playing with these positions suggests an ability to transcend the slag/drag binary, becoming both and neither.

Negotiating sexiness by being able to demonstrate enough cultural capital around notions of sexual knowledge was not the case for all women. In the following section, we further explore how this subject position of the knowledgeable expert sexual consumer was defined against those "other" women who were place outside this identity.

Getting It Wrong

The pleasure pursuers used their expertise of sexual consumerism to demonstrate their legitimate claims to new sexual subjectivities. To do so, they also had to evaluate other women's ability to take up new sexual subjectivities. This process allowed them to "other" certain women by constructing them as failing to live up to the appropriate standards of knowledge, experience, and authenticity of the sexually discerning consumer.

As we discussed in Chapter 1, consumption may be experienced as one of the few sites for the modern subject to exercise freedom, constructed as it is through discourses of choice, autonomy, and pleasure; but it is not a risk-free adventure. Our material possessions and consumption practices come to represent

3. The slag/drag binary has also been discussed in terms of Madonna/whore, virgin/whore, and good girl/bad girl.

something of our true, authentic, and individual selves. Given that we have the "choice" to consume, with the aim of becoming the best person that we can be, this also means that if our consumption is deemed inappropriate we are vulnerable to being constructed as inauthentic and failed subjects.

The discursive act of positioning a group of people as different (and usually inferior) has been explored through the notion of "othering" (e.g., Said, 1978; Hall, 1997) and articulates a process whereby people can assert their own claims to authenticity by undermining other's claims (see, for example, Riley and Cahill, 2005; Widdicombe and Wooffit, 1995; discussions of othering in relation to sub-cultural identities). Here, two figures emerged in our pleasure pursuers' talk of those who "get 'it' wrong": first, in the image of an excessively heterosexual working-class female and her bad taste and ignorant consumption choices; and second, in the figure of the woman who laid claim to the identity of the new sexual subject, but who was not yet "dirty" enough to fully inhabit this subject position. These women were therefore deemed as getting it wrong by either being too sexual or not sexual enough. Moreover, these "other" women were often imagined as having the audacity to believe that they were actually getting it right.

THE HEN NIGHTER

Abjection is the process through which disgust operates to form a boundary between the self and the other, through a fascination with those things that disgust us (Kristeva, 1982). Academic accounts of abjection have previously high-lighted the abject others' transgressive qualities, for example in the figure of the grotesque female body, "abject" art, or in theories of the monstrous feminine (see Creed, 1993; Russo, 1994). Others, however, have highlighted forms of abjection that are much more social (Hook, 2006; Tyler 2009). When actual people become the object of another's disgust, the affective response forms a social boundary of "us" and "other." And for many, discourses of the "classless" society have provided a new cultural space in which such forms of abjection have come to operate (Ringrose and Walkerdine, 2008; Skeggs, 2005; Tyler, 2008, 2013).

Neoliberal Britain has long promised a "classless society" (from John Major's Conservative government in the 1990s, through to New Labour, and now the Conservative-Liberal Democrat Alliance; see, for example, David Cameron's association between a classless society and "modern/liberal conservatism"[4]). These discourses of the "classless" society construct individual choice as free from social structures, so that social disadvantage becomes an individual and personal failure, thus tying neoliberalism to a new class hatred (see Chapter 1).

Within a wider social discourse in which class is apparently no longer seen as influencing one's life chances, class disgust has been able to proliferate with figures such as the "lazy dole scum," the "racist white working class," the "yob," the "hoodie," and the "chav," reproduced in a range of media and in the public imagination (Haylett, 2001; Jones, 2011; Walkerdine, 2003; Walkerdine, Lucey,

---

4. http://www.guardian.co.uk/politics/2006/jan/30/conservatives.davidcameron

and Melody, 2001). Markers of working-class femininity, combined with prior constructs of gender and sexuality, have also taken on a particular form within this fallacy of the classless society (Skeggs, 2005). Within these discourses of class hatred, a particular construction of working-class femininity has emerged that combines hyper-femininity, excessive heterosexuality, and an "inappropriate" take-up of masculine behavior, in terms of, for example, alcohol consumption or aggressive behavior. The figures of the "pramface" and "chavette," for example, are emblematic of a new gendered class hatred, as are media representation and "celebrity chav" images of this classed and gendered subjectivity—in the United Kingdom the most striking and memorable being *Little Brittan's* Vicky Pollard[5] (McRobbie, 2009; Skeggs, 2005; Tyler, 2008; Tyler and Bennett, 2010). The bachelorette or hen party has been linked to this form of working-class femininity, not only because it represents an excessive and tasteless consumption of heterosexuality, but because this "loud vulgar display" is publicly visible and instantly recognizable (Skeggs, 2005, p. 966).

These constructs of class, gender, and sexuality were provocatively reimagined in the focus group. The women's sense-making of those who used novelty and hen night products, for example, were often reproduced in the image of loud and vulgar heterosexual display. These women understood the concept of the hen night as a bad form of consumption that expressed inexperience, unknowingness and poor taste. Through this consumption, the working-class hen night was made the pinnacle of what these women couldn't stomach. For example:

Extract 4

AMY I hate all the hen nighty stuff
[Awws, no's]
AMY Like I can't stand those girls who go down town and they've probably never had sex in their lives. *Ever*. And then they go out, oh my god, like those stupid cock straws and things
    [
ZOË Yeah cock straws with like yeah
AMY I just, I just find it like embarrassing like
LAURA Like teeny boppers with like little knobs on
AMY Like yeah, and I just, it's usually like some woman who's like fifty and it's like her third wedding
LAURA It's grim
AMY She's got loads, she's like out with her daughters or like her best friend. And it's just wrong. And they go and try and pull the same bloke, and then, in my head I've got like a whole story about their lives. That's the, that's what makes me cringe
    [

5. http://www.bbc.co.uk/comedy/littlebrittain/characters/vicky.shtml

ZOË Yeah I hate that sort of stuff

AMY Anything else, there might be stuff that personally I do not, that wouldn't do
     anything for me. But I'd kind of think, well fuck it if you're into it like anything
     then it doesn't bother me. But that kind of tacky like. It's like showing off that
     you have sex

     [

LAURA '^wee we're so funny because we've got straw willies^'

     [

AMY It's like, yeah, everyone has, everyone does it, it's not like a novelty. People
     that find it that, kind of, just makes me cringe. So anything else I don't mind.

In Amy's construction of the imagined image of the hen night and the "whole
story about their lives," working-class femininity was constructed through a
combination of discourses of age, class, and experience. Interestingly, the contradictions contained within the claim that a woman who was entering "her
third wedding," and out on a hen night "with her daughters," might not have
had sex was completely missed. So that, in the extract above, "showing off"
your excessive heterosexuality through the consumption of hen night para-
phernalia was constructed as a demonstration of a woman's inexperience. In
the women's framework of new sexual subjectivity, sex must be stylish, appropriately consumed, and sophisticated, where the " 'classiness' of female sexual
activity is extremely important here both as a way of establishing its legitimacy
and of linking sexuality to a range of other contemporary bourgeois concerns"
(Attwood, 2006, p. 85; Smith, 2007). For these women, this classy consumption included consuming for the pursuit of knowledge. The subject position of
the hen-nighter was discredited and stigmatized, unable to authentically take
up the pleasures of this sexually active liberated femininity because her sexual
consumption represented novelty. The hen-nighter had a trivial and humorous perspective on sex. For these sexually discerning consumers with the
knowledge to back up their identity constructions and their search for more
extreme representations of sex, such a public, excessive, and meaningless way
of consuming produced the affective reaction of blatant mocking disgust—as
in Laura's actively voiced imitation, ""wee we're so funny because we've got
straw willies.' "

In extract 4, it was almost as though these working-class women were insulting
because they were not taking sexy consumption seriously enough. The women's
talk in extract 4 became of form of abjection, where the working-class hen night
had to be othered in a gut reaction to their consumption that was beyond language—as seen, for example, when the women are able to produce their disgust,
but unable to put it into linguistic terms, so that the imagined story becomes
cringe-worthy. Combined with this class disgust, the extract above also constructed the "tackiness" of the hen night as making it the most intolerable of sexual practices—in a context, as discussed above, of scat pornography and sex with
dogs and foxes. So that our participants were able to argue that while they could
condone any sexual practice, they effectively drew the line at tackiness—as Amy
says, "Anything else, there might be stuff that personally I do not, that wouldn't

do anything for me. But I'd kind of think, well fuck it if you're into it like anything then it doesn't bother me. But that kind of tacky like."

The notion that "anything goes"—except the hen night—again works to highlight the capital that these women held in relation to overt heterosexuality. The women in our focus group did not need to work on their respectability. For these women, with their social position of power and their heterosexual desirableness secured through their relationship status, they were exempt from having to negotiate the slag/drag binary in relation to their "tasteless" working class counterparts (Cowie and Lees, 1981; Ringrose and Barajas, 2011; Storr, 2003).

The privileging of the slag subject position was also evident when discussing the second group of women, who were positioned as getting "it" wrong. This second group could be considered masquerading connoisseurs, who while otherwise middle class and serious about the pursuit of sexual knowledge, failed to "make the cut" through having misconceived their own level of "dirtiness." In the following extract, for example, a self-defined sexual connoisseur was revealed by Fay to be inauthentic relative to Fay's own experience. As such, the construction of these other women who mistook themselves for sexual connoisseurs were otherwise able to maintain the appearance of being sexually experienced. But their naïveté and lack of authenticity became apparent when faced with the "reality" of sex.

Not Dirty Enough

Extract 5

FAY I want my cousin to read it [*Intimate Adventures of a London Call Girl*], because my [relative]'s always been really weird. 'Cause she's like... older, she's always been like "Oh, but I love sex." Like I was reading this article about, like, a hundred things to do with sex, and I was like, "Ah, it's wicked," and she went "Oh, I wouldn't need to read that because I know it all." And she's always just been really obnoxious about it. *But,* she doesn't like porn, 'cause she thinks porn's dirty. And then, like, we were [abroad], and she like she was like "Uh, he did something to me last night that I've never had done. I feel, like, so naughty." And I just thought there's *nothing*, like, there's nothing that I would get up the next day and go, "Oh my god, I can't believe it, no one's ever done that before"

ZOË Yeah. What was she doing?

FAY So I just thought

AMY What was it she was doing

FAY I don't know. I think it's anal, really. I just think that she needs to read this [*Intimate Adventures of a London Call Girl*] and know what real people do. 'Cause I don't think. I think she just gives blow jobs and thinks she's a dirty cow

These women read the *Intimate Adventures of a London Call Girl* as part of their activity for the first meeting. Fay used this text in the extract above to identify a woman who had undermined Fay's own search for knowledge. This "other" woman was constructed as masquerading connoisseur status, having reportedly told Fay she wouldn't require the same sexual guidance in the magazine article Fay was reading—" 'Oh, I wouldn't need to read [the article] because I know it all.' " However, this other woman's reported dislike of pornography and disclosure of new experience identified her as disingenuous.

Fay's narrative created the response by other members of the group to "know" which sexual practice this disingenuous consumer found so "naughty." The call for more information about the other woman's inexperience permitted Fay to further invalidate her relative in the context of what "real people do." Through normalizing the sexual practices found in the Belle de Jour account of prostitution, "giving blow jobs" just didn't cut it. Given that Fay constructed herself as a person for whom no new sexual practice would be considered shocking—"I just thought there's *nothing*, like, there's nothing that I would get up the next day and go, 'Oh my god, I can't believe it, no one's ever done that before' "—there was no discursive space for other women with anything less than fully expert knowledge of the sexual culture to claim new sexual subjecthood.

The construction of other women, who had gotten new forms of sexually assertive femininity wrong, worked in a powerful way to the benefit the women in the focus group. Through these constructions the women were able to classify "normal" sexual behavior and reassert their own authenticity in the process. There was playfulness in this talk, and much of it was directed toward creating a sense that these women were alike: close friends who were trying to make each other laugh. But in a wider societal context, such talk could be understood as being at the loss of the "solidaristic bonds between women on the basis of perceived interests and shared oppression...noisily disavowed in favour of what seems like a more 'modern' set of behaviours including competitiveness, bitchiness and verbal violence" (McRobbie, 2009, p. 127). Despite the feminization of sexual consumption potentially bringing women together and allowing discourses of pleasure to proliferate (Plummer, 1995), there still exists a "vicious sexual stigmatization against other women" (Storr, 2003, p. 203). What the discourse of "getting 'it' wrong" entailed, in part, was the maintenance of these women's own powerful position above those who are already socially illegitimate or did not fit into the framework of the new sexual subject.

The preceding analysis sets the scene for exploring how the women in the younger cohort of our study laid claims to new sexual subjectivities. For these women, the practice of sexual consumption was a means of producing identities that were constituted as knowledgeable, powerful, and agentic. What emerged from these women's talk was the pursuit of pleasure and the management of those who could participate in this pursuit. The women were able to position themselves as (s)experts through the display and demonstration of knowledge and by speaking against co-constructed social mores in an attempt to extend constructs of acceptable social attitudes. And they delineated who could participate in this pursuit of pleasure. Inexperience or "tastelessness" didn't make the cut, so that a symbolic violence was practiced upon those subjects whose class and attitudes marked them out as inauthentic. Knowledge and privilege was also provoked through these women's constructions of space. As we document next, through the analytic of heterotopia, the feminization of sexual consumption became a space to enact these women's knowledgeable subject position.

PART 2: FEMALE SEX SHOPS AS POSTFEMINIST HETEROTOPIAS

In the previous section we identified how the women in the pleasure pursuers group presented themselves as consumers of sexualized goods in ways that promoted their own sexual knowledge and expertise. In doing so, the women created a discursive space to police the boundaries of who could take up the identity position of the new sexual subject. The construction of these boundaries were often maintained along the lines of class, age, experience, and authenticity. This practice of inclusion and exclusion was maintained through the material construction of space. In the following section, we outline how the new sexual subject located herself in space, and delineate how Foucault's concept of the heterotopia may help in unpacking our understanding of the new sexual subject further. Through the analytic of heterotopia, the following analysis shows how the discourses of safe and seedy coalesce with discourses of power, sexuality, gender, contemporary femininity, and rights and privilege to reproduce power as a material space on the British high street.

Mapping the Sex Shop: Safe and Seedy Maintained

Before turning to our analysis, it is helpful to place the female friendly UK sex shop in context. Legislation relating to "sex establishments" in the United Kingdom is vague, leaving much of the licensing and regulation of sex shops up to local government. The main law regulating British sex shops today is the Local Government Miscellaneous Provisions Act 1982. This act defines a sex establishment as a premise that sells a "significant degree of sex articles." In the case of the sex shop, this has conventionally been interpreted to mean that stores require a license if more than 10% of profit comes from the sale of pornographic magazines and videos. Local government has the discretion to set its own fees and to refuse any license, with license renewal required every 12 months or less. A fine of up to £20,000 can be made for permitting persons under the age of 18 into the store or for displaying "sex articles" in the store window to the general public.

These legal regulations have led to sex shops being situated on city outskirts, usually in rundown areas, due to the financial responsibility of paying and keeping a license. The law also necessarily impacts on the traditional sex shop image, with its identifiable age-restriction signs and blacked-out windows, which limit the passing public's view of the store's stock. Traditional sex shops are thus geographically segregated; they are located on the periphery of shopping areas and appear to be sealed-off spaces to those outside them. This geographic segregation has created an understanding of sex shops as sleazy and inadequate spaces, requiring legal regulation to protect the general public from their obscenities.

In the 1990s, however, seismic shifts occurred in how sex shops were located both geographically and psychologically within British public life. These shifts occurred through a particular interpretation of the 10% rule of sex shop legislation, combined with a changing view of femininity that constructed women's sexuality as active and autoerotic through discourses of neoliberalism, postfeminism, and hedonistic rights of pleasure (Gill, 2007b; Harris, 2004). The market leader of the new sex shop is "Ann Summers."

Ann Summers's shops are situated centrally in many British high streets and specifically address women. Originally bought in 1971 as a traditional sex shop, the owner's daughter, Jacqueline Gold, implemented the female-oriented Ann Summers Party Plan in 1981, which sold lingerie and sex toys via a Tupperware-style sales technique (see Storr, 2003). Amid the success of the Party Plan, Gold rebranded Ann Summers with a view to addressing female consumers. With this target audience, the 10% understanding of the Local Government Miscellaneous Provisions Act 1982 was strategically manipulated, since stock largely consisted of underwear and novelties. This has meant financial freedom from the license,[6] less limits on location (allowing centrally placed high-street stores), and the ability to display stock in the window. The company now boasts over 140 high-street stores located in the United Kingdom, Ireland, and Spain, as well as over 7,500 party organizers, a highly successful website, and sales of around £150 million in the 2012–2013 economic year (with the British press claiming that the economic downturn will see Ann Summers's profit rise due to a new "stay at home" ethic, and Gold suggesting further economic success due to the popularity of E. L. James's *Fifty Shades of Grey* series[7]). For many in the United Kingdom, Jacqueline Gold is a household name, regularly appearing on "business women of the year" lists and synonymous with go-getting, spirited female entrepreneurial attitude. Gold is often credited with introducing the "Rabbit" vibrator to UK homes and consequently is constituted as having sexually liberated the British woman (Attwood, 2005; Smith, 2007; Storr, 2003).

The success of Ann Summers can be attributed not just to shifts in location and shopfront enabled by legislation, but also by its ability to address women in particular ways. The store layout, for example, is structured in combination with the law that forbids presentation of sexual products to the public, so that underwear appears at the forefront, with sex toys and a limited range of videos and magazines positioned toward the back. Chandeliers, pink walls, and subtle black-and-white prints of heterosexual couples and individual women deepen the experiential connotations that semiotically distance Ann Summers from the traditional sex shop image. By employing the discourses of fashion, consumption, and autoeroticism in this way, Ann Summers works by deeming sexual consumption easily

6. The exact price of each license is decided on an individual basis by the local government.

7. http://www.theguardian.com/business/2013/mar/14/ann-summers-fifty-shades-trilogy

accessible, highly individualized, and intrinsically tied to feminized consumer practices.

The pleasure pursuers constructed Ann Summers as a safe space for female consumers by coupling forms of appropriate feminine consumption with the shop's position on the high street, the store layout, and the style and aesthetic of the products within. In extract 6, for example, femininity was symbolically represented through décor and color, with the contrasting male position having an almost unspoken but implied presence.

Extract 6

LAURA I think that they're like geared towards women, aren't they? Like look at what you can wear to feel sexy and look at these toys you can use. And I always look at vibrators as more aimed at using on your own

FAY Yeah

LAURA It's about you, it's not about pleasing your partner I think. That's the vibe I get

[

AMY And all the catalogues are like

LAURA Very women friendly I think

AMY Yeah

LAURA It's like Love Honey and stuff. It's like all bright and nice and you know girl's colours and just directed to women

[

AMY 'Cause the girls in the catalogue they don't really look sexual. Even though they're wearing like sexual clothes, their expressions and that are really quite like innocent, aren't they, and they look quite friendly

LAURA So I'd definitely say that it's good

FAY Yeah

LAURA And not that coarse and seedy element

The internal appearance of Ann Summers was affirmatively interpreted by the women as addressing female consumers in highly autoerotic and individualistic ways. Such constructions of femininity challenged the focus on the heterosexual couple by reinstating a postmodern self-for-itself, producing a hedonistic consumer of her own desire. Emphasizing this self-for-itself, colors, and style added to this experiential femininity. Thus, as Laura made clear, the sexual self was constituted more by individual pleasure seeking and "feeling" rather than looking sexy; thus sexiness was over and above the aim of "pleasing your partner," embodying a femininity that was "not another, or for another, but herself for herself" (Radner, 1995, p. xi).

Also identifiable was the non-sexual nature of this sexual consumption space. For example, Amy identified the catalogue models as "friendly" precisely because they appeared to be "innocent" and non-sexual. The construction of a female-friendly space had been achieved through the women's non-sexual construction, which excluded the masculine "coarse and seedy element" and incorporated the "bright and nice" aesthetic of female-focused shops. Through this discursive removal of sex from the sex shop space, "safe" and "seedy" were maintained.

As extract 6 demonstrates, the sex shop space was effectively being constructed by these women through notions that emphasized the non-sexual nature of this space, a contradiction that seems characteristic of many postfeminist consumption spaces. For example, in our individual interviews, pole-dancing classes were understood as containing none of the referents of sex, despite their distinctly sexualized history. Others have similarly noted the "schizoid sexy" of sexualized icons such as the playboy bunny, a symbol that at one and the same time comes to symbolize both sex and innocence (Renold and Ringrose, 2011). And as we have documented earlier, extreme sexual representation was made non-sexual because it was used as something gross that needed to be passed around. The extent to which the claim that current constructs of contemporary sexiness were indeed not sexual meant that, for us, we needed a concept that could make sense of these contradictions, while also remaining critical to the ways these articulations were tied to wider power structures. Reading these women's articulations of sex shop spaces through the concept of the heterotopia makes sense to us, as it allows for an understanding that helped to analyze the materialization of powerful discourses and the way these discourses reflect wider social contexts (Hook and Vrdoljak, 2002).

For Foucault, the heterotopia constitutes those spaces that unsettle because of their relationships with other sites. The graveyard, for example, is unsettling in the way it places people who are living among the dead; the boat or ship unsettles because it is "a floating piece of space, a place without a place" (Foucault, 1986, p. 27). Such spaces hold onto constructs that do not seem to belong and makes the space stand out as spectacular. The sense of unease that such sites communicate through their contradictions do not, however, come from the sites themselves, but from the ways the particular materiality of these sites comes to be constructed in the context of power and discourse. As such, the heterotopia becomes a useful analytical tool for enabling the identification of space as a discursively non-innocent and political construct. Not merely a description of space, but the materialization of forms of discourse and power, the concept of the heterotopia provides a useful analytic lens for making sense of the contradictions produced through the history and discursive formation of female-oriented sex shops on the high street.

Indeed, as we discussed earlier, it is only within a very recent history that such complex characteristics of the sex shop space can be articulated. The heterotopia allows us to understand how the sex shop manifests itself onto the high street, as a space that contains inherent contradictions whose repositories range from the mundane to the extraordinary. What we are witnessing here is the materialization of power and discourse, webbed through the shifting feminization of city centers and male consumer practices. This was evident, for example, when the pleasure pursuers discussed Ann Summers' external appearance as part of being on the high street and the new ordinariness of sex shopping that this engendered. This female sex shop's "other" space, the more male-oriented store, was imagined by invoking notions of seediness, constructing a bleak and desolate space that worked to exclude women.

Extract 7

AMY Like people who would go and shop in La Senza and buy underwear and
then pop into Ann Summers, and then you move further back in the shop,
don't you, as you go along
FAY Definitely
ZOË It's so nice. It's good because it like it's not seedy anymore. Like just walking
into the old, like even walking into the old Ann Summers you did feel a bit like.
'Cause it's all blacked-out windows
[
LAURA Yeah and then the doors won't open
ZOË And you feel really bad. And you would just go up to it and go "aw no no I'm
not gonna go in." But, especially now 'cause they've made them all really big
and it's right there on the high-street, and it's just another shop. So you're not
like embarrassed or ashamed walking in there you're just like "oh yeah, just
shopping"

Here, safety was indicated by the store's high-street position and the mundan-
ity of the shopping trip. The ability of Ann Summers to be viewed as just another
high-street shop, rather than an establishment selling sexual products, disengaged
it with the more typical sex shop connotations, thus constituting it as "not seedy
anymore." Indeed, this was a clear example of the rewriting of sex shops within the
everyday routine (Juffer, 1998).

Through defining Ann Summers as "just another shop," constructions of public
and private space were also present in the historical discourses of safe and seedy.
Indeed, the older store was imagined as impenetrable to the point where the
doors may not open. In contrast, movement between regular high street underwear store La Senza, which was figured by Amy as a construct of normalcy, and
into the "big" sexual consumption space was just part of being on the high-street.
These movements between spaces were figured as normative actions, "scripts"
with no irregular or defining feature, producing frictions between Ann Summers's
normative and extraordinary identities (Evans, Riley, and Shankar, 2010b; Hook
and Vrdoljak, 2002). Where the stereotypical male sex shop requires "furtive-
ness, secrecy and anonymity" in a society where "sexuality is a problem to be kept
within guarded environs" (Smith, 2007, p. 170), female-friendly spaces appeared
as having little to do with sex, with the focus on the normalcy of shopping.

However, also notable were the layers of public and private. "Old"[8] Ann Summers
was constructed as a private space in the public domain, seen from the outside as
having blacked-out windows. In comparison, Ann Summers on the high street
was "big" and public, yet its layout provided the potential for privacy, as in Amy's
observation that you could move "further back in the shop." Movement toward
the back implied that more seedy/sexual products were both physically and

8. "Old" Ann Summers was a reference to a store in the city that predates Jacqueline Gold's
rebranding.

psychologically hidden in the more private areas of the female-friendly consumption space. It is within such constructions of space that Ann Summers became connected with other spaces, while simultaneously producing contrast and difference (Evans, Riley, and Shankar, 2010b; Hook and Vrdoljak, 2002).

Safe and Seedy Refigured

The discourses of safe and seedy that our participants drew upon to construct the sex shop space can be interpreted as largely maintaining gendered expectations. However, the heterotopia is highly pliable; it is able to change its social meaning and therefore has the quality of social change and power beyond itself. This was evident in the ways the pleasure pursuers found ways of extending notions of safe and seedy that reflected their new sexual subjecthood. Alternatives to "safe" and "seedy" were produced in one of two ways. First, by employing a "developmental discourse" through which the women constructed themselves as having developed from a naïve to a sexually discerning consumer; and second, by critiquing the "female-friendly" Ann Summers as "tame," thereby constructing imaginary and desirable "seedy" female spaces—"a need for seed."

All the women's "first-experience" narratives of Ann Summers involved themselves as teenagers, often entering the store "for a laugh." However, the women constituted entry into Ann Summers as always initially problematic, overcome by the subject positions made available with the construction of increased experience.

Extract 8

AMY ...You do feel like its somewhere you're not meant to be going sort of thing. And go in and sneak in and sneak out. But I've always had this thing where, if I'm anxious I don't actually look around. So I knew what I was gonna get and I ran in and go and buy it and just come out. But I think as I've got older, and the more stuff you look at the more you think, actually, I'm probably dirtier than this shop

[Laughing]

AMY So it doesn't worry you so much, does it? Whereas like cause when you're younger you're like in your head it's like, "oh my god all these people are like doing things and I don't know what they're doing." And like it's all stuff I don't know about. But I think as you get older you don't really care, do you?

The extract above was representative of a common theme within the women's talk, whereby they constructed themselves as having developed from naïve to well-experienced pleasure seekers who had become desensitized to sexual consumption, and as such, "dirtier than this shop." Importantly, knowledge did not bring excitement, which might indicate that Ann Summers was still novel, but instead incited indifference, so that "you don't really care, do you?" Through the developmental discourse, this construction of indifference reduced the anxiety and threat of being figured as ignorant. The developmental discourse also further distanced these women from their "other" denounced subjects—the inexperienced hen-nighter or self-deceptive and insincere sexual consumer, who still found novelty in her new sexual experiences. Rite of passage in this postfeminist heterotopia was thus formed by the construction of developmental time and increased knowledge, allowing these women to claim increased expertise over their younger (and "othered") selves through which the "discursive strategies of entitlement operate" (Hook and Vrdoljak, 2002, p. 214; also see Foucault, 1986, 1997).

Supporting the developmental discourse, the call for seedier spaces for female consumers was represented in two mutually supportive ways: by critiquing Ann Summers for its safeness; and by constructing imaginary utopian spaces that worked to extend seedy sexual consumption for women. Below for example, extracts 9 and 10 reproduced Ann Summers as a safe space, but critiqued it for being "tame." Extract 9 occurred in Amy and Zoe's discussion of their ideal sex shop, "Deviant Dungeon and Porn Emporium," in which they critically reflected on the Ann Summers experience. Extract 10 was produced at the closing of the focus group, when the first author Adrienne (Ady) concluded the meeting by asking the women to summarize their feelings of Ann Summers in one word.

Extract 9

AMY Well the thing is, I think that's exactly the thing that probably puts me off Ann Summers now. Is that it's quite tame. Whereas when I first liked it I really liked it. Whereas now when you've seen it and done it. If it was like quite an experience going somewhere.

Extract 10

LAURA I thought of one [word] in the end
ADY Which one?
LAURA Tame
AMY Yeah
LAURA I thought in the end actually, although we all used to think it was a dirty naughty shop, when we go in we've all sort of thought
AMY Yeah
LAURA Aw, I want something a bit more hard-core than that
[Laughing]
LAURA That seems to be a general feeling for everybody
ZOË Yeah that's true

Amy described Ann Summers as "tame," evoking notions of safety and lack of excitement, whereas the sex shop ideal should provide the consumer with an "experience." Thus, Ann Summers was constructed as a mundane space. Laura also summarized Ann Summers as "tame," a statement that sought and drew consensus. Her desire for "something more hard-core" that needed to be sought in more extreme places than the female-friendly space Ann Summers (one that had previously been experienced as positive and exciting) can be read as an attempt to extend the gender boundaries of sexual consumption. These extracts remained within their developmental discourse of increased knowledge; thus the women's construction of Ann Summers as a female-friendly space in which sexual reference was apparently absent, and within which they placed the hedonistic female consumer, was therefore constituted as failing to fully enable them into the subject position of the new sexual consumer. The Ann Summers space needed to be rewritten and expanded considerably for these women to demonstrate their higher level of knowledge and experience.

The women produced a solution for the problem of a developing sexually experienced identity that was not fulfilled by female-friendly spaces in its later stages, by imaging spaces that could rework notions of safe and seedy. In "Heaven and Hell" (Figure 4.1), for example, we see an extended feminization of typically seedy notions of sexual consumption. Designed by Laura and Fay, this image occurred

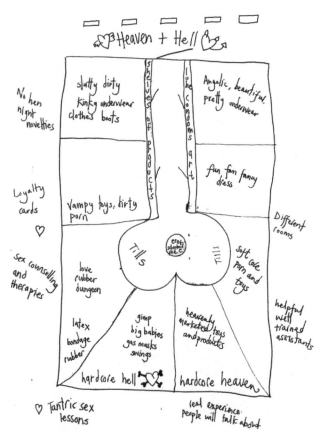

Figure 4.1 Heaven and Hell.

in the data when the women were provided with colored pens and two sheets of paper and were asked to design their "ideal" sex shop.

Heaven and Hell (Figure 4.1) was described by the women as providing a seedy element in an inviting space. The layout, structured by a penis and expressing the overt heterosexuality of these women's contemporary femininities, allows the consumer to experience increasing amounts of seediness as they walk down the length of the store. The products contained within each room were thus suggestive of what was considered more safe than seedy. For example, underwear appeared at the safest end of the store/penis, with it being conceivable that by "underwear" they were referring largely to women's items. The store was also divided into two halves. "Heaven" was described as having "nice girl's colour" and "glitter," gradually directing the consumer of safety to "hardcore heaven." "Hell," in comparison, was dedicated to seediness. Described as a strategy to make "hard-core" products increasingly accessible, this image constructed dissatisfaction with the available discourses of Ann Summers, and presented an identity that desired both safe and seedy spaces.

This alternative spatiality, as an imaginary utopian and thoroughly fantasmatic space, was the making of this space into their own (Evans, Riley, and Shankar, 2010b; Foucault, 1986; Hetherington, 1996). But despite its fantasy, and despite the pleasures of this space, it still plays on its own exclusion. Only some women were enabled within this normative framework of sexual knowledge and experience. Taste discourses were reproduced along classed constructions, represented, for example, through Heaven and Hell's insistence on "no hen night novelties" (see Attwood, 2005; Storr, 2003; Smith, 2007). The privileging of male sexual desire, and therefore potential exclusion of lesbian identities within this image, is also notable. Thus, this resignifying was always in relation to power, so that the postfeminist heterotopia worked to both extend the linguistic possibilities of female sexuality by blurring gendered spaces, while simultaneously reproducing this power in other ways through organizing space around privilege and "right" to enter (Foucault, 1986, 1997; Hetherington, 1996; Hook and Vrdoljak, 2002).

Masculinity Maintained, Raincoater Refigured

As demonstrated in some of the extracts above, the consumption of sexual material has often been constructed as problematic, for example, as abnormal, dangerous, or clandestine (Attwood, 2007b). Such understandings inform the public imagination of the kinds of people who do this consuming, which in turn map onto discourses of gender and age. Historically, two dominant figures of the sexual consumer emerge: the old male "raincoater," a persistent figure of perversion, and the adolescent male, whose problematic hypersexuality has featured more heavily in the public consciousness with the rise of the Internet (Attwood, 2007b). The problematic nature of men's sexual consumption is further reinforced by discourses within academia and broadcast media that associate sexual consumption with emotional and physical violence toward women (for example, see Paul, 2005;

Wolf, 2009). Men who consume sexual material are therefore typically under-stood as sexual, seedy, and problematic, whereas, tied into the history of feminin-ity, women are typically understood as sexualized and objectified by men, and have therefore been figured subjectively as non-sexual agents.

But these women were not constructing themselves as non-sexual agents. And in a similar shift, the problematic seedy male sexuality discourse also underwent a reworking that was linked to notions of privilege and "rights" to enter. While the male "raincoater" remained for these women a figure of perversion, the women constructed other new masculinities that, in a neoliberal postfeminist context, needed rights to the pleasurable aspects of sexual consumption afforded to female consumers (see Tuck, 2009, for an argument supporting the need for positive representations of male sexual consumption). As evident in extract 11, this con-structed men as having an unequal opportunity to consume in these sexual con-sumption spaces *for themselves*.

Extract 11

AMY Don't you think it's weird that there's like a main, like a high-street chain that's like sex toys for women. But there's not really anything for men, is there? The same. I mean like...if you think of people like women buying vibrators and things like that, you buy like a rampant rabbit and things like that, your seen as quite like, you know, you could be quite an outgoing, confident sort of woman. But then, if a man went and bought one of those vibrating vagina things, you imagine somebody that's socially inept don't you. And who's got some problems

[Sounds of agreement]

AMY It's not really, it's gone the opposite way in equality, hasn't it? Because men can't go out, "cause really nothing, there shouldn't be anything for Pete going out and going, 'yeah I bought this vagina"

[Laughing]

AMY "It's amazing." And it's, you know, he probably wouldn't. He probably wouldn't be able to do that. And he might get as much pleasure from that as you get from your vibrator

LAURA Yeah

AMY So it's kind of gone like, like where do men go to buy stuff. It's not really. I mean there's other dirty sex shops, but there's not like the same sort of sex toys things is there for men, I don't think

In the extract above, the pleasure pursuers suggest that there is an absence in spaces for male consumers. The physical space of Ann Summers is on the high street because postfeminism so heavily ties discourses of femininity into sexual agency (Evans, Riley, and Shankar, 2010a). Yet the history of heterosex also ties masculine discourses with sexual agency—but this is a different type of sexual agency, characterized by power and domination. As we suggest above, this dis-cursive tie has created the construct of the "male raincoater," where male sexual agency is also deemed pathological and perverse. Thus while a high street space for women associated with the confident sexually liberated woman has emerged, we are much less likely to see a "boyfriend" section, or discourses of "doing it for himself." Indeed, this phrase easily conjures up an imaginary "socially inept" male "who's got some problems," a figure used in contrast with men Amy knew who were seen to defy these labels and yet who also owned sex toys. The inequality in gendered sexual consumption is thus constructed, with Amy's reversal of the domestication of vibrators discourse. A man stating, "yeah I bought this vagina…it's amazing," worked as evidence of this inequality: a shared understanding in the group as evidenced by their laughter at this reversal.

This construction of the male consumer as having done badly out of the feminization of the high street, and having unfair unequal access to sexual consumption practices, is tied into the recent construction of (appropriately hegemonic) men as shoppers. A growing consumer culture incorporates male consumers in a way that men now engage in practices that have been traditionally marked as feminine (Nixon, 1997). For example, many high-street and typically female shops include concessionaires that target the male consumer (for example, in the way Topshop has a Topman). We have also witnessed a growing trend for female products sold to men through changes in the linguistic organization of products; "man"-bags instead of handbags, and makeup and other beautification practices are sold to men through products such as "guy"-liner or "skin protector" (which clearly still draw on older notions of what it means to be a man). But as evident in the advertising of these products, the claims to new equality and feminization of the male consumer product is still shot through with exclusions. For example, L'Oreal's advertisement for their "Expert Hydra Energetic" moisturizer, rather than appearing feminine, includes shots of actor Gerard Butler riding a motorbike over a car and playing rugby, before finally embracing a beautiful woman, proving to the audience that neither his strength, dare-devilish nature, nor his heterosexuality are challenged in the act of applying moisturiser. His white masculinity is left unscathed by his participation in a hitherto feminine beauty practice. Echoes of this context appear in the preceding extract: a call for the feminization of sex shopping for men (in a previously male-only space), which is nevertheless not too feminine as to compromise a man's heterosexuality.

So while the existence of the "dirty" and the safe "high-street" sex shop were maintained, the connections and juxtapositions between these sites also permitted the women to explore some of the apparent exclusions that the relationships between these places seem to engender. Since discourse about the inequalities of space often relate to women's fear of violence and men's control over women's spaces (Green and Singleton, 2006), the extract's postfeminist reworking contradicted common-sense notions, making sense more within a discourse of neoliberal detraditionalization of masculinity. As such, in an apparently "genderless" society in which all things are now equal, men can be positioned as having "lost out" to the feminization of the sex shop (Riley, 2002; Ringrose, 2007, 2013). What was presented, therefore, was the construction of a double standard, in which men were neither permitted positive active sexual identities, nor the safe space in which to produce such identities. Thus, in contrast to the male position being problematic for the implication of seedy autoeroticism, the presentation of a contemporary masculinity was problematic instead through the social exclusion and inequality produced by the dominance of female-oriented spaces.

Through the focus on female enjoyment, the pleasurable aspects of Ann Summers addressed these women through discourses of femininity, neoliberal individualism, and autoeroticism, serving as a space for the construction of sexually active identities. And yet within this mainstreamed sexual address, Ann Summers also functioned to maintain historical notions of sexual consumers. Through its construction as mainstream and non-sexual, even "innocent," its available discourses maintained the hedonistic consumer as a non-sexual agent. In this analysis, we have shown how the women's reworking of "safe" and "seedy" went some way to questioning the gender divisions of the sex shop. However, resistant use of Ann Summers still left the sexual consumption space somewhat intact, in that any variation necessarily recites the norm in its production (Butler, 1999). Indeed, in this analysis, "safe" and "seedy" were left in place—these distinctions were not themselves challenged. The women's reworking of "safe" and "seedy" into their own normative framework of the white, heterosexual, and middle-class consumer was tied into the gendered history of sex shops in a way that took "safe" and "seedy" for granted, as assumed natural. Thus, while the postfeminist heterotopia can be used in ways that alternatively order space, this alternative ordering neither assumes radical political action nor escapes the laws of gender (Evans, Riley, and Shankar, 2010b; Foucault, 1986; Hook and Vrdoljak, 2002).

So where are we now with our new sexual consumer? These women appeared throughout their talk to always reposition themselves as powerful, agentic, and confident, and to construct themselves in ways that were knowing and experienced. This does appear at first glance to be the embodiment of what feminist modes of sexual empowerment might look like, as well as something the women themselves clearly took pleasure in. But in doing so, their talk ultimately appeared to highlight insecurity. By having to appear sovereign and powerful, the pleasure pursuers spent a lot of time making sure others could not take their place. Positioning themselves so firmly within postfeminist sexualized culture, as being about self-transformation and never about achieving the ideal, these women created a doubled entanglement for themselves. In the final section of our narration of these women's talk, we show how their powerful self-constructions came undone; how, by postfeminist standards, these women's self-constructions only ever amounted to the pursuit of pleasure, and never possession of it.

PART 3: CELEBRATING WOMEN

To reiterate a key point, the pleasure pursuers articulated pleasure and power in taking up new sexual subjectivities. Postfeminist rhetoric was used as a discourse of pleasure to challenge what the women together conceived of as the dominant discourse and socially acceptable attitudes of contemporary society. This sense of resistance can also be seen more broadly, for example in the way that pole dancing is advertised as a practice against the "restrictions imposed" on the female body (Walters, 2010, p. 5). We also see resistance in the group's discussion of gross-out pornography, which is discussed not as a legitimation of "extreme" sexual practices, but to demonstrate knowledge about it. As Foucault (1976, p. 7) has stated, "[w]hat sustains our eagerness to speak of sex in terms of repression is doubtless the opportunity to speak out against the powers that be." However, identifying restrictions created ruptures in the women's accounts, particularly around the postfeminist requirement to constantly transform the self. These ruptures are discussed below in relation to moments where the pleasure pursuers celebrated the bodies of other women.

One discursive space in which this speaking against was practiced was in relation to beauty standards. For example, in the next extract, Fay described why she had found a YouTube video of burlesque so enjoyable. In this context, the practice of burlesque was constituted as a liberatory practice that spoke against thin-ideal beauty standards through its representations of "real" women.

Extract 12

FAY I really liked the video that I watched where it was like real sized women, just being really beautiful and sexy. And it actually looked good when they actually had a bit of cellulite. And their arses did wobble a bit. And I was like, *yes*. Yeah, definitely. 'Cause it's so real

AMY And it's like their confidence, isn't it. Like you don't have to be perfect, or you can love yourself if you can love yourself

LAURA Yeah, definitely

In the extract above the women constructed burlesque as a space in which they could talk about other women in terms of beauty and sexiness (see also Commane, 2010; Holland and Attwood, 2009; Whitehead and Kurz, 2009; Willson, 2008). Each of Fay's truth claims spoke against an absent dominant discourse. The video represented "*real sized* women…[who] *actually* had a bit of cellulite. And their arses *did* wobble a bit" (emphasis added), in contrast, we can assume, to the mainstream media representation of unrealistic women who didn't have cellulite or wobbly "arses." What seemed to be at stake in Fay's insistence of real women was the "tyranny of slenderness" and "beauty myth" (Chernin, 1982; Wolf, 1990). This extract challenged the societal discourse of "thin" by finding pleasure in the "authentic" representations of confident "real" women. Extract 12 could therefore be understood as engaging with an embodiment that was liberated from the need to constantly work on the self (although still requiring postfeminist notions of "confidence"), where the "real" woman can dismiss social norms so that, as Amy stated, "you can love yourself if you can love yourself."

Similarly, certain female celebrities were celebrated for using their bodies for money in ways that were assertive, despite their levels of attractiveness. In extract

13, for example, the women in one of the focus groups discussed British glamour model and media personality Abi Titmuss.

Extract 13

AMY I do like Abi Titmuss though. Even though she's a biter. I still like her

ZOË It's because she's a nurse or she was a nurse

AMY No she's just I think its cause she's like really quite not attractive and not deviant looking and she's made loads of money out of it hasn't she

ZOË She's not attractive actually is she

AMY She's not she's got no ass at all and massive shoulders

LAURA Wasn't she one of the first ones to realize um like if I own the rights to all my pictures then every time they use a picture

AMY Yeah, I get paid

LAURA Yeah I you know so she has all the profit off them

ZOË She's not an idiot I don't think

LAURA So she has basically all the every single magazine and paper, whenever there's a picture of her she just phones them up and says "Right, that's a picture of me, I own the rights, thank you very much"

ZOË Yeah, she's no fool

In the extract above the women in the focus group constructed Titmuss as a likable celebrity. The reasons given for her likability included the similar pre-celebrity-status career to one of the women in the group and Titmuss's appearance. The identification of Titmuss as unattractive and/or simply ordinary in comparison to most female celebrities made her both unthreatening and more like these women. Her appearance was framed as an "against all the odds" scenario in which, despite not being attractive or deviant looking, Titmuss had created financial revenue for herself through her body as a cultural signifier of sexiness. Moreover, her perceived money-making skills and business strategy added to the creation of Titmuss's postfeminist celebrity. The agency in this extract was placed firmly in the hands of Titmuss, which Laura actively voiced in the extract in a way that was presented as unhesitant and direct.

Not only had Titmuss, this fairly ordinary woman, managed to make it as a celebrity sex symbol, she was was figured as a savvy and independent woman who could navigate the business of celebrity in new ways. It was less that the "[m]edia entrepreneurs want celebrities involved in their projects" (Turner, 2004, p. 34)—in a neoliberal twist on the economy of personality, Titmuss fulfilled multiple roles as entrepreneur, celebrity, ordinary woman, and "no fool," savvy, self-made business woman.

Immaculate Consumption

There are many ways of interpreting the pleasure pursuers' various discourses about women's body size. Contradictory discourses of embodiment in the media that celebrate both slim and "real," or that reclaim "curves" while simultaneously reproducing images of straight firm bodies, abound, as is evident in our participants' talk in extract 13.

Some scholars have warned of the problems associated with assuming a single oppressive "thin" beauty standard (see, for example, Johnston and Taylor, 2008, on the implications of the "real" in the Dove Campaign for Real Beauty). The celebratory discourse represented in extract 13 reproduced a wider social discourse in which women's attractiveness was still tied to their bodies (Gill, 2007b; Probyn, 2008; see also Chapter 1). Moreover, the societal discourse that celebrates the "real" body is often coupled with contradictory discourses about what the "ideal" attractive body might actually be. We would suggest that such concern over "thinness" and the celebration of cellulite, wobbly bodies, and curves have increased through the lens of postfeminist sense-making. If perceptions of both "fat" and "thin" are equally denounced, it makes it even more unclear what body size one is attempting to achieve. Although we would not suggest that there should be an "ideal," the lack of any clear ideal creates uncertainty. The postfeminist discourses around the "real" body might be understood, therefore, as not producing one ideal but many. Within a postfeminist framework, the proliferation and contradiction over what constitutes the ideal body means that women are always vulnerable to positioning themselves as somehow failing. If the "ideal" body norm is constantly shifting, there is always work to be done.

This kind of uncertainty and contradiction was represented by the women in the focus group (see extract 14). Despite moments in which power and pleasure worked together to enable an agentic identity for the women, this agency was also regularly contradicted. To take the example of burlesque, the construction of a practice in which "real" body norms were celebrated was coupled with praise and admiration for those burlesque performers who seamlessly fitted into the image of perfection that these women otherwise challenged. This was particularly true of burlesques' celebrity icon Dita von Teese.

Extract 14

AMY But don't you think it's [the burlesque image] just as unobtainable

LAURA Yeah

AMY It's any it's not like more achievable. It's just that more like girlfriend look

ZOË [Laughs] Girlfriend look, yeah. They're probably less achievable really, 'cause you kind of think strippers, 'Oh yeah,' you know, 'they're a bit'

AMY Yeah

ZOË 'Oh.' you know, 'anyone can get a stripper.' They're gonna be a bit easy. Whereas burlesque dancers, you're like, 'Oh wow, they're really glamorous, and they're really like untouchable'

AMY Yeah, there's more effort in it. Your average porn star is just like a bit of fake tan, isn't it. And bleached hair and, like, massive tits. And she's [Dita von Teese] like probably takes ages just doing hair and makeup

LAURA And she, there's no way I think she could ever would even ever allow herself
        to walk outside the house with=

ZOË Oh yeah, definitely=

LAURA With like not completely, not completely done. You know, you don't see
        pictures in Heat magazine, of Dita at the coffee shop looking rough. You know,
        in a jumper

[Laughing]

LAURA She just wouldn't got out with a jumper on, she always

ZOË 'Cause that's part of her job isn't it. She has to maintain that

LAURA And, you know, you're like '*Wow*'

ZOË I just wouldn't have the time to do it

On the surface, the burlesque dancers' image, as found on the Internet, was more
attainable than celebrities reproduced in the media. But on closer inspection, every
idealized version of femininity (even the girl next door, the "girlfriend look") was
constructed as hard work and unachievable for the "ordinary" woman. In their talk,
the burlesque dancer was no longer the figure of imperfection and reality; instead,
her bodily performance of femininity became "unobtainable" and "untouchable."
She was displaced by the stripper and the porn star, whose classed consumption
of "fake tan... And bleached hair and, like, massive tits" were deemed easily repli-
cable but undesirable and too sexually available. The fantasy of constant feminine
beauty maintenance that was evident when discussing such "icons" of postfeminist
sentiment produced a tension with the reality of material bodies and the pressures
of contemporary life, in terms of time and money. Furthermore, this extract constructed the existence of neoliberal entrepreneurial careers that required constant
beautification practices that these women could not realistically engage with in the
same way (similar discussions appeared throughout the Belle de Jour meeting). To
quote Zoë, "I just wouldn't have the time to do it."

Such contradictions in the women's talk seemed to highlight the limitations
of postfeminist discourses of the "real" body. Revealing the need to always be
working on the body, in ways that were necessarily uncertain in a context where
mixed messages about body ideals circulate, extract 14 underscored the women's
privileging of the constant pursuit of pleasure, hedonism, and knowledge. And
it undermined the celebratory discourse of bodily imperfection so that all desirable feminine bodies required diligent work. As such, these women's own sexually
discerning identities were always ultimately incomplete and non-agentic; they did
not have the resources to work on beauty constantly, a requirement for truly valued embodied femininity.

In this chapter we have analyzed the dominant discourses of the younger cohort
(25–35) of women—the "pleasure pursuers." In our analysis we have made sense
of their engagement with and take-up of new sexual subjectivities in three ways.
In part 1 we outlined the pursuit of pleasure through the subject position of the
new sexual subject. Here, through the construction of expert sexual consumption,
these women practiced taste, knowledge, and authenticity. The new sexual subject

was demonstrated through these women's ability to "rate" products and by seeking to extend the discursive boundaries of acceptable social attitudes through "shock" and "grotesque." The new sexual subject was also a privileged subject position within an otherwise discursive social space in which the consumption of sexuality was normalized. These women laid claim to a unique and distinctive identity in the context of normalized sexual consumerism by delimiting who could take up this knowledgeable position. We suggest above that both the working-class hen night and the insincere masquerading sexual connoisseur were violently refused participation within these women's constructs of taste, knowledge, and authenticity. These four women thus took pleasure from their engagement with and take up of new sexual subjectivities, but in the process they participated in a form of individualist competition with other women, neutralizing the threat of these women through othering practices.

To further explore this sexually knowledgeable pursuit of pleasure, we sought to analyze the women's constructions of the Ann Summers sex shop space. The second section of this chapter drew on Foucault's concept of heterotopia to analyze the materialization of space, power, and discourse. This theory of space suggests an analysis of how space is practiced as a discursively non-innocent and political construct that makes sense within the broader sociopolitical context of postfeminism and neoliberalism.

As a postfeminist heterotopia, Ann Summers was a space constituted by these women through contradictory discourses that construct the subject in complex ways, producing a heteroglossia of competing meanings. For the women in the focus group, the Ann Summers space reproduced gendered consumption through its construction as safe, hedonistic, and female-friendly. Pleasure was constituted through contrast with the seedy sexual and problematic male sexuality, situated in the space of the traditional sex shop. However, these women challenged this gendered consumption: first, through creating alternative utopian spaces that drew on discourses of masculine seedy sexual consumption; and second, through the construction of gender discrimination and inequality where the "new" man should be afforded equal access to culturally acceptable modes of sexual consumption. But despite this challenge to the gendered expectations of sexual consumption, "safe" and "seedy" were maintained as assumed truth constructs. The women resisted passive feminine sexual subjectivity through their constructions of the sex shop space. But this construction relied on gender binaries (including the figure of the male raincoater) for this spatial reworking to be intelligible. And the women denied access to certain subjects through privilege and "rights" to enter (e.g., they were "dirty" enough, and so could frame Ann Summers as "tame").

The final subsection of this chapter has explored the doubled workings of power and pleasure. Social norms were constituted as opposed to these women's pursuit of pleasure and sexually hedonistic identity constructions. Through the construction of morally conservative societal restrictions and the celebration of bodies that spoke against the "thin" ideal, these women practiced agency as a "kicking against." However, this practice of agency was doubled through the desire to constantly transform the self. Taking up new sexual subjectivities allowed these women to become knowledgeable, righteous, authentic, agentic, boundary pushing, and pleasure-seeking—consumer citizens of sexual consumption par excellence. But this pursuit fell short of the ultimate achievement: the practice of this subject position with the time and money required to maintain itself.

What we have presented in this chapter is just one aspect of how new modes of femininity were constituted by the women in our study—by looking at how the sexualization of culture appeared to provoke the pleasure pursuers into embodying the position of the new sexual subject. And what appeared from this talk was a sassy and confident woman—a self-construction that is daring, hedonistic, exciting, adventurous, and knowlegable. But the benefits gained by this group of women are tempered by certain rights to pleasure.

First, our participants made sense of their sexual subjectivity with reference to other women—and often by excluding other women from the construct of new sexual subjecthood. The technologies these women were drawing on are embedded within a nexus of contemporary and historical gender relations—including what we would identify as a recent refocus of competition with other women. This sense-making also reinforces neoliberal and postfeminist notions of the self, which make the links between femininity and competition stronger. As we identified it in Chapter 1, neoliberalism may be said to priviledge sucessful economic participation and encorage competition through reimagining the self as a "company of one" (Read, 2009). So that in the preceding analysis, we see an individualism that masks inequalities and locates inequalities as a person's own failure. And we witness feminism called into account, in that the pleasure pursuers were performing an expressive femininity. This is something to be celebrated, where these women were imagining new spaces and were attempting to resist sexist assumptions of what women's sexual subjectivity should be. But this was done in a way that negated membership to those who weren't consuming or weren't consuming correctly, and so destroyed any sense of female camaraderie that these new disocurses might otherwise permit.

And second, the pleasure pursuers' sense-making was tempered by the rights to pleasure simply through the logic of postfeminism. In drawing on this sense-making, we have shown how these women then find themselves wanting in comparison to celebrities. Notions of self-transformation managed to make even our new sexual subjects fail in their own identity constuction as always knowledgable and knowing: because they did not have the time and money required for the constant maintenace of new sexual subjectivities.

5

Functioning Feminists

Nostalgia, in fact, may depend precisely on the irrecoverable nature of the past for its emotional impact and appeal. It is the very pastness of the past, its inaccessibility, that likely accounts for a large part of nostalgia's power.... This is rarely the past as actually experienced, of course; it is the past as imagined, as idealized through memory and desire. In this sense, however, nostalgia is less about the past than about the present.

HUTCHEON, *1998, n.p.*

This chapter analyzes the discourses drawn on by our older group of women who, because of their identification with a particular form of feminism, we've called the "functioning feminists." The names given to the four women in this group were Helen, Tessa, Natalie, and Kerry. These women were between the ages of 48 and 54 at the time of the focus group meetings. All were white, identified as heterosexual, and had professional careers in health within the areas of psychology, counseling, and care. Their friendships seemed to be largely based on their related careers, the similar age of their children, and the close proximity of their homes (in a relatively middle-class area of a city in South West England). They strongly identified as middle class (during one meeting, Helen, for example, described herself as "entrenched" middle class, while Tessa called herself "irredeemably" middle class, descriptions that seemed to resonate with the group as a whole). All the women were in a relationship, and all had children in their teens or older.

The women were recruited opportunistically, as an already existing friendship group, interested in taking part in the study, and whose age meant that they were part of a generation who had grown up in the "pre-postfeminist" discursive space of second wave feminism. Following the same procedure as the pleasure pursuers group, our older group meet three times for research purposes to explore their ideas and experiences of contemporary sexiness through cooperative inquiry-inspired focus groups. As part of these meetings, the members of the group were encouraged to explore aspects of the topic that they found significant through individual reflection, group discussions, and individual and group activities set during and between the meetings.

Although these women were not recruited for their feminist positioning, their talk during these focus groups seemed heavily influenced by their identifications with second wave feminism. Second wave feminism therefore functioned as a framework for making sense of their own and others' sexual and feminine identities, thus giving us the title for this group.

In the following analysis we document the women's sense-making in relation to contemporary sexiness in three ways. To position these women within the book, part one of the chapter outlines the general theme of the women's talk. The functioning feminists produced sentiment and nostalgia for a romanticized historical feminist informed sexual identity, which they constituted as more politically motivated than contemporary female sexualities. Their construction of nostalgic feminist modes of consumption allowed these women to position authentic "real" sexuality as historically viable. Contemporary forms of femininity, by comparison, were constituted as cold, mechanical, inauthentic and—above all—consumerist. These accounts of new sexual subjectivities were embedded within a highly emotive framework, so that our older participants were moved into "feeling" by sexualization discourses, and spoke about these feelings very passionately.

We use the second section of this chapter to explore these feelings by drawing on concepts of affective technologies of the self as analytics for making sense of the identity management these women engaged in as a response to the sexualized media and culture. We explore the way that threat and anxiety were their central responses to postfeminist consumer culture, and how they managed this threat through a process of othering (younger) women and a policing of each other around potentially complicit statements. These affective modes of being seemed to tighten the hold of nostalgic feminism, making it virtually impossible to consider engaging in contemporary culture as an authentic act that closed down alternative ways of understanding the self.

Following the structure of our pleasure pursers' analysis (Chapter 4), the third section of this chapter explores the ruptures in the functioning feminists' sense-making. Here we explore these women's most ideal ethical individualities and "good" feminist selves by looking at the unexpected consequences of the nostalgic feminist subject position, and the difficulties of policing other women that this subject position entailed. The women's feminist values seemed challenged by the consumption of goods that did—at first glance—conform to these women's feminist values. We explore vibrator ownership as an example, showing where the women's feminist selves and contemporary consumer-oriented femininities coalesced. In doing so, we show where the ways these women were constructing themselves through various technologies of the self were undone, as well as the potential discursive spaces from which to open up (and shut down) alternative ways of seeing the self.

PART 1: ALL IN THE PAST: HISTORY, FEMINISM, NOSTALGIA

This section introduces the functioning feminists by considering the way that these women created authentic identities by drawing on constructs of history, feminism, and nostalgia. These themes underlie the ways the functioning feminists made sense of contemporary forms of sexiness, and help make sense of the tensions within these women's discussions. For our older group of participants, the right way to produce sexual identity was constituted through the subject position of the "feminist" and the construction of "real" gritty sexual experience. These modes of femininity were always positioned as a historical possibility of nostalgic and melancholic remembering. This nostalgic remembering worked to effectively cut off any possibility of authenticity in today's consumer-mediated culture. In this context, contemporary expressions of sexiness—with their lack of history, feminist ethic, or romantic sentiment—were set in apparent contrast to what these women valued.

Nostalgic Feminism

Our older group of women identified with historically situated sexual identities in two ways. First, these women drew on a historically nostalgic account that constructed their own youthful sexual identities as feminist and authentic. Authenticity was bestowed by locating their youthful identities historically within the sexual revolution of the 1960s and 1970s, which enabled them to construct sexual identities in the past as meaningful because they were complex, political, and, as it were, uncorrupted by consumerism.

A second way that these women bestowed authenticity on previous eras' sexual identities was by drawing on a discourse of sexual realism. "Real" sex occurred in these women's talk in accounts of gritty (but nonetheless innocent) working-class media representations and in personal anecdotes of sexual awakening set against a backdrop of the bleakness of the 1970s and 1980s. What appeared from the women's talk was a heady mixture of innocence, naiveté, gritty reality, political depth, and sexual importance. Such talk of sexual historical identities became the emotionally charged ideal and discursive framing against which to assess sexuality in the present as always falling short. What emerged in our analysis, then, was a "nostalgic feminist," a position we explore next, before going on to outline some of the functions of taking up this subject position given that it positions authentic sexuality as only possible during a point in time that has already passed.

Feminism: The Lost Paradigm

In making sense of their own youthful sexual identities, our older group of participants celebrated their participation in the sexual revolution during the 1970s, and its folding in with feminist ideals, new ideas for women's roles within society, attempts at radical reform, and the fun of scandalizing the older generation. This sense-making allowed our participants to place their youthful selves as having political weight, so that their sexual subjectivities were constructed as tied to historical political identifications that lent them authenticity. For example, in the following two extracts, Tessa created a nostalgic image of herself in her youth. In the first of these extracts, Tessa does this by calling on all the women in the group to locate themselves at a distance from postfeminist modes of sexuality.

Extract 1

TESSA I'm just wondering if it's, if we could agree. Maybe we can't agree. That when we were young, um, sexuality giving having sex had had had a different, for many people had a different, was not just about having fun. It was about, uh something that was more, um, complicated. It was about liberation and it was about giving something away and it was about being different to your mother. And it was about a different paradigm.

In this extract, Tessa contrasts sexualities that are "just about having fun" with historically located sexualities that are complex and are associated with a politicized social change agenda of liberation and rebellion. In the process, she calls for and lays claim to a collective feeling of difference between the women in this group and the (implied) younger generation, so that while she discursively offers the opportunity for the other women to disagree with her, she does so within a set of constructs in which disagreement would have been to accept an inauthentic and frivolous sexuality. The effect is to construct and contrast a specific, historically located sexuality as authentic and meaningful through being politicized, in contrast to contemporary sexualities that are devoid of political meaning.

The older group of participants idealized their historical sexuality, in contrast with anything that had gone before or after, through repertoires of "paradigms" and "uncovered territory." For example, the construction of a history of "paradigms" in this extract made it possible for Tessa to construct sexuality as a series of historically contingent ideas, distinct and contrastable from each other. In this paradigmatic shift of perspective, contemporary sexuality is constructed as being about "fun"; the sexual revolution sexuality of Tessa's generation is defined as something different, complicated, and authentic; and the sexuality of the previous generations, in turn, is construed as something else (which is not, in this extract, given definition, other than to be associated their mothers, and perhaps we can surmise from the following discussion, as something other than free). Constructing sexuality in this way allows Tessa to position the functioning feminists as effectively having done something "different": from those only out to have fun and from their mothers before them.

Tessa places her and the group's understanding of sexuality as a historical magical moment between the changing roles of women, in contrast to their own mothers' identities, on the one hand, and to current consumer-oriented contemporary femininity, on the other. These women thus positioned contemporary young women's sexual femininities as categorically different from those of their youth because contemporary young women were not considered to have an agentic, political, social change agenda.

Extract 2

TESSA I think the, why one thought one was doing it [sex] in the seventies was totally different to why people think they're doing it now. In that, I as, I remember walking the streets of [small town, Southern England]. You know very nice, uh, very nice sort of moderate hippie gear with no shoes on and a scarf wrapped round my head and a long dress on…It was all about, it was about peace and love. It was about radical politics…You know you weren't gonna wear bloody shoes because you wanted to scandalise people. And you wanted to be flowing and beautiful=

NATALIE And free

TESSA Free and, you know, Fairport Convention or whatever. And it had a completely, and it was about taking the power of your sexuality.

In extract 2, Tessa again contrasts contemporary sexuality with that of her youth. She relates a memory of her youthful self, tying in her hippie appearance to a politics of peace, love, and freedom, which in turn is tied into a politicized, agentic sexual identity. She offers us an image of herself as a "nice" and "moderate hippie": an image that seems to need upgrading, with its subsequent association with "radical politics," so that a moment of her youth is given sexual authenticity through its political orientation to second wave feminism, while being vividly evoked through clothes, music, and the unconventional act of not wearing shoes.

Extract 2 reproduced a romantic view of 1970s counter-culture, such as having a focus on radical politics, peace, and love, and of understanding sex as a form of power to be (re)claimed through this political framework. This romanticized image was used as a counter to contemporary understandings of sexuality. Tessa's description of sexuality in the past as "totally different to why people think they're doing it now" is taken as self-evident. But, while it is not articulated explicitly in the extracts we have presented, we will show that what emerges as the impasse for authentic contemporary sexual identities is their association with consumption.

We analyze the accounts drawn on by the functioning feminists as technologies of a feminist storytelling, tied into the premature death of feminism that positions the teller as having access to a time of political depth (Hemmings, 2005). The women in this group were able to claim the loss of this historically enabled identity moment, binding themselves together through nostalgia in the face of the "death" of the feminist paradigm (Hawkesworth, 2004). And, in the way that loss can be experienced as ambivalent, these women described a sexuality optimistically identical to progressive politics, but located this progressiveness as only possible in the past (Berlant, 2011; Hesford, 2005; Jagose, 2010). We would suggest that this death of the (second wave) feminist paradigm was experienced as a "haunting" in the sense that it was "felt rather than comprehended" (Hesford,

2005, p. 230). That is to say, these women's accounts were often contradictory about the history of feminism, for while there was a feeling of feminism in the room when these women spoke, we would argue that their talk was sometimes not in keeping with the ethics of second wave feminism (for example, in these women's praise of romantic relationships and the need to give "something away").

The concept of "haunting" has been seen as liberatory, as haunting implies a "something-to-be-done" (Hesford, 2005; Gordon, 2008). But, in exploring the effects of this talk, we analyze our participants' relationships with the "dead feminism" they describe as more melancholic than liberatory. To proclaim one's "paradigm" as dead had two effects within these women's discourses. First, nostalgia refused to acknowledge the historical progression between feminism and postfeminism: as though to say, "it's nothing to do with us." This sense-making thus denied any alliances between older and younger women in their attempts at developing their own agentic, powerful sexualities.[1] Second, by always positioning authentic sexuality as part of a bygone era, the feminist subject position was resolutely denied within the current cultural landscape. These two effects of the functioning feminists' ways of speaking were further supported by another historical locating of authentic sex, this time in the 1970s and 1980s in contexts that often contradicted these women's identification with feminism, but which served to define authentic sex as incompatible with contemporary forms of consumer-oriented sexiness. The functioning feminists were thus able to construct their nostalgia and historical location of authentic sexuality through how they constituted consumption, placing the right way to consume sexuality firmly in the past. We explore the locations that these women identified as authentic sex in the following section, demonstrating how these articulations make sense within the framework of a left melancholia (Brown 1999).

Authentic Sex

The functioning feminist's representations of the gritty and the "real" were often used in contrast to today's polished stylization and glamorous consumer-oriented femininity. For example, in extract 3 the women discussed the film *Rita, Sue and Bob Too* (1986). The film depicts the story of two working-class girls from a run-down estate in Bradford in the United Kingdom. In the film the two girls enter into a sexual relationship with a married man for whom they have been babysitting. The film *Rita, Sue and Bob Too* may be seen as an odd film for these women to celebrate. First, these women's socioeconomic positioning as "entrenched middle class" would make this representation of sexuality difficult for these women to inhabit, or at least difficult for these women to speak about as part of their own construct of sexual authenticity (although see extract 4). But also some of the

---

1. Despite the pleasure pursuers' celebration of themselves as active, different, and sexually agentic, which we could imagine would fulfill some of the functioning feminists' desires for young women.

film's misogynistic depictions of gender relations in the 1980s could have provoked critique from these women, rather than commendation.

However, the use of the film *Rita, Sue and Bob Too* in the extract can be comparable with the pleasure pursuers' use of the Internet meme *Two Girls, One Cup* in the previous chapter (see part one of Chapter 4). As with *Two Girls, One Cup*, the functioning feminists' discussion of *Rita, Sue and Bob Too* was used to delineate and define what was authentic. Similarities in the sense-making of both groups was evident, since neither used these visual texts to navigate sexual pleasure; instead, they were made significant by allowing the participants to locate themselves as authentic and knowing consumers of images, of the past or the present, respectively. These visual texts thus functioned in terms of claims to knowledge. But what made *Rita, Sue and Bob Too* different from *Two Girls, One Cup* was the film's representation of the unknowing subject as an indication of its authenticity.

Extract 3

HELEN What's the film on the telly that I saw recently? Well probably a year ago now, I don't know, time goes by so quickly. And it was these two women who were living in an estate in Yorkshire walking to baby-sit in this house, and then, it's a famous film, and then they baby-sit, and then the couple come back from baby-sitting and the man takes the two women off to have sex with them

[

TESSA Oh Harry met Sally, no no, you know

[

NATALIE No no its not

TESSA Bill, Bill, Jill, and Sue, too

NATALIE Yes yes

TESSA Sue, Jill, Fred, and Bill, too, four people's names

NATALIE Yes, yes, four people's names, but we're not sure what the names are

TESSA Rita

[Sounds of agreement]

NATALIE Yes Rita's one of them. That's it, yeah. Rita's one of them

ADY I I have never heard of it

HELEN The thing about that film is when I saw it, I can't remember when it was, um, but that's more credible than Belle de Jour to me

TESSA Yeah

NATALIE *Yeah*. Of course it was because there was more emotion

[

TESSA   More credible. And more real

HELEN Yes. It was set in Yorkshire, it was these Yorkshire lasses, you know, with this guy and they fancied him and they wanted, they didn't know what sex was about, and they wanted to find out

[

TESSA And they drove off and they shagged

HELEN They did fancy him and they were gonna find out and they did. One sat in the back of the car, one in the front, and they both got fucked, you know, and they were then they sort of, you know, it was like=

NATALIE Cause it was more honest wasn't it

HELEN Well it was somehow, it was more *real*

NATALIE Yeah. And more live

HELEN You know, yeah, and more emotion. And there was something something quite=

NATALIE Excitement. Yeah

HELEN Yeah, it was alright, it was just alright

NATALIE But it was emotion, there was some emotion

In the extract above *Rita, Sue and Bob Too* was held up as representing a "real" and emotionally authentic sexual encounter. Helen hails this historical mode, noting how in her own life "time goes by so quickly." Helen's discussion of the film led the women to collectively identify the film, which is variously described as "more real," "more honest," "more credible," and having "more emotion." Used in contrast to the contemporary narrative of high-class prostitution in Belle de Jour, the gritty reality of *Rita, Sue and Bob Too* in which the "Yorkshire lasses...both got fucked" was deemed more "credible" through the film's attributes of emotion, honesty, and excitement.

We would suggest that what the women find more authentic about this representation of sex is in the working-class cultural location of the film. The women's construction of historical working-class femininity in this extract fits in more broadly with a social discourse in which the working-class subject is depicted erotically for the purpose of authenticity. A classic example of this discourse is represented in the sexual relationship between the working-class Oliver Mellors and Lady Chatterley in *Lady Chatterley's Lover* (see Johnson, 2008, for more examples). The working classes are imagined as unmediated, unhindered, and uninhibited by their innate sexual drives and unable to control themselves. In contrast to the uptight civilized bourgeois subject, working-class sexual expressions of identity are deemed more genuine (Johnson, 2008).

In our participants' talk, the working-class figures of Rita and Sue were more authentic not only because of their uninhibited working-class sexuality, but also their naiveté and the simplicity of their attraction to Bob: they "didn't know what sex was about and they wanted to find out." In contrast to the knowing sexuality of the postfeminist narrative of high-class prostitution represented in the best-selling memoir by Belle de Jour, Rita and Sue's historically unknowledgeable and uninhibited working-class sexual subject positions are constructed as all the more genuine and legitimate.

But this characterizing of working-class sexuality as authentic sexuality was historically located and did not get translated across to contemporary representations of the working class. The naiveté, unknowingness, and lack of consumer-oriented sexuality in *Rita, Sue and Bob Too* set these characters apart from more recent discourses of working-class sexuality, whose erotics are tied into notions of excessive consumption (Johnson, 2008; Skeggs, 2005), or, as Kerry in our group described it, who engage in consumer practices that leave them "looking like prostitutes."

Contemporary working-class sexuality was thus not valorized, nor did it hold attraction for our functioning feminists, who did not want to see their imaginary sex shops in working-class areas like the main shopping precinct (although in a very self-aware way, as Tessa says, "when I'm thinking of my perfect sex shop, *I'm not thinking* of that sex shop being in Little Street at all. I'm thinking of it being down by the Theater... [laughs] and that's *so bourgeois* isn't it. That's so, um, you know, um, irredeemably middle class about me"). For the functioning feminists, the authenticity of the working-class subjects depicted in films such as *Rita, Sue and Bob Too* came to represent a "return as the objects of nostalgia, longing and fascination" (Stallybrass and White, 1986, p. 191). Authentic sex was thus located in the past—and, importantly, a past that was not consumer-oriented.

The account of the authentic sexual experience represented by *Rita, Sue and Bob Too* was considered significant enough to be returned to later in the focus group discussion. In returning to the "realness" represented by the film, Tessa was then reminded of her time as a university student in the 1970s, which she retells to the group as an anecdote regarding her own "gritty" and authentic sexual experience.

Extract 4

TESSA I was sharing a room with this girl from the valleys [a rural working class area of Wales] with black hair. And, um, sweet girl. And, um, and I didn't know her at all. And I was a [Humanities] degree student at that time and, um. And we were both virgins. And then one night I had to go to the loo through the kitchen, and the loo was outside. It was a real sort of damps-worth sort of house. And I went through the kitchen, and there she was having sex with this guy on a chair. And she looked at me, and I just walked passed her like, "Oh my god, what"s going on.' And she said "Aw, Tess," she said, "He's got a *stonking* hard on.'

[Laughing]

TESSA And it was just really [laughs]

NATALIE Nice

TESSA Just thought, *yes.* Wahay

NATALIE Honest

TESSA Yeah yeah

       [

HELEN Completely. That's just fine, you know

TESSA [Laughs]

NATALIE Yes

HELEN That's all right. There's something fine about that cause it's real

In the extract above, Tessa used the group's recent authentification of gritty sexual experience in *Rita Sue and Bob Too* to recount an anecdote of sexual awakening from her own youth. What is highly evident in the extract above are the discursive techniques and work put in by Tessa to set the scene. The information provided about Tessa's old roommate includes details on the nationality (and class, given the rural and working-class context of "the valleys" in Wales), hair color, and temperament. All this work is then followed up by an act of distancing: "I didn't know her at all."

The story above was made willfully downbeat; it occurred on her way to "the loo...outside," creating an image of the kind of house without indoor toilets, which is reinforced with her description of it as a "damps-worth sort of house." Here Tessa witnessed the couple having sex "on a chair." And again, innocence and the unknowingness of the situation took center stage—"we were both virgins." There was simplicity; the man had a "stonking hard on" and his sexual desire was met. The recounted anxiety experienced as part of Tessa's youthful stumbling across the copulating couple—"Oh my god, what's going on"—was diffused in the context of the focus group through the use of humor. It was an unexpected witnessing of a sexual incident in a non-commercial, commonplace, and modest space within the historical context of Tessa's youth. The mundane and unmediated incorruptibility of the situation as recounted by Tessa allows the group collectively (in their interjections and comments) to construct the experience as "real" and "honest."

As well as the pleasure in remembering developing sexual identities, what struck us about how these women talked about their history was the way it was used to undermine the present. In their historicizing there was no desire to return to the past, no call for it to be reinvigorated, but only a nostalgic longing for the past. In Brown's (1999) discussion of the melancholy of the political Left, she describes this backward-looking attachment to feeling as a form of narcissism in which the Left comes to terms with the present by remembering the past nostalgically, with the effect of immobilizing political action in the present. Drawing on Brown's (1999) theorizing of this left melancholy, and replacing the "Left" with "feminism," we could argue that within these women's formations was:

> a [feminism] that has become more attached to its impossibility than to its potential fruitfulness, a [feminism] that is most at home dwelling not in hopefulness but in its own marginality and failure, a [feminism] that is thus caught in a structure of melancholic attachment to a certain strain of its own dead past, whose spirit is ghostly, whose structure of desire is backward looking and punishing. (Brown, 1999, p. 26)

But as Brown (2003) argues, in proclaiming feminism dead, the dead feminism (which for our participants was a particular version of second wave feminism) still rules in this moment, so that we interpret the functioning feminists as having "more than a minor attachment to the unhappy present" (p. 4). What seemed to trap these women into this "unhappy" present was how the framework of what we could call a "nostalgic feminism" allowed our participants to construct their own (historical) sexualities as agentic and authentic, in comparison to contemporary young women who engage in non-politicized consumer-oriented sexiness (despite there being a historical relationship between feminism and consumerism see Scott, 2005, for an overview). This meant that there was satisfaction to be gained from their melancholy, allowing them a privileged place in comparison to contemporary young women.

But by insisting on the past as the space for authentic sexuality, these older women's sexual subjectivities were fixed historically. There was little talk by these women of their own contemporary sexuality, as people living today—that is, little in the way of thinking about being sexy now or being older, sexy women. And any talk that discursively moved their sexual identities into the present without this sense of nostalgia was effectively policed within their group interaction. But before we discuss this process of policing, we first turn to the role of consumerism in delineating authentic (historical) sexuality in contrast to contemporary femininity.

The Pac-Man of Goodness

The nostalgic feminist can be seen as an anxious and uncertain response to a modern era defined by a sentiment of "modernization." Our analysis of the functioning feminists resonates with Hutcheon's description of feelings of nostalgia in the contemporary moment, where the "simple, pure, ordered, easy, beautiful, or harmonious past is constructed (and then experienced emotionally) in conjunction with the present—which, in turn, is constructed as complicated, contaminated, anarchic, difficult, ugly, and confrontational" (1998, n.p.). For the pleasure pursuers in the previous chapter, the authenticity of their sexual identities was enabled through claims to knowledge and a comparison with those who'd gotten sexiness wrong because of "bad" (working-class or inauthentic) consumer practices. But for our functioning feminist group, sexual authenticity in the current cultural context was constituted as simply impossible and unimaginable—not because certain people had gotten their consumption wrong, but because everyone was a consumer and consumerism was wrong. So that, like the abjection of working-class and inauthentic consumers from the identity position of the new sexual subject, the functioning feminists expelled contemporary consumer identities from their own. For example:

Extract 5

TESSA Well it's [sexuality's] happening in a different environment where things are much more commercialised, commodified
    [
NATALIE Yes it's the commercialisation of it isn't it, *yeah*
TESSA And capitalised
NATALIE *Yes.* Like capitalism's taken over everything hasn't it. That's how it feels to me. Capitalism has to do, has to do, demands, demands a new product all the time
    [

TESSA Yeah, capitalism, yeah

   [

NATALIE Yeah, like "what can we sell"

TESSA Capitalism's hideous really=

NATALIE "What can we sell now"

TESSA Capitalism's like a bloody great munching, you know, Pac-Man or something that sort of devours everything that's good, you know, I just think it's
really, it's really very cynical. And that makes me sad

[Sounds of agreement]

In extract 5, contemporary culture was positioned as "different" from the wom-
en's historically authentic identities because of the all-encompassing and saturating
commodification of everyday life. The anthropomorphic all-powerful capitalism
was never satisfied—it was actively voiced as insistent, "what can we sell...what
can we sell now." Capitalism was able to take on a force of its own; it was able to
"demand." As a metaphorical Pac-Man, iconic of Thatcherite 1980s popular culture and one of the most recognizable brands in the globalized commercial world,
capitalism "munched" its way through "everything that's good." In the women's
construction of this destructive ideology of capitalism, they placed their own historical identities as occurring in an environment before such commercialization;
the women are positioned as watching over the devastation from their own position of nostalgic remembering, and not located in this ideology of capitalism.

The women's construction of a "cynical" capitalism was set against their construction of sexuality in the past. Given the passion and emotional intensity with
which they spoke about this ideology of capitalism, we might expect expressions
of anger or a call to arms of the feminist and anti-capitalist discourses that these
women were using to narrate their emotions. However, the critique of capitalism
became "sad" and we are left with questions about why this emotional response is
so downgraded.

We suggest that one answer lies with Brown's (1999) discussion of left melancholia, in which she suggests that the state of melancholia represents a loss of the
prospect of utopia; "gone is the belief in radically breaking with history; equally
eviscerated is the notion of inexorable progress towards freedom and the related
notion that an innate human desire for freedom is the engine of history. Shattered
too is the conviction that...power, is ever anything but illegitimate" (2003, p. 6).
Reading the functioning feminist's discussions in light of this left melancholia, we
could suggest that despite the ways these women's sense-making seem liberal and
politically oriented, the effect of these ways of speaking stalls any ability to envis-
age contemporary feminist activism. Because these women located feminism in
a sentimentalized past, their melancholy for their feminism refused feminism in
the present. As Benjamin, who first described left melancholia, suggests, "[n]ever
have such comfortable arrangements been made in such an uncomfortable situation" (Benjamin, 1974, p. 30).

In line with our use of Brown's (1999) left melancholia, we would suggest that a
more contemporary politically oriented response would mean that these women

would have to relinquish some of their authority on the discourses of feminism and anti-capitalism. Giving away their feminist identity, and allowing it to proliferate among a new generation of feminist women, would mean that these women no longer held on to the present as a means of creating an authentic identity for themselves; feminism, as they experienced it, would really be dead, in the sense that they would no longer be its main proponents.

The seeming incompatibility of authentic sexuality and consumer-oriented sexiness so powerfully described in extract 5 made the practice of feminist cultural production difficult, if not irreconcilable, in the current cultural context. This was further evident, for example, in some of the women's discussions of vibrators (although their talk around vibrators was also highly complex, at one moment a symbol of feminist liberation, and at other times tied to consumerism and contemporary femininity—we unpack this in the final section of this chapter). First though, we discuss the next extract, which followed a discussion between Helen and Tessa on the availability of vibrators in their youth. The feminist DIY magazine *Spare Rib* was called upon as an appropriately historically located and feminist means of consuming sexuality, and had at one time apparently provided a vibrator as a free gift with the magazine. But the incompatibility between feminism and consumerism was evoked to ultimately question *Spare Rib* on its authenticity and credibility once the women considered the magazines' relationship with capitalism.

Extract 6

HELEN I'm sure it [vibrator ownership] did [happen] but I I never heard about it. I was a good Catholic girl. Um, anyway I wasn't aware of any of it. Spare Rib was the only one. Do you know the magazine Spare Rib?

ADY Mm yeah

TESSA Yeah Spare Rib was pretty good about that sort of thing weren't they, they were quite

HELEN Mm

TESSA But then of course it got taken over by so-called the other side and and capitalism gone mad and [coughs] suddenly Spare Rib were terribly snooty about things like that

HELEN Mm

TESSA I think written more for capitalism rather than sexuality. Or maybe more aesthetic reasons, I don't know, probably more to do with money and business maybe

In this extract, Helen and Tessa discussed the coverage of vibrators in *Spare Rib* magazine. Here innocence again became something to lay claim to, as Helen positioned her youthful identity as having been "a good Catholic girl." This meant that Helen was able to both deny an awareness of vibrator ownership in presenting an authentic sexual identity within these women's logic of authenticity, and also presented herself as genuinely feminist in having known that *Spare Rib* provided a means to acquire a vibrator, while also positioning the younger researcher as potentially outside this (older women's) feminist discussion, as someone who may not be aware of the magazine.

Spare Rib was initially constituted as a means of engaging in authentic and desirable feminist consumption. But the positivity with which these women initially constructed *Spare Rib* was tarnished through its relationship with capitalism. Tessa called the authenticity of the magazine into question, claiming that it was "taken over by so-called the other side and and capitalism gone mad."

In the previous extract, capitalism was identified as a consuming and destructive Pac-Man. Adding another layer to this reviled image, capitalism in extract 6 was constructed as wholly opposed to the side of feminism and through pathological discourses of madness. Tessa's description of *Spare Rib*'s move to "the other side" so that it then becomes written "more for capitalism rather than sexuality" articulates a clear dichotomy between capitalism and feminist sexuality. Her talk thus constructed capitalism and feminist sexuality as incompatible. Within this logic it becomes impossible to maintain authentic feminist sexuality within a capitalist framework, a form of sense-making that delegitimizes new sexual subjectivities, which, as demonstrated earlier, are constructed by this group as embedded within consumption and capitalism (see for example, extract 5).

The analysis thus far has explored the dominant ways that this group of women spoke about authentic sexuality and how their talk functioned to negate contemporary forms of female sexuality through the discourses of history, feminism, and nostalgia. Authentic sexuality for these women was located in the past—it was in their ownership of the feminist counterculture of the 1970s and in the gritty realism of mundane historical representation through film and personal experience. Within these accounts, unknowingness, innocence, naiveté, and the pure and unmediated identity were privileged. This authentic sexual identity, mediated through history, feminism, and nostalgia, was a contradiction: complicated and simple, politically goal-oriented and unknowing, liberatory and conservative— but what held this sense-making together was the tying in of historically authentic sexualities with non-consumerism.

The functioning feminists variously appealed to emotion in both what they spoke about and the way they spoke it. We have suggested earlier that one way to make sense of this emotion is to recognize its hauntingly melancholic character, and to understand it as fixing these women in place as having some agency in the current social context of sexiness by virtue of these women's nostalgia. But, this nostalgia nevertheless refutes any attempt to revive feminism as a paradigm and meaningful critique, given its inherent incompatibility with the contemporary landscape. This melancholia and its nostalgic place in the past left the functioning feminists "functionally crippled" (Reiss, 1983, cited in Hutcheon, 1998), apparently unable to imagine their current selves as authentic sexual beings and unable to identify or celebrate with a younger generation. For if authentic sexuality was located in the past and outside consumer culture, how could the functional feminists make sense of women who do take up contemporary sexual subjectivities, other than to problematize them? In part two of our analysis of these women's talk, we explore this problematization and ask: What are the identity-effects for older women in making sense of younger women in this way?

PART 2: POSTFEMINIST CONSUMER CULTURE AS THE ABJECT

In the following analysis we map the ways in which the women in the focus group managed their feminist identity. If the way these women spoke about the past was through a nostalgic feminism, characterized as melancholic in its refusal of the present, then contemporary postfeminist consumer culture was treated as the threatening abject that meant there was no way back to the past. There was a general expression of anger, dismay, and sadness by the women in the focus group about the emergence of consumer-oriented sexualized femininity. In exploring how contemporary postfeminist (hetero)sexualities were problematized, we first show the way that these women saw icons of postfeminist culture as inherently anti-feminist. Second, we explore how the threat that this anti-feminism represented was managed through placing themselves as different from young women. We argue that young women represented the threat of exclusion, to which the functioning feminists responded by holding young women at a distance, while equally showing a desire to understand. As in the pleasure pursuers accounts in Chapter 4, we thus identify a process of othering in women's negotiations with postfeminism, but for the functioning feminists, we read an abjection of postfeminist consumer culture in relation to left melancholia to explore the exclusions, boundaries, and ruptures that the emergence of a postfeminist consumer culture engenders.

The anger that these women felt toward postfeminist consumer culture was particularly evident in their discussions of Belle de Jour's *The Intimate Adventures of a London Call Girl*. One of the pre-meeting activities had been to read this text, which sits within a contemporary boom in the publication and controversy surrounding "erotic fiction" for women (e.g., *Girl With a One Track Mind*, *The Sexual Life of Catherine M.*, *One Hundred Strokes of the Brush before Bed*, *Wetlands*, *Fifty Shades of Grey*). *The Intimate Adventures of a London Call Girl* began as a blog in 2003 and documented the high-class prostitution of its author, Belle de Jour (later revealed in 2009 as Brooke Magnanti). The blog was subsequently turned into a series of books (*The Intimate Adventures of a London Call Girl* and *The Further Adventures of a London Call Girl*) and a television dramatization (*The Secret Diary of a Call Girl*, ITV; Showtime). The franchising of this story of high-class prostitution was noteworthy for the speculation that the narrative attracted in relation to the author's anonymity.

For the functioning feminists, who were discussing Belle de Jour before her identity was revealed, the narrative of high-class prostitution provoked an anxiety over the loss of feminism. The women's identification with feminism became more steadfast in the context of this account of prostitution, providing a space to reaffirm what they found disruptive in contemporary culture. For these women, Belle de Jour became a figurehead of contemporary forms of youthful female sexuality and a threat to their feminist values, so that the emotions that moved these women when discussing this book were also able to hold them in place as those with a genuine feminist identity (Ahmed, 2004). For example, in extract 7, Belle de Jour was positioned as a central protagonist and ally to anti-feminist practices.

Extract 7

NATALIE And if we say like after feminism, why do we still have so much domestic abuse. Well *why not when there's all this going on*
[General agreement]
NATALIE So that's what I feel. I just feel like, and that's why I'm sad about it
HELEN And I do think, you know, there is this whole culture of misogyny that is so endemic in our society
NATALIE Well this [*Intimate Adventures of a London Call Girl*] is part of it, isn't it
    [
HELEN And this is *absolutely* part of it

The women in the focus group regularly drew upon the critique of a sexualization of culture through feminist expert discourses of patriarchy, misogyny, and objectification. In extract 7, the women practiced the "kicking against" of an assumed dominant discourse (Foucault, 1976). In a position of watching over the "culture of misogyny," Natalie called on the emotionally charged nature of domestic abuse. Indeed, as a rhetorical strategy, the discourse of violence against women positioned the character of Belle de Jour as beyond reprimand—linked to domestic abuse in such a way, it would be impossible to celebrate a woman who colluded in the maintenance of such a practice. Belle de Jour was positioned as "absolutely part of" the saturating culture of misogyny, and as such was constructed as relinquishing liberatory feminist politics—a position that could only generate negative emotion from those of a "truly" feminist identity. Here, feminism (and, as such, their own subjectivity) was depicted as something in the past, having failed in the light of characters such as Belle de Jour. It was not the emergence of patriarchy but the loss of feminism that was provoked by Belle de Jour and the sexualized culture that she came to represent.

The most emotive account, however, appeared when the women began to discuss the practice of genital hair removal. In the following extract, the relationships between the sexualization of young girls and Belle de Jour's beauty practice of genital hair removal was linked ferociously to the reproductions of patriarchy.

Extract 8

TESSA But what that says to me, is it says, power and control, *men over young girls*
    [bangs hands on table]
NATALIE *Yes*, because that's what they all=

TESSA Young girls who are too young to have pubic hair
Natalie Yeah
Tessa That is what's really sick about the dominant discourse today, it's about
  pedophilia
  [
HELEN I couldn't agree more
NATALIE It is about pedophilia
HELEN Yes
TESSA Because men, the backlash against feminism is because men are not pre-
  pared to be, in their eyes, controlled by women
HELEN So they'll be, so they go for the younger women
  [
NATALIE Little girls yeah
TESSA So they, the dominant discourse is about [bangs hands on table again] look-
  ing as young you can. And if that means you look twelve, great
NATALIE The younger the better
TESSA It's sickening really isn't it
KERRY Really isn't it
HELEN I was actually quite horrified

In the extract above, Belle de Jour and the practice of genital hair removal are described as "sick," with these women making sense of this sickness in relation to a broader culture of sexism. As with the construction of Belle de Jour as a woman who represented the continuation of violence against women, the drawing of Belle de Jour into the discourses of pedophilia constituted a distancing: an "exaggerated affect that comes with the reflex urgency of the wish to divide the self from the other" (Hook, 2006, p. 11). In the extract, the "exaggerated affect" and the "reflex urgency" of Tessa's repeated banging on the table was here testament to the extent to which Belle de Jour disrupted these women's identities, followed by further repetitions of how much this situation disgusted them. Terms are used to keep the affect going—"little girls," "and if that means you look twelve, great," "the younger the better." Constructed as a move toward acceptable "corporate pedophilia" through the beauty-complex, Belle de Jour's beauty practices were figured as both pressuring women to represent themselves as "young girls," while encouraging a particularly vilified sexual and "patriarchal" practice. To speak in the way that Belle de Jour did was therefore constituted as a doubled violence toward women, both physically and emotionally.

Tessa's use of "the backlash" discourse draws on a top-down theory of power in which "men are not prepared to be...controlled by women" and so have imposed the beauty practice of genital hair removal in order to reinscribe their own dominance over women. In this way, although the pedophile was still within the larger social discourse of disgust, the figure of the pedophile was not positioned as an abnormality in the women's talk. Here, instead, the pedophile was representative of all men's desire to maintain power over women.

The women in the focus group also compared their own nostalgic construction of sexuality in the past with their interpretation of what the Belle de Jour account represented of contemporary culture. For example, in the following extract, the women began by discussing how relationships were organized in their youth. Relationships in the past were constructed as romantic and relational. Comparing this idealized construction with Belle de Jour, the women in the focus group drew on an image of autoeroticism with inanimate objects to create a figure of postfeminist subjectivity of narcissistic selfish individualism, disgust, and degradation.

Extract 9

HELEN It was about commitment as well on a certain level

TESSA And it was about in intimacy and expecting something

HELEN Mm mm

TESSA Whereas this, the Belle de Jour dominant discourse about relationships between men and women isn't about intimacy, it's not about love

    [

NATALIE Nothing about intimacy

TESSA That word that intimate is such a lie isn't it

HELEN Yeah

TESSA It couldn't be *less intimate*

HELEN No it isn't intimate

TESSA It's like having a blimming, you know, bottle and wanking into it. I mean it just hasn't got any intimacy at all, by my definition of intimacy

In this extract, the women compared two forms of relationships: the intimate, committed, and loving relational relationship (see Illouz, 2012; Wetherell, 1995) and a sexually cold, mechanical, and detached relationship with the self. There was a stark contrast in which these ideas were described, and the powerful way in which the non-intimacy of contemporary relationships was depicted through a sexual act with an inanimate object intentionally aroused abject feeling. (This description of autoeroticism also appears to impersonate a controversial incident on the reality television program *Big Brother 6, UK* (2005), which received hundreds of complaints to Ofcom after contestant Kinga Karolczak simulated sex with a wine bottle).

It would be wrong to call the act described in extract 9 "autoerotic." Indeed, the very notion of "wanking" into a bottle worked doubly in this extract. It was both a metaphor of the anti-relationship, and discredited—through the reference to a bottle—any "erotic" sentiment of postfeminist consumer culture. The likeness of the anti-relationship to a container, a bottle, brings to mind the liquid and fluid of bodily functions to make the act appear disgusting (Kristeva, 1982; Tyler, 2009). There are alternative discourses that could have been drawn on in order to construct this narrative. For example, the women could have discussed the pleasures and politics of masturbation and the analysis of power imbalances within the heterosexual relationship evident in many feminist critiques—which they do draw on at times, see Autoerotic Paradox. But in this instance what was more important—and urgent—in the extract was the dis-identification with postfeminism through the construction of a symbolically dirty, degrading, and emotionally inhuman sexual act (Ringrose and Walkerdine, 2008). Both groups draw on a postfeminist discourse to make sense of Belle de Jour, one doing so in a way that embraces postfeminist sentiment, and the other doing so in ways that critique it.

Within the analytic of abjection and melancholic nostalgic feminism, we could interpret the anxiety produced by Belle de Jour as having challenged these women's subjectivity, allowing the women to reassert their own historically located social order (Tyler, 2009). Postfeminist consumer culture threatened to break down the meaning of these women's own subjectivities, and required a forceful affective response to reassert themselves (Harradine, 2000; McAfee, 2004)—even if this dis-identification required abandoning the feminist discourse and claims to progressive politics in their own youth by, for example, absenting notions of violence against women in intimate relationships. This process of creating a boundary between themselves and postfeminist consumer culture is demonstrated further in the following analysis. Taking a stand against postfeminist consumer culture was evident in more than simply speaking against it—it involved both refusing to let "others" take up the feminist identity and collectively policing each other's potentially complicit sentiments.

Identifying "The Other"

The process of abjection to form a boundary between these women's sense of self and sexualized culture permitted both the expression of being the "other" and of othering "others." "Young women" were regularly called upon within the women's meetings. The figure of the "young woman" held a doubled position. First, she was excluded from being and seeing from a feminist perspective, and therefore was problematic because of her "false consciousness." Yet, second, she held a powerful position of being discursively placed within the dominant discourse and able to reject the older women's feminist subjectivity. Managing this inclusion/exclusion also represented itself in complex discussions about how much interest in new sexual subjectivities one should show, in which postfeminist consumer culture became both "fascinating" and threatening. These accounts therefore attempted to complete the process of abjection by sealing off their identities into a "seamless boundary" (Butler, 1999, p. 182).

Young Women, Exclusion, and Threat

From very early on in the meetings, the functioning feminists made age matter. They were very eager to differentiate themselves from the other younger group of women, who they knew were similarly taking part in the research. Their desire to represent themselves as having a "different slant" on sexualization meant that young women (both the other participants and young women more generally) were often treated within their discussions as an "other." Indeed, in talking about age, more often than not the language used was about generational difference rather than the women's age as they experienced it in the present. The comparison between generations clearly structured much of the women's talk about young women into a "them" and "us" divide.

The figure of the young woman that materialized within these women's discussions was one who was unable to see how power worked in society. This meant that the functioning feminists were able to position young women as more dupable than themselves (see also Chapters 2 and 3 for discussion of feminist analyses of new sexual subjectivities). The women in the focus group, on the other hand, had a "gods eye view" of society (Haraway, 1988, 1991). Through discrediting the "young woman," these women were able to discursively create a position for themselves as authorial and powerful.

Extract 10

TESSA Well if I, well patriarchy is not going going anywhere. Now, we live in a very
     very patriarchal society. But young women, they don't seem to see patriarchy
NATALIE *No exactly,* they *don't*
     [
TESSA They they don't seem to see=
HELEN They don't connect
TESSA They they the connections between power and in in society and and going to
     war and all kinds of things, so incredibly, religion is so *incredibly patriarchal=*
     [
HELEN Yeah, yeah
TESSA Throughout the world and yet it seems to be invisible
NATALIE Yeah, yeah, well it's like, maybe that's why when you're thirty you're ok
     about this. They they don't see the links between the misogyny in society, like
     the links with domestic abuse with like all the those things. *They don't see it.*
     And you see where I, I'm sorry, but where I've been really, like, what's the word
     used, you said aw because you don't like the noise in clubs
     [
KERRY Yeah, yeah
NATALIE And I so I don't know if I'm just being old-fashioned, but I I don't care

The functioning feminists constructed young women as unable to see the power that worked within society. In this extract there were assumptions made about the younger group of participants—the younger group were "ok about this" because they were unable to see the power that the older women had privilege to through their feminist positioning. Using the metaphor of vision, this extract therefore constructed a false consciousness on the part of the young woman. Not only did this discourse of the young woman allow a powerful "seeing" identity for the women in the focus group, but this construction of the young woman who was unable to see patriarchy meant that she was ultimately unable to lay claim to a feminist position herself.

However, despite the "power of seeing power," the fragility of this position was also made clear. To identify oneself as old-fashioned is to place one's ideals in a past value system that no longer holds weight in today's society. Therefore, Natalie's description of herself as "old-fashioned" seemed to work differently from defining a dominant discourse to then refute it so as to gain a sense of agency (Foucault, 1976). To have an old-fashioned point of view was to no longer count (part of these women's melancholic feminism). So that the identification of power that others cannot see became an almost pointless endeavor.

As well as "blind" to power, the figure of "youthful" femininity was also deployed as a figure of potential exclusion. As with the pleasure pursuers, these women were also invited to take part in a shopping trip to Ann Summers (although only two members, Helen and Kerry, participated). The helpfulness of the staff that Helen encountered in Ann Summers produced a tension in her narrative of this experience. Helen's anticipation of being othered was countered by her account of quite a pleasant shopping experience aided by the Ann Summers staff. In the context of the Ann Summers store, the anticipation of exclusion by the "young" members of staff was considered an object of anxiety. Describing her pleasant experience with the young member of staff as "shocking," Helen was questioned by Tessa in extract 11 as to why this might be:

Extract 11

TESSA What did you think she [the member of staff] was gonna be like?
HELEN I probably would have thought, I probably, distant, probably a bit=
TESSA Snooty
HELEN Yes, a bit like, "What are you in there," you know, "who do you think you are?" And she wasn't at all
ADY What about the um
      [
HELEN Because I was old enough to be her granny
TESSA They're obviously well trained
HELEN Yes, very very well trained, very well trained
TESSA It's interesting isn't it, how how how willing we are, we are to feel comfortable

The "distant" and "snooty" exclusionary practice of the anticipated figure of the young woman was constructed as forbidding Helen from Ann Summers through the imagined questions her presence would evoke: "Who do you think you are?" Such questions were constituted as resulting solely from Helen's age, as a person who was "old enough to be her granny." The construction of the opposite response from the member of staff, however, broke down the expected generational distinctions within new consumer-oriented sexualities. Helen's account is thus one that has the potential to challenge the functioning feminists' rejection of the possibility of authentic and positive consumer-oriented sexual identities. But this possibility is shut down through Tessa's reframing of Helen's account in which Helen's "connection" with the member of staff becomes rationalized by Tessa as an inauthentic relationship enabled by Ann Summers having trained their staff well. Tessa's account of Helen's positive shopping experience thus positions Helen within the ideological/consumerist dupe position that had previously been applied to younger women. And the threat to their feminist nostalgia is thus negated.

Managing threatening situations also became an opportunity to reassert agency. As Hook (2006) suggests, part of the process of sealing off the individual self from the threat of the other to define one's autonomy happens through the identification of "borderline" objects. Such borderline objects defy me/not-me categorization and threaten to dissolve the integrity and separateness of "self" along with the broader social system of identity" (p. 11). By identifying certain material practices as threatening, the women laid claim to both non-agentic "this is not *for* me" statements, and more agentic "this is not me" ones. Me/not-me categorizations secured the women's autonomy from the "broader social system" of new sexual subjectivities (Hook, 2006, p. 11). The experience of the Ann Summers store in the following extract, for example, was expressed within a very spatially aware discourse. Tessa constructed a sense of foreignness and trespassing in which "this is not me/for me" represented both the threat of and the challenge to the commercialization of femininity within the sex shop space.

Extract 12

ADY What about you, Tess. I know you didn't go in there but you said=

TESSA Not recently, um, when I went in there in, um, in [city in Southern England], it was a few years ago. Um, no, I just I just had a very, um, I just did feel quite uncomfortable um, self-conscious I think um

ADY Of what

TESSA Um, exposed. Um, am I the right sort of woman? You know, should I be here?
         [
HELEN Mm

TESSA Have I got any right to be here? Is is this what sexuality's about? Um, and yet I don't remember, you know, I don't remember anybody being unpleasant. Or I don't remember them being pleasant, but I don't remember them being unpleasant. And it's in a very exposed place, funnily enough, Ann Summers in [city in Southern England]. It's right by the [street] which is the very throbbing heart of the shopping center. It's on a corner so when you go past it's sort of hmm, I remember that
         [
HELEN [Laughs]

TESSA And I remember feeling like that inside as well feeling like, "Aw I don't want to get *too close to that*" [laughs].

In this extract, Tessa is the "other," evoking a sense of being vulnerable and lacking legitimacy in this space; she describes herself as "exposed" and asks, "am I the right sort of woman…should I be here?"). This heavy sentiment of discomfort and self-consciousness, coupled with Tessa's stuttered speech throughout this extract, was reiterated within how she narrates her experience of being in the store, where not wanting to get close to the products was related to Tessa's notion that these commodities were not part of sexuality as she understood it. Tessa appeared therefore to be engaging here in a doubled abjection: she was neither the intended addressee, nor does she want to get too close to this abject other. Tessa spoke of both being threatened by the store in her asking "Am I the right sort of woman?" and "Have I got any right to be here?"; but equally she threatened the store by critically evaluating it through hypothetically asking "Is this what sexuality's about?" and, reversing claims for legitimacy in this space, she questions if the store, rather than her, had a right to be in its "exposed" and central location (its busyness and proximity to many people metaphorically constructed as "very throbbing heart of the shopping center").

"This is not me/for me" rhetoric appeared regularly in the women's talk and in their negotiations of the construct of threat that the new sexual subjectivities held to their sense of self. Drawing on Hook, we argue that these women were able to apply "this is not me/for me" sense-making "to secure the integrity of a given structure [their nostalgic feminism], be it bodily, psychical or social in nature" (Hook, 2006, p. 218). As we have argued earlier, the functioning feminists constructed positive subjectivities for themselves by locating their sexuality in their historical youth; any talk that threatened these positive identities, for example, by moving their sexual identities into the present, was rejected. Similarly, the "not me/for me" accounts worked to protect their nostalgic feminism, because they allowed them to position themselves outside contemporary sexual culture. Thus, the construction in extract 12 of a completely different sexuality, a highly commodified sexuality represented in Ann Summers, was constructed as not only "not for" Tessa, but also "not" Tessa, permitting an articulation of her separateness from new sexual subjectivities and a strengthening of the integrity of her feminist identity.

What we want to highlight here is the pleasure associated with speaking in these ways. These meetings were enjoyable. There was a considerable amount of talk, both about sexiness, but also how much they enjoyed the chance this research had given them to talk, think, and reflect on the current state of sexiness. So that, despite their critique of contemporary culture and articulations of a general sense of pointlessness and sadness, these women were enjoying their rhetoric and the way they positioned themselves within it. As we've outlined above, we suggest that the pleasures in this talk come from a certain sense of power, even while this power is tied to a political inertia (Brown, 1999; Benjamin, 1974). The functioning feminists were thus invested in maintaining a distinction between themselves and younger women and between themselves and new sexual subjectivities; and they were able to do this through a process of "othering" and abjection.

Fascinating Other

Abjection is something that needs to be cast off from the self. But the flip side of abjection is fascination and desire (Harradine, 2000; Hook, 2006; McAfee, 2004); and a discourse of fascination was regularly drawn upon within the focus group meetings. When discussing contemporary sexualities, this group of participants regularly employed words such as "fascinating," "curious," and "interesting," and articulated a desire to comprehend "young women's" engagement with this culture. There were also complex negotiations on the level of interest that the women themselves should show toward sexualized culture, highlighting the slipperiness of keeping the other at bay. For example, in the extract below, Helen's narrative of her first encounter with the Rampant Rabbit™ vibrator through a late-night television program shifts from initial fascination and interest, to a distancing discourse of exploitation and difference.

Extract 13

HELEN ...I'd heard about Rabbits, and um, I heard about it first one night when I couldn't sleep. I looked at the, put the telly on, and made myself a cup of tea and I put the telly on at about three o'clock in the morning or something. And there was this whole program, panel of about three or four women, maybe more, I can't remember now, talking about the Rabbit. *Well I'd never heard of it.* So of course I was glued, you know. Anyway, and so I was telling Kerry [during the shopping trip to Ann Summers], "Aw," you know, "I knew about them and blah." And um, so we were sort of giggling about that a bit, about the clitoris and the g-spot and the, um, but it was fairly vacuous. I mean the whole thing was fairly vacuous. I mean we were doing it because we'd made this commitment [to be part of the research], do you know what I mean. I mean the reason why I wouldn't go back [to Ann Summers] probably is because actually it doesn't interest me, you know. That's the thing. I mean I was doing it because I was doing this. And and I could so easily get to the exploitation of women. And I was trying to stay this side of that, you know, by thinking, you know, "Oh, there are lots of younger women here," and, you know, that's different because I couldn't *imagine* me as a twenty-year-old going into an Ann Summers. I mean we just didn't have them, did we.

Helen's narrative of the experience of Ann Summers and the Rampant Rabbit™ had different subplots. Helen constructed herself as having first heard of the Rampant Rabbit™ when viewing a late-night television program. Helen's position within this anecdote was of someone who had been thoroughly interested in hearing about and understanding this sexual commodity. She claimed that she was "absolutely glued," and exaggerated her shock at having never heard of this branded vibrator. Such "gluing" could be identified as a "sticky" signifier, with the associated risk that by being "glued" Helen's interest in the vibrator could stick to herself (see Ahmed, 2004; Ringrose, 2013). However, through the account of being "glued," Helen positioned herself as not the designated audience of this culture, but as an anthropological voyeur overseeing the practices of a different culture. And yet while this account presented Helen as excluded from the culture more generally, her knowledge of the product through the television program allowed her to briefly present herself in a position of power—as a somewhat authoritative insider who could share her knowledge with Kerry on their shopping trip ("so I was telling Kerry, 'Aw', you know, 'I knew about them' ").

Thus, in the first part of Helen's account she takes up a subject position of excluded but interested, which starts to slide toward a position of being included and knowledgeable. But, there is a sudden turn in this narrative; the desire to understand became "vacuous" and the store irrelevant ("it doesn't interest me"). We analyze this shift in terms of Helen managing the threat to the group's collective feminist identity that is produced by her becoming too involved with the other (see also extract 12 for similar risk management). The discursive tactic employed to counteract this threat and maintain difference between the group and new sexual subjectivities was to agentically lay claim to not having any interest in this culture (the vibrator became "not me" rather than "not for me"). And rather than considering the contradiction between her articulation of both fascination and lack of interest, Helen evokes and lays claim to a feminist identity through her discourse of exploitation ("I could so easily get to the exploitation of women. And I was trying to stay this side of that"). Thus, in the last part of this extract, Helen creates a complicated identity that works to neutralize any threat of sexualized culture for their feminist identity, precisely because sexualized culture had already been negated (Hook, 2006). To do this, she constructs two opposing "sides" and herself as attempting to explore the other side for the purposes of research (and not personal interest). In exploring the other side, she seeks to imagine the other, but is unable to. Her feminist analysis of the position of young women (exploited), and their age and sociohistorical consumption-oriented location (they are young and have Ann Summers shops) makes them so "other" to each other that any attempt at imagining the younger other becomes an impossibility for members of this group.

Managing Complicity: The Internal/Policing Feminist

The loss of feminism hailed by the discourses of postfeminism meant that the women in this group could not celebrate any aspect of new sexual subjectivities. As in Helen's extract 13, there appeared to be much identity management around any complicit sentiments toward postfeminist sexiness. The policing of potentially complicit statements appeared to take place both within the group dynamics, through the shutting down of alternative meanings, and also where women constructed a sense of guilt at having found aspects of contemporary sexiness pleasurable. What the policing of these complicit sentiments entailed was the closing down of any sexually self-subjectifying discourses so that these women seemed unable to talk about their contemporary selves in relation to sexual pleasure or sexiness.

Discussions on Ann Summers were particularly interesting in terms of the policing of complicity. As suggested by our earlier analysis, the trip to Ann Summers to spend their £5 voucher was less successful with the older group of women, with both Tessa and Natalie declining to take part in this activity. Helen and Kerry did arrange to spend their vouchers, choosing to engage in this pre-meeting task together. However, as Kerry did not attend the Ann Summers meeting, Helen was the only woman with recent experience of the Ann Summers store. As discussed in relation to extracts 11 and 13, Helen was able to articulate relatively positive aspects of her Ann Summers experience. The positive recounting of this experience included her enjoyment of the shopping trip as a shared experience between Kerry and herself, the "connection" she made with the sales staff, and the insider knowledge she had about the products from having seen the Rampant Rabbit™ discussed on a late-night television show. So, although Helen also talked about her nervousness and hinted at her critical perspective and distance from the store (as "not your usual Ann Summers people"), Helen's early narratives were largely uncritical of Ann Summers. But as with extract 11, we see in extract 14 how Tessa reinterpreted and problematized Helen's positive narrative, in this case, about the dynamics between her and the shop staff:

Extract 14

TESSA It's funny isn't it. Because part of my brain is going, "aw, how clever of them to get, you know, to get friendly Marks and Sparks style," you know. Part of me's quite cynical about that. Maybe they pay, I was even thinking maybe they pay them a pound an hour more, so they'll be really nice to people and good quality shop assistants. 'Cause that's what they need, isn't it. They *need* that 'cause they absolutely need to get people through that door
[
HELEN Absolutely
TESSA And that's quite scary. There's a whole load of people like me and you. And maybe you. Who wouldn't go through the door

In the extract above, Tessa's cynicism toward Helen's enjoyment of the shopping experience appeared as part of the critique of capitalism. Tessa positioned the Ann Summers shopper as a cultural dupe, being tricked by the conglomerate of Ann Summers who may be paying more for friendly staff who resemble shop assistants at the ironically British middle-class (and non-sexual) shop "Marks and Sparks" (Marks and Spencer). Helen's relational account of the pleasure experienced by herself and Kerry at a personal level was thus revised so that the company was positioned at the center of the narrative with its imagined company policies becoming concretized as real and "quite scary." It thus became very difficult for Helen—who agreed that as a shop there was a need to get people through the door, and who also was identified by Tessa as someone who, like Tessa, "wouldn't go through the door"—to continue on the positive narrative with which she began the meeting. Regular querying of Helen's experience by Tessa (see also extract 11) thus led Helen to revoke some of her original sentiments around pleasure and the shopping experience (see, for example, extract 13).

As such, Helen questioned her own enjoyment of Ann Summers, and by the end of the meeting had re-inscribed many of her earlier discussions about the focus on female pleasure. These reworked concepts finally built toward the end of the meeting. In a confessional mode, Helen expressed "guilt" at having enjoyed the Ann Summers experience.

Extract 15

HELEN I suppose, um, I'm curious. And I suppose I'm curious because the most, the thing that's curious the most curious thing for me is the fact that I wasn't uncomfortable in there. And yet, if I actually just remove myself slightly from there, every single thing in the shop was horr, was really quite uncomfortable and quite horrible really. In a way, you know, horrible. But, I suppose exploitative of women, and yet when I was in there I didn't experience that. So it was kind of I did remember tonight while I was sort of just opening the packets of smoked salmon I was thinking, well, I'm gonna have to say that I wasn't uncomfortable. Because I wasn't.

Appearing right at the end of the meeting when asked to summarize their feelings of Ann Summers in one word, this extract showed Helen distancing herself from outwardly condoning Ann Summers while simultaneously reasserting her enjoyment of the shopping trip after the repercussions of its feminist critique. Helen related this tension through describing herself as "curious" rather than, for example, "confused" or "challenged," which might suggest that the nostalgic feminist might need revising, meaning that the sense-making around the horribleness and exploitativeness of Ann Summers remained intact. And Helen drew on her own experience—"when I was in there I didn't experience that [uncomfortableness]"—so that the authenticity of her feelings cannot be undermined. But by "actually just remove[ing] myself slightly" Helen was able to see the "reality" that Ann Summers had hidden in her moment of complicity. Furthermore, Helen constructed her own reflexive thinking as problematic in the knowledge that she would have to report her experience of relative "comfort" to the group. If confession produces "truth" (Foucault, 1976), then through Helen's construction of "guilt" she was able to manage her complicity by reasserting the "reality" of Ann Summers; Helen's true self was maintained. She was able to both reclaim her enjoyment of the shopping trip (reframed as a simple curiosity and an experience that was comfortable) and position Ann Summers as incompatible with her feminist identity (and ability to theoretically critique it).

The functioning feminists' discussions often cycled down to a tension between complicity and critique, which required the employment of various rhetorical strategies that worked to keep young women and postfeminist consumer culture as the other to themselves. But these strategies were not completely successful, and tensions in the distancing and othering of themselves from younger women emerged, particularly when they talked about autoeroticism and the mainstreaming of masturbation. Drawing on the same model of analysis that we applied to the pleasure pursuers, in which the third part of our analysis employs a deconstructive turn to explore the counterpoints in our analysis thus far, we next explore such ruptures in the functioning feminists' talk of "difference." But, whereas for the pleasure pursuers, vulnerability to being othered was the counterpoint to their confident othering, for the functioning feminists any counterpoint enabled by the ruptures in their othering were forestalled, foreclosed, and ultimately forbidden.

PART 3: AUTOEROTIC PARADOX

This section concludes the analyses of our older group of women's talk by exploring the crossovers between aspects of sexualized culture and these women's feminist values. A good example of this parallel between postfeminist sentiment and the feminist identity was vibrator ownership. The postfeminist focus on autoeroticism employs a feminist discourse of the pleasures and politics of masturbation since the "by women, for women" rhetoric of the current consumer market for vibrators can be said to reflect a second wave feminist focus on female sexual pleasure (Smith, 2007). Thus, despite the history of vibrators also drawing on notions of female sexual pathology and the vibrator's own inherent phallocentrism, both second wave feminist and postfeminist sensibilities construct the vibrator as an emancipating technology of sexiness (Juffer, 1998; Smith, 2007; Storr, 2003).

In accordance with the way these women discussed other aspects of postfeminist consumer culture, it was precisely the vibrator's relationship with feminism that was placed under scrutiny. Combined with the functioning feminists' nostalgic feminism and the policing of postfeminist complicity through disgust, the possibility of collusion between consumer culture and feminist ideals became a difficult ground for these women to negotiate. Accepting aspects of postfeminism, with its consumer-oriented sexuality, could not be done without also significantly shifting standpoints in relation to their feminist identity. Again we see a pattern in which these women were able to find some commonality and positive development in relation to gender relations and feminism, followed by the group pulling back to reframe the situation from a less "dupable" position, as in extract 17:

Extract 17

HELEN Yeah, well, that's the thing I did think when I was there [in Ann Summers], there are quite a few sort of young women around. I did think, I thought that was good. There was something quite good about that I felt as though, if they were sort of thinking about, and of course you don't know if they're doing it for their boyfriends. You don't know. I mean obviously I didn't ask them. But I did get some sense that they were there for themselves. And I thought, well I thought things had moved on a bit that's what I thought, you know. And I was quite pleased about that.

In this extract the mainstreaming of vibrators was constructed as potentially forming a bridge between the generations, in the sense that young women who shopped in Ann Summers could be considered by this group as "something quite good" (Helen): perhaps because these young women, like the functioning feminists in their youth, were consciously engaging with their sexuality—implied in Helen's statement "[as] if they were sort of thinking about." In contrast to the negation of sexualized culture in much of the preceding analysis, the mainstreaming of autoeroticism enabled by consumerism was framed in extract 17 as a potentially positive development in women's sexuality. Those women were shopping in these spaces "for themselves," rather than "for their boyfriends," and even though Helen underscored this with uncertainty, she evaluated their actions as "good" and part of a positive cultural shift in which "things had moved on a bit."

But Helen doesn't elaborate further on why women in Ann Summers could be thought of as "good." Instead she shifts the focus onto identifying a problem with the scene—"doing it for their boyfriends." This statement develops an argument (in this extract and the next) for the need to ascertain whether contemporary vibrator consumption was done for oneself or for a man (throughout these discussions of vibrators, the focus remained firmly located within heterosexuality). This concern over for whom the consumption was being done became central for these women, and a measure of validity and value of the sexual practice. What is particularly interesting about this yardstick of who was receiving pleasure was that it was not applied to their own youthful stories (the couple having sex in the kitchen, for example) or the historicized media portrayals of what they considered real and authentic. Only contemporary relationships required evaluating in relation to who was likely to receive pleasure from this purchase.

Vibrator ownership has clear links to a second wave version of feminism, potentially providing a space for women to know their bodies and to explore giving themselves sexual pleasures. In order to de/validate contemporary young women's consumption of vibrators, the functioning feminists constructed a criteria based on who the vibrator was bought for: if young women were buying for themselves, it could be aligned with second wave feminism; if for a boyfriend, it was part of a postfeminist false consciousness, or indeed perhaps something more overtly patriarchal. But, despite not having any way of making this judgment, they collectively decided that young women were purchasing these products for a male partner. The outcome of this logic was to reduce any connection between these young women's sexual consumption and their own form of feminism. It also avoided or closed down further questions: for example, is it impossible for vibrators to be positive in a heterosexual relationship? And, are vibrators celebratory if bought for "themselves" in the context of the wider individualizing discourse that postfeminist autoeroticism is part of, which locate women's failures as personal failures without recourse to their social context? Thus, as in the next extract, any form of understanding or celebrating young women's vibrator buying was re/framed as problematic.

Extract 18

HELEN Yeah, and really I think that fact that I don't want to go back [to Ann Summers], that I have no desire whatsoever to go back there. Because probably in the core of myself I was uncomfortable. But superficially I sort of, um, conducted myself in such a way that I wasn't. And I wasn't uncomfortable, you know, my conscious feeling was not one of uncomfortableness. But I think actually, somewhere I was. Because you know, I now just scan the shop and there wasn't anything in there really that. Well, you have you do you wonder how much of it was about. I think only a small amount of it would actually have been about women discovering their own sexuality. I don't know because I didn't speak to the women. But I just wonder how many of them were there. It was great, I was very pleased to see younger women there. Do you know what I mean, in the numbers. There was no question about that. But actually if you take it to the next step you have to think, how many of them were there for them. And how many of them were there because maybe their bloke had said something to them. You just don't know. And you have to wonder whether quite a large proportion of them were there, something to do with satisfying=

ADY Somebody else

HELEN Somebody else. And probably a man.

The anxiety surrounding the mainstreaming of autoeroticism—which we read as produced by its ability to allow these participants to make connections between their feminist identity and young women's sexual consumption—can clearly be witnessed in the extract above through Helen's constant re-framing and the to-and-fro summarizing of counterarguments. The amount of discursive work to identify her own level of un/comfortableness demonstrates that this was a diffi-cult series of ideas for Helen to communicate to the group. We get a sense in this extract of the fear of being "tricked" or of providing the "wrong" account.

Helen again discussed her inability to infer for whom the women were shop-ping, because she had not asked them, which draws on the assumption that these women would be able to at least recognize that their shopping was for somebody. Yet in extract 18 Helen's assessment takes on a more critical tone. This more criti-cal interpretation was gleaned by "take[ing] it to the next step"; it was constructed as requiring a more thoughtful in-depth process of interpretation in which young women were there under some form of explicit or implicit coercion: "how many of them were there because maybe their bloke had said something to them." The men in young women's relationships, and thus heterosexuality in general, are identified as the culprits—as all women in this account were figured as in a het-erosexual relationship in which they acted to please their male partner over and above themselves (even while this willingness is celebrated in relation to *Rita, Sue and Bob Too*).

The intersection of feminist discourse and consumer culture produced a double-sided discourse, in which the women evade questioning the connections between feminist notions of sexual liberation (their own second wave framework) and female self-pleasure framed without feminist politics (a postfeminist one). This concern about who was being pleased in the context of vibrator ownership was complicated further by these women's involvement with the nostalgic femi-nist subject position, on the one hand, and a commitment to the concept of the emotional heterosexual relationship, on the other. For example, in the following extract the women maintain their discourse surrounding the commodification of sexual relationships evident elsewhere. The notion of vibrator ownership was critiqued here *because* it was framed as being at odds with commitment and intimacy in the heterosexual relationship: *because* it was done for oneself in the interests of capitalism.

Extract 19

KERRY Is it [vibrator ownership] something to do with, I wonder, it's not this not wanting to not need men so much. You know trying to push men out of the picture

NATALIE Not needing to have any emotional link with men

KERRY Not needing

[

TESSA So having a commodity instead of a=

KERRY Yeah. So actually it's almost like a sort of protective thing

ADY Yeah

TESSA Well that's interesting for

[

KERRY The more we can the more we can do ourselves, and we don't need the male just the safe safe security. The, I don't know

[

NATALIE Well maybe it's the

TESSA I think it might be like a dominant discourse of capitalism. That you'll never be satisfied

NATALIE You've got to buy more

In this extract, Kerry began to construct vibrator ownership as a coping mechanism and a means for women to gain independence from men, in a way that allied with Helen's discourse and both women's emphasis on the postfeminist rhetoric of "the more we can do ourselves" as a potential site of feminist and postfeminist collusion. In doing so, Kerry also reproduced gendered expectations by positing a pseudo-psychological hypothesis in which women may use vibrators as a means of "protecting" themselves and providing "security" in their sexual pleasure. Indeed, such an interpretation of women's desire for vibrators as a way of protecting themselves was unsurprising given the group's careers centering on the psy-industries of counseling.

However, Natalie and Tessa concurrently worked on Kerry's "defense mechanism" theory of vibrator ownership. The discourse of postfeminist independence became conflated with not needing an emotional relationship. In contradiction to Helen's concern that women may be buying vibrators to please a man in extracts 17 and 18, the emotional heterosexual relationship with a man was held up as ideal. Vibrator ownership became about not needing a valued emotional attachment. In this sense-making, the ideal emotional relational heterosexual relationship was undermined by consumerism, which the women had previously identified as emotionless. The anti-capitalistic discourse in this extract meant that "having a commodity" instead of a romantic and emotionally relational relationship with a man was framed as a "cold" intimacy in which contemporary consumer culture was constructed as producing an endlessly unemotional culture of narcissism (see Illouz, 2007). The feminist notion of doing it for or by one's self was thus variously positioned by these women in contradictory discourses—vibrator ownership was a potentially significant improvement on gender relations, impossible in the context of the heterosexual relationship, framed as colluding with capitalism, and also deeply problematic in relation to their construct of the "real" emotional heterosexual relationship.

Drawing to a close this three-part chapter of the functioning feminist's negotiations of sexualized culture, we note that for these women the sexualization of culture was at odds with their ideal selves. The construction of a feminist identity for these women involved authenticating themselves by framing all contemporary female sexualities and relationships as bad, anti-feminist, cold, vile, and toxic. We have argued that the positioning of contemporary culture as toxic was done in three ways. In the first subsection of this chapter, we have argued that the women constructed authentic sexuality as having occurred historically. Through nostalgic constructions of hippie feminist youth and gritty portrayals of mundane and unglamorous sexuality, sexual unknowingness and "innocence" functioned as a means of closing down and shutting off contemporary culture as anything but authentic. Consumer culture was positioned as the antithesis of real, honest sexuality. It was mad, bad, all-consuming, and all-saturating, and it produced subjects whose sexuality was cold and mechanical.

We have analyzed their construction of contemporary culture as inauthentic as a means of securing for these women a sense of agency, in which they were choiceful and political in regard to their youthful sexuality identities. But, this agency was produced through a nostalgic feminism that was melancholic and unable to move from the historical location in which it positioned itself. And it provided these women with a vocabulary for critiquing and negating sexualization, working as a mechanism for pushing it away and not letting it become part of themselves.

To further open up these identity-effects, we have argued that a concept was needed to take account of the emotionality of these women's talk about the sexualization of culture. We have drawn on a notion of feminist melancholia to understand the regulation practiced in this context, and have argued that the processes of othering and abjection might also be useful for understanding the feminist response to postfeminist consumer culture. This othering was employed to make sense of this emotionality and the process of managing their (older women's) feminist identity, to seal it off from perceived threats to power and identity in the context of a postfeminist consumer culture.

The social and emotional abjection of postfeminist consumer culture allowed these women to reject and negate any historical contingency between feminist ideologies and the development of postfeminist consumer culture. The final section of this chapter further reflects this rejection. Here we showed how aspects of postfeminist consumer culture seemed to make sense and support these women's feminist values. Taking a stand against these corresponding ideologies often created uneasy ground and contradictory discourses. For example, the women negotiated vibrator ownership by presenting a critical discourse in which buying vibrators was simultaneously incompatible with feminist discourses, given the likelihood that the practice was ultimately for a man *and* that it undermined the honest and real emotional heterosexual relationship.

Not all feminist positions entail the sort of sense-making we have described. This analysis seems to evidence the alternative technologies of the self that are used to perform identity in the contemporary matrix of neoliberalism, consumerism, and postfeminism. So that, like the new sexual subject, what the functioning feminist subject position entails is a response to and within postfeminism. This was a resistant identity in relation and response to postfeminism. But also this subject position is not radically different from some of the sense-making taking place in the wider public sphere—especially in those accounts that figure young women as problematic for the way they take up femininities in a new "postfeminist" context (see Chapter 2 for our discussion of these). For our older group of participants, there was a refusal to engage on many levels, from the practicalities of the focus group meetings (such as the fact that two of the women didn't engage in the trip to Ann Summers), to the policing of complicity between the group members. The sexualization of culture was experienced as highly threatening to these women's ways of making sense of the world, so that the only response was to try by any means to exclude any positive ways of figuring it and to refuse to take part. The threat represented by this lack of engagement was managed not only through an older mode of feminist critique, but also by declaring this same feminism a dead critique in the contemporary discursive landscape, thereby also locating themselves this way.

The declaration of the loss of feminism was "a means of identifying a perceived danger in need of elimination, a way for a community to define itself through those it symbolically chooses to kill" (Hawkesworth, 2004, p. 963). For us, the discursive-emotive frame with which these women made sense of postfeminist consumer culture worked on two levels. In one sense, feminism has always required something to kick against, what Ahmed (2010) has termed "the politics of unhappiness"—and therefore the development of a postfeminist consumer culture was a reason to remain angry, as a way of keeping feminism "alive" by declaring it a has-been in the contemporary context. These women's negotiations of sexualized culture perhaps also point toward the need to consider the "exclusion" engendered by new sexual subjectivities and the sexual cultures of which they were a part. Although already in a socially privileged position—that is, these women were white, heterosexual, able-bodied, and middle class—the group's collective exclusion from the sexualization of culture formed the foundation of their ethical sense of self and provided other ways of constituting identities that were agentic and sexually assertive—even if this pleasure was only available through nostalgic remembering. Their position as nostalgic feminists was not a reflective desire to be addressed by this sexualization, but a reason to distance themselves from it. But the politics of unhappiness in the functioning feminist group also prevented these women from being able to talk about their own desires, pleasure, and wants, and their own subjective feelings of exclusion. And ultimately the abjection of postfeminist consumer culture constituted a shutting down of alternative ways of seeing the self (particularly, it seemed, for Helen).

6

Constant Regulation, Constant Repositioning, and Finding Hope in "Othering"

Jane was very nervous about attending her first pole-dancing class. She was worried about what other people would think of her body. But once she got there she found the experience fun. It felt empowering—until she noticed another woman scrutinizing her cellulite.

Sasha felt uncomfortable passing the adult-only store a few streets away from her house—it just wasn't the same as the High Street sex store she shopped in.

Loretta couldn't believe her eyes when her 11-year-old daughter's part in the school show involved a grinding dance with the other girls in her class that imitated a hip hop video currently in the charts. Her daughter looked like a lap dancer.

We began this book with the above stories because they introduced some of the forms of contemporary sexiness—and anxieties around sexiness—with which we wanted to engage. The rise in the visibility of sex and of sexual cultures has created a great deal of anxiety, as we evidenced in our discussion in Chapter 2 of the number of government reports, media commentaries, academic analyses, and other public discourse (see for example, the amount of concern over "the sexualization of children" on the popular British website mumsnet). But the new sexual subjectivities that have emerged out of this contemporary sexiness have also elicited celebratory accounts of a dawning new era of liberated female sexuality. How to make sense of this contradictory social landscape and analyze the dynamics between sex, identity, and consumer culture has been the focus of the book. In this final chapter we draw our findings together and outline our ideas for new lines of fruitful inquiry.

Our focus throughout has been on employing a poststructuralist informed analysis of contemporary sense-making around new female sexual subjectivities. From this standpoint, how women come to understand themselves and their sexuality is structured by cultural understandings that are sociohistorically located and which are (re)produced through social processes. Our analytic has been to explore these cultural understandings as discourses that construct female sexuality in particular ways, and the consequences for women in taking up these discourses and making them their own.

Applying this approach to thinking about new sexual subjectivities, our intention has been fourfold: to analyze the sociohistoric context that has given rise to new sexual subjectivities (see Chapter 1); to outline a way of theorizing women's negotiations of sexiness within this context and to do so while avoiding some of the limitations of the debates that have come to characterize much of the contemporary discourse of sexualized culture (Chapters 2 and 3); and then to apply our theorizing to analyze how two groups of women negotiate their very different positioning within contemporary sexiness and the implications this has for their subjectivity and relationships with other women (Chapters 4 and 5). Here we draw together this work by highlighting and developing key aspects of our arguments. In doing so, we create a position to move to our fourth intention for this book, using a deconstructive process in line with Lather (2007) to identify ways of thinking that move us not just to a more nuanced analytical framework (as we argue for in Chapter 3), but into a new space altogether—one that might enable a more hopeful feminist analysis.

OVERVIEW: TECHNOLOGIES OF SEXINESS

At the beginning of this book we highlighted a synergetic coalescing of neoliberalism, postfeminism, and consumerism through analyzing the sociohistoric context that has given rise to new sexual subjectivities (see Chapter 1). Within neoliberal sense-making, the self is understood as a project to be worked on, an understanding that requires the person to participate in self-surveillance and scrutiny in order to identify aspects of themselves that need improvement so as to perform the desired form of self-transformation (such as "exercise to produce a sexy body!") or the maintenance of that transformation ("more exercise so you don't let yourself go!").

Technologies for such transformations are usually individualistic and consumer-oriented. For example, one might seek to address body image concerns through cosmetic surgery rather than join a feminist conscious-raising group. Thus, neoliberal subjectivity is individualist, self-motivating, consumer-oriented, and underpinned by a sense-making in which the person is understood as exercising freedom and choice as she makes rational, autonomous, consumer-oriented decisions with which to transform herself into "who she wants to be." As such, neoliberal subjectivity operates in a similar manner to the economy of the neoliberal market, through forms of freedom enabled by the process of consuming oneself into being (Walkerdine, 2003).

However, what we have documented in preceding chapters is a sense of never fully feeling complete or secure in one's consumption. This is because consumerism is constantly on the move, providing too much choice, even while there is a limited range of things that we can physically buy. Desire is created but not sated within consumerism. Whatever we "chose" is done so in a framework where there is always something else that you could have had, meaning that individuals within this framework are never content. No matter how we construct ourselves in relation to those technologies of subjectivity that define the contemporary moment, there is a constant deferment of completeness, happiness, pleasure, and other valued markers of the good life. Taking up neoliberal subjectivities that require people to create a sense of self through consumerism and lifestyle thus sets people up to fail, while encouraging them to locate these failures as their own individual failures (to consume appropriately) rather than as failures of the social structure, or in the logic of neoliberalism itself.

Neoliberal rhetoric dominates contemporary Western sense-making in constructing the ideal subject and citizen, and for women, it produces a specific set of sense-making around femininity and sexuality that coalesces within postfeminism. The postfeminist sentiment focuses subjectivity onto the body, creating for women an intensity of attention on the body and a coupling of femininity with bodily practice—the outcome being that for many women normative femininity requires constant beauty work and a deployment of consumer products to enable this transformation.

Despite the need to deploy a range of resources (time, skill, money) to facilitate beauty work (see, for example, Riley and Scharff's [2013] analysis of the cost of lip preparation alone by a well-known makeup manufacturer), women's beauty work is reconstituted as pleasure. The normative requirements to participate in such transformations are constructed as choiceful acts of rational, autonomous women exercising consumer freedom. Thus in media, such as women's magazines and advertisements, beauty work is presented as a form of pleasure and pampering through re-appropriated feminist-informed discourses of autonomy and pleasure ("because you're worth it!"), while feminism itself is repudiated and no longer needed in an age of individualism (McRobbie, 2009; Gill, 2007b; Ringrose, 2013).

Within this context a certain new kind of sexual subjectivity has emerged, one that, in contrast to earlier constructions of women's sexuality as passive, celebrates an agentically sexual woman, who seeks and enables her own pleasure and sexual autonomy. But this new sexual subjectivity is Janus faced, offering both a vision of sexual liberation serviced with a range of consumer products, and acting as a disciplinary force, requiring women to always be "up for it" and to participate in a form of choiceful sexual objectification. Postfeminist sexual subjectivities articulate further contradictions since its neoliberal informed address speaks to women across the world as individuals able to be hailed by postfeminism (see, for example, the internationalization of women's magazines like *Cosmopolitan*) while simultaneously, structural inequalities are reinforced since the dominant figure of postfeminist subjectivities is youthful, white, middle class, slim, and able-bodied.

The apparent contradictory nature of postfeminist sexual subjectivities, of being liberating and disciplining, available to all yet exclusionary, is perhaps the underlying reason for the polarization and subsequent stagnation of debates on how to make sense of women's engagement with sexualized cultures. One form of stagnation has occurred around a call to (often older) feminists to celebrate (often younger) women's choices and pleasures in participating in new sexual subjectivities, while these (often older) women question the idea of celebrating a form of disciplinary sense-making. At the reverse (often younger) women are stigmatized for failing to take up the (often older) feminist ideal of sexual liberation. Both stagnations mask the structural inequalities of this sexualization around a range of factors including age, ethnicity, class, sexuality, and body shape/size/ableness.

Trying to move through these debates in Chapter 3, we drew on Foucault's idea of technologies: technologies of subjectivity, the broad sense-making from which subject positions are enabled, and technologies of the self, the practices which we can employ to perform ourselves into these subject positions. Drawing on a range of poststructuralist and psychosocial theory, we considered how a "technology of sexiness" might enable certain new sexual subjectivities that "hail" or resonate with some women, who then engage in technologies of the self in order to successfully produce themselves as new sexual subjects. We suggested that our technology of sexiness framework allows for an analysis in which postfeminism could be understood as a doubled movement that both opens up and closes down possibilities for how women can make sense of themselves. And in relation to women's engagement with sexualized culture, we argued that there were at least three of these doubling moments.

First, women who take up new sexual subject positions may employ a range of technologies of the self and take pleasure in how they then experience themselves (as sexy, agentic, autonomous women, for example). But to do so, women have to draw on technologies that are available to them, which are embedded within a nexus of contemporary and historical gender relations. So when women, for example, consume porn as part of being modern agentic sexy women, they're also participating in a consumer culture with a history of objectifying women. This doesn't mean that women are self-objectifying, because when women take up new sexual subjectivities they reiterate or perform these subjectivities, and, drawing on Butler, we argued that this reiteration opens up possibilities for parody and subversion. Women, for example, can use sexual subjectivity to subvert notions of passive femininity; but where we see the second doubled moment is that in order for subversion to be readable it has to repeat dominant discourses of female sexuality, including objectification. So, in order to subvert older notions of femininity, women have to invoke them.

Our third doubled moment was that, although different iterations of women's sexuality can allow challenges to the gender order, the media could recuperate these in reactionary ways. For example, it has been suggested that Madonna's various TV kisses with other women worked to reinforce heterosexuality (Diamond, 2005).

Within our technologies of sexiness framework, then, women are conceptualized as being able to act agentically, but not in the context of their own making, nor with technologies that are discursively or symbolically neutral (see Chapter 3 for further discussion). Applying our technologies of sexiness framework to help us think through how women are negotiating new sexual cultures, Chapters 4 and 5 explored the sense-making of two groups of women.

In Chapter 4 we explored how a friendship group of women, embodying young, white, heterosexual, and middle-class femininity, had been able to take up postfeminist discourses of female sexuality, and in Althusser's terms had been hailed by them. In analyzing how this group of women made sense of themselves, their sexuality, and other women, we explored their pursuit of pleasure and, tying it to Berlant's (2011) concept of cruel optimism, examined the implications for them in taking up new sexual subjectivities, and the pleasures and vulnerabilities that this entailed.

In Chapter 5 we took a similar approach to explore the sense-making of a group of older white, heterosexual, and middle-class women. Although the discursive location of this group of women meant that they were not the dominant focus of postfeminist discourses of sexuality, the variation in and contradictory nature of postfeminist discourses meant that it was possible that they might have been hailed by new sexual subjectivities. For example, the term "mummy porn" evokes a subject position of an older, sexually agentic woman (a term used particularly in media discussions of older women reading E. L. James's BDSM fantasy novel *Fifty Shades of Grey*). In this way, older women have also been hailed, and "[t]he discourses of positive aging have created the sexy ageless consumer as a personality and socially responsible citizen" (Katz and Marshall, 2003, p. 12).

But the group of women we recruited constructed themselves as deeply resistant to any postfeminist sentiment, accounting for this resistance through their feminist identification. We drew on Brown's (1999) interpretation of leftist melancholia to analyze how this group of "functioning feminists" made sense of themselves, their sexuality, and other, younger women. Here we also developed an analysis of the pleasures and vulnerabilities that our participants' "feminist resistance" entailed. Next we examine our findings for each group of women. We follow this with a discussion of the commonalities in an attempt to think through these dichotomies and, in a deconstructive turn, to identify new productive spaces for thinking about contemporary sexiness (Lather, 2007).

VULNERABLE LOCATIONS

Sexiness has been resold to women as liberating, empowering, and self-determining: a form of sexiness that permits women to understand themselves as desirable and desiring. Our young group of women had embraced these ideas, and taking up new sexual subjectivities enabled the pleasure pursuers to construct themselves as being sexually powerful, agentic, confident, knowledge-able consumers. This self-construction was clearly experienced as positive, allow-ing for a form of femininity firmly located within postfeminist, neoliberal, and consumerist discourses. But there were other aspects to taking up this subject position. Looked at from another angle, it was a vulnerable and insecure place to inhabit: given that desire is created but not sated within consumerism, mak-ing sense of oneself through a discourse of individualist consumption meant that these women could never be a finished product themselves.

The technologies of the self that these women were drawing on to produce them-selves into the valued position of sexual connoisseur meant that they were always in pursuit and never in possession of pleasure. Analyzing their sense-making through the theoretical frameworks of technologies of sexiness and cruel opti-mism, we understood these women as producing themselves into the new sexual subject through their use of a range of consumer products and consumption prac-tices (the cock ring, the seeking of ever more extreme images on the Internet) that were made sense of through neoliberal and postfeminist discourses. Their technologies of sexiness at once gave them a dominant position to some women (the working-class hen nighter, the cousin who didn't get it right), while requiring them to constantly push their boundaries, actively working on themselves, so as to enable their continued claims of being sexual connoisseurs.

Always on the search for the next thrill, and othering those who consumed in less classy ways, these women were also vulnerable to seeing themselves as the "other," since they could not compete with the consumption practices required for the kind of postfeminist sexiness they saw embodied in contemporary celebrities. Thus othered and othering, the vulnerabilities in the pleasure pursuers take-up of postfeminist sentiment emerged in line with the theory of cruel optimism, in which our participants could be understood as forming an attachment to a sub-jectivity that allowed them to "keep on living on and to look forward to being in the world" (Berlant, 2006, p. 21) that was, however beautifully packaged, not in their interest or in the conditions of their own making. To some extent, all con-temporary Western ideologies function through consumerism, and we are not necessarily arguing for or attempting to imagine a sexiness that is located outside consumerist discourse. Yet, for us, the question arises: Why embrace this notion of sexiness if it evokes such vulnerabilities?

Perhaps this new sexual subjectivity is so appealing because it provides a pow-erful dream of ideal subjectivity: a dream of a sexy, powerful, agentic woman that so many women (to a certain extent and in different ways) wish for and buy into. The new sexual subject seems to be so compelling because it folds a particular idea of what womanhood should be into morality discourses, beliefs in a just world, and technologies of subjectivity pertaining to sexuality, employment, beauty, capitalism, and feminism. Postfeminist discourses evoke the idea that this form of womanhood is attainable and desirable for all women, who, through agentic self-determined choices, hard work, and effort, can reach ethical individuality and create themselves as good people, good consumers, good feminists, and good women.

Yet, this dream of being a sexy, powerful, agentic woman is undermined by the logic of postfeminism that absents other ways of making sense of sexiness outside individualist consumption and that requires a level of constant self-surveillance, self-monitoring, and self-disciplining that feeds into forms of insecurity, aggression, and hatred directed at the self and at others (Gill, 2007b; McRobbie, 2009). To quote one of the women we interviewed, making sense of oneself through new sexual subjectivities involves "constant regulation, constant repositioning. Um, but with no resolution. There there's never a kind of, phew I can relax, I know what I have to be now....But there is none of that. It's just this constant search" (Jay, individual interview, aged 35). This powerful dream of sexual subjectivity and the notion of the strong confident woman thus appears to evaporate into a sense of goal posts that are continuously on the move, and an underlying lack of hope, an outcome of the cruel optimism of contemporary capitalism that makes consumerism both the problem and the perceived source of solution.

Of course, some women may instead resist the allure of postfeminist discourses, such as our older group of women, who rejected a role for consumerism in the production of their sexual identities, or indeed any women's sexual identity that could be construed as legitimate. Their accounts constructed capitalism and feminist sexuality as so incompatible that imagining an authentic feminist sexuality within consumer culture was impossible. This resistance to those technologies of sexiness that prevail in the contemporary context engendered nostalgia for earlier times. In this nostalgia, the past was recollected in terms of relationships being more central, and understood in political terms, with sexiness more "real" and gritty because it was innocent, naive, and unmarked, as it were, from consumerism. For this group, the dreams of sexual liberation developed within second wave feminist consciousness had not been realized, and younger "pleasure pursuers" could only be constructed as participating in some kind of consumer-oriented false consciousness, unable to experience authentic feminine sexiness and pleasure. From this standpoint, our older group identified as authentic, older, wiser, political feminists in comparison to younger women who participated in postfeminist sexual cultures.

Taking up a position of older, wiser, authentic feminists provided these women with an apparently powerful and pleasurable subject position, but it also meant that they denied themselves and other women pleasure in any participation in postfeminist sexual subjectivities. In comparisons to the pleasure pursuers, who drew on consumer technologies in the production of agentic, sexual selves, yet were unable to claim full or completely confident membership of this identity, our older group of women were "functioning feminists." They were able to create positive identities for themselves in relation to a politicized sense of sexuality, but in the process excluded themselves from any form of consumer-oriented sexiness, and so any chance of participating in new sexual subjectivities that may have been exciting or pleasurable were lost (see hints of this in Helen's talk of Ann Summers, which were closed down by other members of the group).

In relation to technologies of subjectivity, our older group of women were caught in a double bind. Taking up a "functioning feminist" position and constructing contemporary sexiness as consumerist and inauthentic made them vulnerable to rejecting their own sexual selves in the present. An alternative option may have been to take up new sexual subjectivities, yet this strategy would have made them vulnerable, too, not just to ageism and the "fear" of the sexy oldie, but to their ability to claim authority from age and experience. Thus, at a time in their life when they might expect to lay claim to knowledge, they are the ignorant; the matriarch must turn to the younger woman for help to navigate a foreign terrain and give up the pleasures and power associated with a position of authority. We speculate that their resistance to this option suggests that it was deeply threatening—a threat that perhaps underpins so much of the defense of their own melancholia, inasmuch as they abject the figure of the "young woman" from any feminist identity, and police anyone with an alternative point of view—as, again, with Helen's enjoyment of Ann Summers.

The doubled nature of discourses, in that they simultaneously open up and close down possibilities for subjectivity, is thus evident in the sense-making employed by our older group of women. The expert position that they created was clearly a powerful position that they could carve out for themselves, but within it was the risk of not just excluding others, but excluding the very notion of a possibility that contemporary women—themselves or others—might be able to carve out as a space of authentic, feminist-acceptable female sexuality.

Pleasure instead took the form of melancholia, with authenticity located in the past and articulated through historic remembering. The effect of this melancholia was political inertia; no solutions were offered or hope for the future evoked. "[T]here is a certain capacity for self-poisoning in the structure of feminism" (Colebrook, 2010, p. 330), and for our functioning feminists we see this toxicity actualized through the closing down of our participants' own sexual identities and a resistance to exploring the new; a failure to connect across the generations and empathize or celebrate young women's attempts to take ownership and pleasure in their sexuality; and a closing down of possibilities for thinking about how social change could be facilitated, a process that, as Berlant (2011) argues, negates hope. Thus, both the functioning feminists and pleasure pursuers produced their subject positions in part through the othering of women, so that whether one rejected or embraced new female sexualities enabled through postfeminist consumerism, part of the identity taken up involved threat, anxiety, and the policing of other women.

The women we spoke to did not take up the technologies of subjectivity that they did in unthinking or uncritical ways. In their talk of their negotiations with new sexual subjectivities there was critical thinking, humor, parody, pleasure, and agency. But the pleasure pursuers were stuck in the grip of the promise of consumerism that simultaneously guaranteed their claim to knowledge while undermining it, while the functioning feminists were attached to a history that they understood as having no relevance to the contemporary landscape. Both groups were unable to find a place where they felt confident about their current sexuality, but both groups understood themselves as right. The pleasure pursuers believed that they were doing sexiness the right way, the functioning feminists thought their sense-making was self-evidently correct, and because of this both were able to position themselves as ethical subjects within contemporary culture. But from these positions they were also unable to critically reflect on their own culturally formed ways of understanding or to see any other viewpoint as valuable.

It is this othering of other women that we see as the most problematic nature of women's negotiation with postfeminist sexual culture. The process of othering was a central feature of talk in both groups (such as, the working-class hen nighter for the pleasure pursuers and the pleasure pursuers for the functioning feminists). Othering divided our participants from women perceived as not like themselves and was the process that stopped our participants from feeling confident, either in terms of having gotten it "right" or that they could carve an authentic space for themselves in the here and now.

However, this othering gave us an analytic for identifying and exploring the vulnerabilities of engaging or resisting new sexual subjectivities. In identifying othering in our participants' talk, we were able to turn our analytic gaze onto the object/subject of this othering and to speculate on the nature of the anxieties they evoked. It allowed us to ask: Why did it matter if some women weren't doing sexual subjectivities in the same way? Against what vulnerabilities were these defences being mobilized? These questions helped us to explore the toxic aspects of taking up or resisting new sexual subjectivities, and from this analysis they have allowed us to now address the fourth intention of this book: identifying new ways of thinking about feminist analysis of sexual cultures.

FINDING HOPE IN OTHERING

In Haran's (2010) article on redefining hope as praxis, she specifically addresses how engaging with the "other" may facilitate a feminist "dreaming of and working towards better futures" (p. 393). Her praxis of hope draws on Benjamin's notion of intersubjectivity, a psychoanalytic approach to subjectivity in which becoming a subject is predicated on recognition of the other as another subject, rather than an object. This intersubjective relation entails identification with the other, but in ways that do not revert the other to object or abject. Instead, identification of/with the other as "a mind outside of our own" has to recognize and understand the other as a subject in his or her own right.

Haran (2010) develops Benjamin's work that analyzes the communication between analysts and analysand in the clinical psychoanalytic relationship, and applies it to the dialogue between text and a reader in order for her to produce a feminist close reading of a particular text (Starhawk's novel *The Fifth Sacred Thing*), which Haran describes as an example of thinking about "the possibility of embodying commitment to unending negotiation amongst the different communities that might make up [such] a better world" (2010, p. 396). What Haran (2010) calls for is a way of thinking "about hope as an ethical commitment to recognising oneself and others as both *desiring subjects* and *vulnerable objects* in the pursuit of social transformation and social justice, and as an on-going practice of *using our fears or anxieties* to deepen and extend our capacity for intersubjectivity and intercorporeality" (p. 399, emphasis added), so that all protagonists are able to recognize their entwined interobjectivity and intersubjectivity by using their common vulnerability as a resource for building more hopeful futures. Building on this transition from therapy to feminist readings, we in turn seek to apply this approach to a different form of communication—that between women hailed in different ways within postfeminism.

Applying Haran's analysis to our own work, such an approach requires people to use their own subjective and emotional investments in the others' accounts conscientiously in a "knowing way." This knowingness could, of course, simply reproduce the knowingness of the pleasure pursuers and the functioning feminists, impeding any sense of recognition. However, as Haran (2010) suggests, reading in a "knowing way" would entail a more relational and empathetic reading between subjects. Among other things, this would involve avoiding simplistic readings by recognizing one's own investments, recognizing the other's point of view as valid, and showing the interconnectedness of life and theory (Haran, 2010). Through this act of recognizing the other, Haran's work implies that we might be able to imagine the possibility of social transformations that allow women to feel confident in their sexuality, a vision of a hopeful future that is absent in both sets of our participants' talk.

In Colebrook's (2010) discussion of the possibilities of feminist hope, she suggests that we are limited in the forms of hope possible in the present precisely because hope is predicated on this present. In relation to our participants, on the one hand we have an intoxication of hopefulness, where the pleasure pursuers appear to hold out for something that then disappoints, and on the other a toxic hopelessness of the functioning feminists, who seem unable to move personally or politically beyond their leftist melancholia. In the light of our discussion of Haran's hope as praxis, we ask: What would our data have looked like if our participants had been able or had worked toward recognizing themselves and the other as both desiring subjects and vulnerable objects in the pursuit of ethical subjectivity? If they had recognized that others have validity and they themselves have investments? Could this strategy have enabled a path out of the double binds of postfeminist negotiations in which they find themselves?

These questions may also be applied to ourselves as feminist analysts. It seems to us that we (as women, feminists, researchers) might benefit from seeing how we also draw on the same sets of ideas and entanglements as the participants in this book. The stagnated polarized debates that we outlined in Chapter 2 among feminist analyses of sexualized cultures reflect remarkably similar patterns to our participants' sense-making: academic feminist analyses often have celebrated or rejected new sexual subjectivities and have othered those differently positioned within these debates. These analyses are also characterized by an absence of hope for a different/better future, despite feminist theory being structured by "commitments to dreaming of and working towards better futures" (Haran, 2010, p. 393).

An absence of hope in general characterizes aspects of feminist theorizing in the "ruins" of what we might think of as "post-post" period in academia (Brown, 2003; Lather, 2007). And in relation to feminist analysis of sexualized cultures, we note that neither those who celebrate nor those who resist postfeminist sentiment evoke hope in terms of "the inevitable triumph of the people over the illegitimate powers of wealth and rule that exploit, dominate or disenfranchise" (Brown, 2003, p. 6). Commercial powers that construct the context not of women's own making may be critiqued, absented, or otherwise negotiated, but both the critics and the celebrants are trapped within the logic of postmodern capitalism in which "the opening of a different future, the ideal illuminating that future—has vanished" (Brown, 2003, p. 7)

From this perspective, the question becomes, how do we find hope in our thinking about women's sexual subjectivities among the "ruins" of postmodernist academia? Our analysis suggests that one way forward would be to ask ourselves what would happen to feminist analyses that refused the pattern of othering that have seen in both our participants' talk and in feminist analyses? What would we get if we engaged in analyses of new sexual subjectivities that took as their starting point a recognition of our own investments, that explored our own vulnerabilities and the anxieties they produced in relation to sexual subjectivities, along with a recognition that the other's point of view is valid?

Considering Haran's hope as praxis in relation to our analysis of sex, identity, and consumer culture, we propose that current accounts of gender relations in the context of postfeminism explicitly work against a conscientious reading, denying the potentialities of "young women" and ignoring the way older women are living through contemporary culture, too—as if they somehow really do live in the past. These accounts of contemporary gender relations prevent thinking differently and more hopefully about women's sexual subjectivities. They render invisible or "other" those women who are either placed or place themselves against sexualization and reproduce, as with our functioning feminists, the idea that young women are subject to their own false consciousness, so that young women become the object (and not a subject) of concern.

One object of concern in feminist analyses is the contemporary young working-class woman and how she is positioned culturally as always having somehow "gotten it wrong" (Harris, 2004; Griffin, 1997). For example, McRobbie argues that a certain "[l]uminosity falls upon the girl who adopts the habits of masculinity including heavy drinking, swearing, smoking, getting into fights, having casual sex, getting arrested by the police, consumption of pornography, enjoyment of lap-dancing clubs and so on" (2009, p. 83); she is analyzed as a phallic girl inhabiting an impossible space, where, on the one hand, she is told she can "have it all" in the face of a worn-out and old-fashioned class system, yet, on the other hand, she is vilified for her disreputable and "tasteless" patterns of consumption and for failing to recognize her place in the social structure (Harris, 2004; see also Chapter 4). And while there's concern for young women living in such "impossible spaces," these women can't do it right for feminists either: such that, for example, McRobbie (2009) questions their engagement in masculine behaviors that are deemed to support the hegemonic masculinity behind this gender performance.

We ask, what might it mean for feminist analysts to position the phallic girl in this way, as an object of feminist concern? What would it mean if we saw this positioning as a form of othering and, when doing analysis, considered it a cue to explore our own anxieties that were being provoked? How radically different would our analyses look if we both made ourselves vulnerable, and valued the other?

We suggest, therefore, that one way of moving beyond the doubled stagnations and stuck places of our current analyses of sexualization discourses would be that we become sensitive to when we, as women and researchers, "other" women, including when we construct other women as objects of concern. Using this as an analytic, we might focus our analysis on identifying our acts of othering, as ways of deepening our analysis by working with them in two ways: first, by exploring how to value that other's standpoint that we find so disagreeable, and second, by examining our own investments and the anxieties being evoked by this "disagreeable" standpoint. We suggest that taking a standpoint of "curious affection," a term used in mindfulness to help process judgments lightly, may allow us as analysts to do the kind of conscientious reading of our thinking that Haran calls for. This process would allow us to recognize the interconnectedness of life and theory: a more doable praxis (Lather, 2007). And it is our suggestion, as we conclude this book, that using our othering as an analytic to develop analysis might provide new lines of hope for feminism within and through the postfeminist sentiment in which so many women are making sense of their sexual subjectivities.

Our participants are fairly homogenous, except in age, and we would not claim that their accounts can be generalized to all women. Their accounts were situated in a British context, and came from women who were all white and largely middle class. Through these accounts, race and ethnicity remain invisible and class implicit (a pattern we also see in feminist academic accounts; see, for example, Riley and Scharff, 2013). We have also been critical of our participants' discussions, but we maintain that these discussions can only be what they are in the technologies of subjectivity in which they happen. We hope that we have shown that this sense-making is not only similar to feminist discussions of sexiness, and that these discussion intersect, but that these ways of understanding the self are a few of a limited number of structures that we can reasonably take up. We also want to have shown how the women's sense-making allowed them to position themselves as good people, but that we need to find ways within these technologies of subjectivity that allow women to both feel good and develop understanding, relationality, and empathy for others—because it is within others that these technologies of sexiness appear to falter. To see the matrix of consumerism, neoliberalism, and postfeminism shift toward more feminist-inspired notions of subjectivity, we need to understand what women more generally are getting from these constructs—what makes them so appealing. This would not mean ever being definitively sure of what we have to be. But recognizing our own anxieties and the value of another's position in the context of what sexiness means today might challenge the sense evoked through neoliberalism and postfeminism of being constantly regulated and constantly repositioned.

REFERENCES

Ahmed, S. (2004) *The Cultural Politics of Emotion*. London: Routledge.

Ahmed, S. (2010) Killing Joy: Feminism and the History of Happiness. *Signs, 35*(3), 571–595.

Althusser, L. (1971) Ideology and Ideological State Apparatus (Notes Towards and Investigation). In *Lenin and Philosophy and Other Essays* (B. Brewster, trans.) (pp. 127–186). New York: Monthly Review Press.

American Psychological Association (2007) *Report of the APA Task Force on the Sexualization of Girls*. Washington, DC: American Psychological Association.

Arthurs, J. (2003) Sex and the City and Consumer Culture: Remediating Postfeminist Drama. *Feminist Media Studies, 3*(1), 83–98.

Attwood, F. (2002) Reading Porn: The Paradigm Shift in Pornography Research. *Sexualities, 5*(1), 91–105.

Attwood, F. (2005) Fashion and Passion: Marketing Sex to Women. *Sexualities, 8*(4), 392–406.

Attwood, F. (2006) Sexed Up: Theorizing the Sexualization of Culture. *Sexualities, 9*(1), 77–94.

Attwood, F. (2007a) No Money Shot? Commerce, Pornography and New Sex Taste Cultures. *Sexualities, 10*(4), 441–456.

Attwood, F. (2007b) "Other" or "One of Us?"; The Porn User in Public Academic Discourse. *Particip@tions, 4*(1), 1–23.

Attwood, F. (2009a) Researching Media Sexualisation. *Sex Roles, 61*(2–3), 288–289.

Attwood, F. (2009b) Introduction: The Sexualization of Culture. In F. Attwood (Ed.), *Mainstreaming Sex: The Sexualization of Western Culture* (pp. xiii–xxiv). London: I. B. Tauris.

Attwood, F. (2009c) Intimate Adventures: Sex Blogs, Sex "Blooks" and Women's Sexual Narration. *European Journal of Cultural Studies, 12*(1), 5–20.

Attwood, F. (2010) *Porn.com: Making Sense of Online Pornography*. New York: Peter Lang.

Attwood, F., Barker M., Bragg S., Egan D., Evans A., Harvey L., Hawkes G., Heckert, J., Holford N., Macvarish J., Martin A., McKee A., Mowlabocusk S., Paasonen S., Renold E., Ringrose J., Valentine L., Watson A. F., and van Zoonen L. (2012) Engaging with the Bailey Review: Blogging, Academia and Authenticity. *Psychology and Sexuality, 3*(1), 69–94.

Australian Senate. (2008) *Sexualisation of Children in the Contemporary Media*. Parliament House, Canberra: Standing Committee on Environment Communications and the Arts.

Ballard, K., Elston, M. A., and Gabe, J. (2005) Beyond the Mask: Women's Experiences of Public and Private Ageing During Midlife and Their Use of Age-Resisting Activities. *Health: An Interdisciplinary Journal for the Social Study of Health, Illness and Medicine*, 9(2), 169–187.

Bailey, R. (2011) *Letting Children Be Children: Report of an Independent Review of the Commercialisation and Sexualisation of Childhood*. Department of Work and Pensions, UK.

Barker, M., and Petley, J. (1997) *Ill Effects: The Media/Violence Debate*. London: Routledge.

Barker, M., and Duschinsky, R. (2012) Sexualisation's four faces: Sexualisation and gender stereotyping in the Bailey Review. *Gender and Education*, 24(3), 303–310.

Bauman, Z. (2000) *Liquid Modernity*. Cambridge: Polity.

Bauman, Z. (2001) *The Individuized Society*. Cambridge: Polity.

Beck, U., and Beck-Gernscheim, E. (2001) *Individualization*. London: Sage.

Benhabib, S., Butler, J., Cornell, D., and Fraser, N. (Eds.). (1995) *Feminist Contentions: A Philosophical Exchange*. London: Routledge.

Benjamin, J. (1997) *Shadow of the Other: Intersubjectivity and Gender in Psychoanalysis*. London: Routledge.

Benjamin, W. (1974) Left-Wing Melancholy (On Erich Kastner's New Book of Poems). *Screen*, 15(2), 28–32.

Berlant, L. (2006) Cruel Optimism. *differences*, 17(3), 20–36.

Berlant, L. (2011) *Cruel Optimism*. Durham, NC: Duke University Press.

Biggs, S. (1997) Choosing Not To Be Old? Masks, Bodies and Identity Management in Later Life. *Ageing and Society*, 17, 553–570.

Blackman, L., and Walkerdine, V. (2000) *Mass Hysteria: Critical Psychology and Media Studies*. New York: Palgrave Macmillian.

Bragg, S., and Buckingham, D. (2009) "Too Much, Too Young? Young People, Sexual Media and Learning." In F. Attwood (Ed.), *Mainstreaming Sex* (pp. 129–146). London: I. B. Tauris.

Braidotti, R. (1994) *Nomadic Subjects: Embodiment and Sexual Difference in Feminist Theory*. New York: Columbia University Press.

Braidotti, R. (1996) Nomadism with a Difference: Deleuze's Legacy in a Feminist Perspective. *Man and World*, 29, 305–314.

Brown, W. (1999) Resisting Left Melancholy. *Boundary 2*, 26(3), 19–27.

Brown, W. (2003) Women's Studies Unbound: Revolution, Mourning, Politics. *Parallax*, 9(2), 3–16.

Brown, W. (2006) American Nightmare: Neoliberalism, Neoconservatism, and De-Democratization. *Political Theory*, 34(6), 690–714.

Buckingham, Willett, D., Bragg, S., and Russell, R. (2010) *Sexualized Goods Aimed at Children: A Report to the Scottish Parliament Equal Opportunities Committee*. Scottish Parliament Equal Opportunities Committee, Edinburgh, UK.

Butler, J. (1993) *Bodies That Matter: On the Discursive Limits of Sex*. London: Routledge.

Butler, J. (1997) *The Psychic Life of Power: Theories in Subjection*. Stanford, CA: Stanford University Press.

Butler, J. (1999) *Gender Trouble: Feminism and the Subversion of Identity* (10th Anniversary Edition). London: Routledge.

Carrol, J. S., Padilla-Walker, L. M., Nelson, L. J., Olson, C. D., McNamara Barry, C., and Madsen, S. D. (2008) Generation XXX: Pornography Acceptance and Use among Emerging Adults. *Journal of Adolescent Research, 23*(1), 6–30.

Chernin, K. (1982) *The Obsession: Reflections on the Tyranny of Slenderness.* New York: Harper and Row.

Church Gibson, P. (1993) *More Dirty Looks: Gender, Pornography, Power.* London: British Film Institute.

Cohen, S. (2002) *Folk Devils and Moral Panics* (3rd Ed.). London: Routledge.

Colebrook, C. (2010) Toxic Feminism: Hope and Hopelessness after Feminism. *Journal for Cultural Research, 14*(4), 323–335.

Commane, G. R. (2010) Bad Girls and Dirty Bodies: Performative Histories and Transformative Styles. In Burkhard Scherer (Ed.), *Queering Paradigms* (pp. 49–64). New York: Peter Lang.

Coupland, J. (2000) Past the "Perfect Kind of Age"? Styling Selves and Relationships on Over-50's Dating Advertisements. *Journal of Communication, 50*(3), 9–30.

Cowie, C., and Lees, S. (1981) Slags and Drags. *Feminist Review, 9,* 17–31.

Craig, M. (2002) *Ain't I a Beauty Queen? Black Women, Beauty and the Politics of Race.* Oxford: Oxford University Press.

Creed, B. (1993) *The Monstrous-Feminine: Film, Feminism, Psychoanalysis.* London: Routledge.

Cronin, A. (2000) Consumerism and "Compulsory Individuality": Women, Will and Potential. In S. Ahmed, J. Kilby, C. Lury, M. McNeil and B. Skeggs (Eds.), *Transformations: Thinking Through Feminism* (pp. 273–287). London: Routledge.

Curtis, P. (2011) David Cameron Backs Proposals Tackling Sexualisation of Children. *The Guardian*, June 6 [available at http://www.theguardian.com/society/2011/jun/06/david-cameron-children-sexualisation-commercialisation].

Davis, K. (1995) *Reshaping the Female Body: The Dilemma of Cosmetic Surgery.* London: Routledge.

de Lauretis, T. (1989) *Technologies of Gender; Essays on Theory, Film and Fiction.* Basingstoke: Macmillan Press.

de Jour, B. (2007) Jeudi, Mars 29, accessed 20 November 2007. Available: http://belledejour-uk.blogspot.com/

Diamond, L. M. (2005) "I'm Straight, but I Kissed a Girl": The Trouble with American Media Representations of Female-Female Sexuality. *Feminism and Psychology, 15*(1), 104–110.

Dines, G. (2011) *PornLand: How Porn Has Hijacked Our Sexuality.* Boston: Beacon Press.

Dines, G., and Murphy, W. J. (2011) SlutWalk is Not Liberation. *The Guardian*, May 8 [available at http://www.theguardian.com/commentisfree/2011/may/08/slutwalk-not-sexual-liberation].

Dow, B. J. (2002) Ally McBeal, Lifestyle Feminism, and the Politics of Personal Happiness. *The Communication Review, 5*(4), 259–264.

Duits, L., and van Zoonen, L. (2006) Headscarves and Porno-Chic: Disciplining Girls' Bodies in the European Multicultural Society. *European Journal of Women's Studies, 13*(2), 103–117.

Duits, L., and van Zoonen, L. (2007) Who's Afraid of Female Agency? A Rejoinder to Gill. *European Journal of Women's Studies, 14*(2), 161–170.

Duits, L., and van Zoonen, L. (2009) Against Amnesia: 30+ Years of Girls' Studies. *Feminist Media Studies, 9*(1), 111–115.

Duits, L., and van Zoonen, L. (2011) Coming to Terms with Sexualization. *European Journal of Cultural Studies 14*(5), 491–506.

Durham, M. G. (2009) *The Lolita Effect: The Media Sexualization of Young Girls and What We Can Do About It.* Woodstock, NY: Overlook Press.

Duschinsky, R., and Barker, M. (2013) Doing the Möbius Strip: The politics of the Bailey Review. *Sexualities, 16*(5-6), 730–742.

Egan, R. D., and Hawkes, G. (2010) *Theorizing the Sexual Child in Modernity.* New York: Palgrave Macmillian.

Evans, D. T. (1993) *Sexual Citizenship: The Material Construction of Sexualities.* London: Routledge.

Evans, A., Riley, S., and Shankar, A. (2010a) Technologies of Sexiness: Theorizing Women's Engagement in the Sexualization of Culture. *Feminism and Psychology, 20*(1), 114–131.

Evans, A., Riley, S., and Shankar, A. (2010b) Postfeminist Heterotopias: Negotiating Safe and Seedy in the British Sex Shop. *European Journal of Women's Studies, 17*(3), 211–229.

Evans, A., and Riley S. (2013) Immaculate Consumption: Negotiating the Sex Symbol in Postfeminist Celebrity Culture. *Journal of Gender Studies, 22*(3), 268–281.

Evans, D. T. (1993) *Sexual Citizenship: The Material Construction of Sexualities.* London: Routledge.

Fairclough, N. (2000) *New Labour, New Language?* London: Routledge.

Filar, R. (2011) Slutwalking is rooted in Riot Grrl attitude. *The Guardian,* May 9 [available at http://www.theguardian.com/commentisfree/2011/may/09/slutwalk-feminist-activism].

Fine, M. (1988) Sexuality, Schooling and Adolescent Females: The Missing Discourse of Desire. *Harvard Educational Review, 58*(1), 29–54.

Fine, M., and McClelland, S. I. (2006) Sexuality Education and Desire: Still Missing after All These Years. *Harvard Educational Review, 76*(3), 297–338.

Fiske, J. (1989) *Understanding Popular Culture.* London: Routledge.

Foucault, M. (1974) Prisons et asiles dans le mécanisme du pouvoir. In *Dits et Ecrits,* t. II. Paris: Gallimard.

Foucault, M. (1976) *The History of Sexuality, Vol. 1: The Will to Knowledge* (R. Hurley, Trans.). London: Penguin.

Foucault, M. (1977) *Discipline and Punish: The Birth of the Prison.* London: Allen Lane.

Foucault, M. (1980) The Eye of Power. In C. Gordon (Ed.), *Power/Knowledge: Selected Interviews and Other Writings, 1972-1977 by Michel Foucault* (pp. 146–165). London: Harvester Wheatsheaf.

Foucault, M. (1986) Of Other Spaces. *Diacritics, 16,* 22–27.

Foucault, M. (1987) *The History of Sexuality, Vol. 2: The Use of Pleasure* (R. Hurley, Trans.). Harmondsworth: Penguin.

Foucault, M. (1988) Technologies of the Self. In L. H. Martin, H. Gutman, and P. Hutton (Eds.), *Technologies of the Self: A Seminar with Michel Foucault* (pp. 16–49). Amherst: The University of Massachusetts Press.

Foucault, M. (1990) *The History of Sexuality, Vol. 3: The Care of the Self* (R. Hurley, Trans.). Harmondsworth: Penguin.

Foucault, M. (1993) About the Beginning of the Hermeneutics of the Self: Two Lectures at Dartmouth. *Political Theory, 21*(2), 198–227.

Foucault, M. (1997) Utopias and Heterotopias. In N. Leach (Ed.), *Rethinking Architecture: A Reader in Cultural Theory* (pp. 350–355). London: Routledge.

Foucault, M. (2008) *The Birth of Biopolitics: Lectures at the College de France*. Basingstoke: Palgrave Macmillan.

Gavey, N. (2005) *Just Sex? The Cultural Scaffolding of Rape*. London: Routledge.

Gavey, N. (2012) Beyond "Empowerment"? Sexuality in a Sexist World. *Sex Roles*, 66(11–12), 718–724.

Genz, S., and Brabon, B. A. (2009) *Postfeminism: Cultural Texts and Theories*. Edinburgh: Edinburgh University Press.

Giddens, A. (1990) *The Consequences of Modernity*. Cambridge: Polity Press.

Giddens, A. (1991) *Modernity and Self-Identity: Self and Society in the Late Modern Age*. Cambridge: Polity Press.

Gill, R. (2003) From Sexual Objectification to Sexual Subjectification: The Resexualisation of Women's Bodies in the Media. *Feminist Media Studies*, 3(1), 99–106.

Gill, R. (2007a) Critical Respect: The Difficulties and Dilemmas of Agency and "Choice" for Feminism: A Reply to Duits and van Zoonen. *European Journal of Women's Studies*, 14(1), 69–80.

Gill, R. (2007b) *Gender and the Media*. Cambridge: Polity Press.

Gill, R. (2007c) Postfeminist Media Culture: Elements of a Sensibility. *European Journal of Cultural Studies*, 10(2), 147–166.

Gill, R. (2008a) Culture and Subjectivity in Neoliberal and Postfeminist times. *Subjectivity*, 25, 432–445.

Gill, R. (2008b) Empowerment/Sexism: Figuring Female Sexual Agency in Contemporary Advertising. *Feminism and Psychology*, 18(1), 35–60.

Gill, R. (2009) Beyond the "Sexualization of Culture" Thesis: An Intersectional Analysis of "Sixpacks," "Midriffs" and "Hot Lesbians" in Advertising. *Sexualities*, 12(2), 137–160.

Gill, R. (2010) Mediated Intimacy and Postfeminism: A Discourse Analytic Examination of Sex and Relationships Advice in a Woman's Magazine. *Discourse and Communication 3*, 345–369.

Gill, R. (2011) Sexism Reloaded, or, It's Time to Get Angry Again. *Feminist Media Studies*, 11(1), 61–71.

Gill, R. (2012a) The Sexualization of Culture? *Social and Personality Psychology Compass*, 6(7), 483–498.

Gill, R. (2012b) Media, Empowerment and the "Sexualization of Culture" Debates. *Sex Roles*, 66(11–12), 736–745.

Gill, R., and Herdieckerhoff, E. (2006) Rewriting the Romance: New Femininities in Chick Lit? *Feminist Media Studies*, 6(4), 487–504.

Gill, R., and Scharff, C. (2011) (Eds.) *New Femininities: Postfeminism, Neoliberalism and Subjectivity*. Basingstoke: Palgrave Macmillan.

Gillis, S., and Munford, R. (2004) Genealogies and Generations: The Politics and Praxis of Third Wave Feminism. *Women's History Review*, 13(2), 165–182.

Gonick, M. (2003) *Between Femininities: Ambivalence, Identity and the Education of Girls*. Albany: State University of New York Press.

Gonick, M. (2006) Between "Girl Power" and "Reviving Ophelia": Constituting the Neoliberal Girl Subject. *NWSA Journal*, 18(2), 1–23.

Gordon, A. (2008) *Ghostly Matters: Haunting and the Sociological Imagination*. Minneapolis: University of Minnesota Press.

Green, E., and Singleton, C. (2006) Risky Bodies at Leisure: Young Women Negotiating Space and Place. *Sociology, 40*(5), 853–871.

Greer, G. (1970) *The Female Eunuch*. London: Paladin.

Griffin, C. (1985) *Typical Girls? Young Women from School to the Job Market.* London: Routledge and Kegan Paul.

Griffin, C. (1997) Troubled Teens: Managing Disorders of Transition and Consumption. *Feminist Review, 55*, 4–21.

Hall, P., and Soskice, D. (2001) *Varieties of Capitalism: The Institutional Foundations of Comparative Advantage*. Oxford: Oxford University Press.

Hall, S. (1997) The Work of Representation. In S. Hall (Ed.), *Representation: Cultural Representations and Signifying Practices* (pp. 13–74). London: Sage.

Hall, S. (2011) The Neoliberal Revolution. *Soundings, 48*(20), 9–28

Hall, S., Critcher, C., Jefferson, T., Clarke, J., and Roberts, B. (1979) *Policing the Crisis: Mugging, the State, and Law and Order*. Birmingham: University of Birmingham.

Haran, J. (2010) Redefining Hope as Praxis. *Journal for Cultural Research, 14*(4), 393–408.

Haraway, D. (1988) Situated Knowledges: The Science Question in Feminism and the Privilege of Partial Perspectives. *Feminist Studies, 14*(3), 575–599.

Haraway, D. (1991) *Simians, Cyborgs, and Women: The Reinvention of Culture.* London: Routledge.

Harradine, D. (2000) Abject Identities and Fluid Performances: Theorizing the Leaky Body. *Contemporary Theatre Review, 10*(3), 69–85.

Harris, A. (2004) *Future Girl: Young Women in the Twenty First Century.* London: Routledge.

Harris, A. (Ed.). (2008) *Next Wave Cultures: Feminism, Subcultures, Activism.* London: Routledge.

Harvey, D. (2007) Neoliberalism as Creative Destruction. *The Annals of the American Academy of Political and Social Science, 610*(1), 21–44.

Harvey, L., and Gill, R. (2011) Spicing it Up: Sexual Entrepreneurs and The Sex Inspectors. In R. Gill and C. Scharff (Eds.). *New Femininities: Postfeminism, Neo-liberalism and Subjectivity* (pp. 52–67). London: Palgrave.

Hawkesworth, M. (2004) The Semiotics of Premature Burial: Feminism in a Postfeminist Age. *Signs, 29*(4), 961–985.

Hayles, N. K. (2006) Unfinished Work: From Cyborg to Cognisphere. *Theory, Culture and Society, 23*(7–8), 159–166.

Haylett, C. (2001) Illegitimate Subjects?: Abject Whites, Neoliberal Modernisation and Middle-Class Multiculturalism. *Environment and Planning D: Space and Society, 19*(3), 351–370.

Hayward, K., and Yar, M. (2006) The "Chav" Phenomenon: Consumption, Media and the Construction of a New Underclass. *Crime, Media, Culture, 2*(1), 9–28.

Hemmings, C. (2005) Telling Feminist Stories. *Feminist Theory, 6*(2), 115–139.

Hesford, V. (2005) Feminism and Its Ghosts: The Specter of the Feminist-as-Lesbian. *Feminist Theory, 6*(3), 227–250.

Hetherington, K. (1996) Identity Formation, Space and Social Centrality. *Theory, Culture and Society, 13*, 33–52.

Holland, S., and Attwood, F. (2009) Keeping Fit in Six Inch Heels: The Mainstreaming of Pole Dancing. In F. Attwood (Ed.), *Mainstreaming Sex: The Sexualization of Western Culture* (pp. 165–182). London: I. B. Tauris

Hook, D. (2006) "Pre-Discursive" Racism. *Journal of Community and Applied Social Psychology*, 16(3), 207–232.

Hook, D. (2007) *Foucault, Psychology and the Analytics of Power*. Hampshire: Palgrave Macmillan.

Hook, D., and Vrdoljak, M. (2002) Gated Communities, Heterotopia and a "Rights" of Privileged: A "Heterotopology" of the South African Security-Park. *Geoforum*, 33(2), 195–219.

hooks, b. (1992) *Black Looks: Race and Representation*. Boston: South End Press.

Hutcheon, L. (1998) Irony, Nostalgia, and the Postmodern [available online at http://www.library.utoronto.ca/utel/criticism/hutchinp.html, Accessed March 23, 2010].

Illouz, E. (2007) *Cold Intimacies: The Making of Emotional Capitalism*. Cambridge: Polity Press.

Illouz, E. (2008) *Saving the Modern Soul: Therapy, Emotions, and the Culture of Self-Help*. Berkeley: University of California Press.

Illouz, E. (2012) *Why Love Hurts: A Sociological Explanation*. Cambridge: Polity.

Jackson, A. Y. (2003) Rhizovocality. *International Journal of Qualitative Studies in Education*, 16(5), 693–710.

Jackson, S., Vares, T. and Gill, R. (2012) 'The Whole Playboy Mansion Image': Girls' Fashioning and Fashioned Selves within a Postfeminist Culture. *Feminism and Psychology*, 23(2), 143–162.

Jagose, A. (2010) Conterfeit Pleasure: Fake Orgasm and Queer Agency. *Textual Practice*, 24(3), 517–539.

Johnson, P. (2008) "Rude Boys": The Homosexual Eroticization of Class. *Sociology*, 42(1), 65–82.

Johnston, J., and Taylor, J. (2008) Feminist Consumerism and Fat Activists: A Comparative Study of Grassroots Activism and the Dove Real Beauty Campaign. *Signs*, 33(4), 941–966.

Jones, O. (2011) *Chavs: The Demonization of the Working Class*. London: Verso.

Jones, S., and Mowlabocus, S. (2009) Hard Times and Rough Rides: The Legal and Ethical Impossibilities of Research "Shock" Pornographies. *Sexualities*, 12(5), 613–628.

Juffer, J. (1998) *At Home with Pornography: Women, Sexuality, and Everyday Life*. New York: New York University.

Kanuga, M., and Rosenfeld, W. D. (2004) Adolescent Sexuality and the Internet: The Good, the Bad and the URL. *Journal of Paediatric and Adolescent Gynaecology*, 17(2), 117–124.

Katz, S., and Marshall, B. (2003) New Sex for Old: Lifestyle, Consumerism and the Ethics of Aging Well. *Journal of Aging Studies*, 17, 3–16.

Kelly, P. (2006) "The Entrepreneurial Self" and "Youth-at-risk": Exploring the Horizons of Identity in the Twenty-first Century. *Journal of Youth Studies*, 9(1), 17–32.

Kendrick, W. (1987) *The Secret Museum: Pornography in Modern Culture*. Berkeley: University of California Press.

Kincheloe, J. L. (2001) Describing the Bricolage: Conceptualizing a New Rigor in Qualitative Research. *Qualitative Inquiry*, 7(6), 679–692.

Kincheloe, J. L. (2005) On to the Next Level: Continuing the Conceptualization of the Bricolage. *Qualitative Inquiry*, 11(3), 323–350.

Kristeva, J. (1982) *Powers of Horror: An Essay in Abjection*. New York: Columbia University Press.

Lamb, S., and Brown, L. M. (2006) *Packaging Girlhood*. New York: St. Martin's Press.

Lamb, S. (2010a) Feminist Ideals of Healthy Female Adolescent Sexuality: A Critique. *Sex Roles, 62*(5–6), 294–306.

Lamb, S. (2010b) Porn as a Pathway to Empowerment? A Response to Peterson's Commentary. *Sex Roles, 62*(5–6), 314–317.

Lamb, S., and Peterson, Z. (2012) Adolescent Girls' Sexual Empowerment: Two Feminists Explore the Concepts. *Sex Roles, 66*(11–12), 703–712.

Lasch, C. (1979) *The Culture of Narcissism: American Life in the Age of Diminishing Expectations*. New York: W.W. Norton.

Lather, P. (2007) *Getting Lost: Feminist Efforts toward a Double(d) Science*. Albany: State of University of New York Press.

Lazar, Michelle M. (2011) The Right to Be Beautiful: Postfeminist Identity and Consumer Beauty Advertising. In R. Gill and C. Scharff (Eds.), *New Femininities: Postfeminism, Neoliberalism and Subjectivity* (pp. 37–51). London: Routledge.

Levin, D. E., and Kilbourne, J. (2009) *So Sexy So Soon*. New York: Ballantine Books

Levy, A. (2005) *Female Chauvinist Pigs: Women and the Rise of Raunch Culture*. London: Simon and Schuster.

Lloyd, M. (1999) Performativity, Parody, Politics. *Theory, Culture and Society, 16*(2), 195–213.

Mackiewicz, A. (2013) New Femininities in the Culture of Intoxication: Exploring Young Women's Participation in the Night-Time Economy, in the Context of Sexualized Culture, Neoliberalism and Postfeminism. Unpublished PhD thesis, University of Bath.

Maddison, S., and Storr, M. (2004) The Edge of Reason: The Myth of Bridget Jones. In J. Hands and E. Siapera (Eds.), *At the Interface: Continuity and Transformation in Culture and Politics* (pp. 3–16). Amsterdam: Rodopi B.V.

Martin, L. S., and Gavey, N. (1996) Women's Bodybuilding: Feminist Resistance and/or Femininity's Recuperation? *Body and Society, 2*(4), 45–57.

Measham, F., and Brain, K. (2005) "Binge" Drinking, British Alcohol Policy and the New Culture of Intoxication. *Crime, Media, Culture, 1*(3), 262–283.

McAfee, N. (2004) *Julia Kristeva*. London: Routledge.

McKenna, S. E. (2002) The Queer Insistence of Ally McBeal: Lesbian Chic, Postfeminism, and Lesbian Reception. *The Communication Review, 5*, 285–314.

McNair, B. (1996) *Mediated Sex: Pornography and Postmodern Culture*. London: Arnold.

McNair, B. (2002) *Striptease Culture: Sex, Media and the Democratization of Desire*. London: Routledge.

McNair, B. (2009) From Porn Chic to Porn Fear: The Return of the Repressed? In F. Attwood (Ed.), *Mainstreaming Sex: The Sexualization of Western Culture* (pp. 55–73). London: I. B. Tauris.

McNay, L. (2000) *Gender and Agency: Reconfiguring the Subject in Feminist and Social Theory*. Cambridge: Polity Press.

McNay, L. (2009) Self as Enterprise: Dilemmas of Control and Resistance in Foucault's The Birth of Biopolitics. *Theory, Culture and Society, 26*(6), 55–77.

McRobbie, A. (1994) *Postmodernism and Popular Culture*. London: Routledge.

McRobbie, A. (1999) *In the Culture Society: Art, Fashion and Popular Music*. London: Routledge.

McRobbie, A. (2004) Notes on "What Not To Wear" and Post-feminist Symbolic Violence. *Sociological Review, 52*(2), 97–109.

McRobbie, A. (2008) A Response to Susie Orbach: On Generation and Femininity. *Studies in Gender and Sexuality, 9*(3), 239–245.

McRobbie, A. (2009) *The Aftermath of Feminism: Gender, Culture and Social Change.* London: Sage.

Miller, P., and Rose, N. (1997) Mobilizing the Consumer: Assembling the Subject of Consumption. *Theory, Culture and Society, 14*(1), 1–36.

Morgan, R. (1980) Theory and practice: Pornography and rape. In L. Lederer (Ed.), *Take back the nigh: Women and pornography* (pp. 134–140). New York: Morrow.

Morley, D., and Chen, K. H. (Eds.) (1996) *Stuart Hall: Critical Dialogues in Cultural Studies.* London: Routledge.

Moseley, R., and Read, J. (2002) "Having it Ally": Popular Television (Post-)Feminism. *Feminist Media Studies, 2*(2), 231–249.

Mulvey, Laura. 1975. Visual Pleasure and Narrative Cinema. *Screen 16*(3), 6–18.

Negra, D. (2009) *What a Girl Wants?: Fantasizing the Reclamation of Self in Postfeminism.* London: Routledge.

Nixon, S. (1997) Exhibiting Masculinity. In S. Hall (Ed.), *Representation: Cultural Representations and Signifying Practices* (pp. 291–336). Thousand Oaks, CA: Open University Press.

O'Farrell, C. (2005) *Michel Foucault.* London: Sage.

Ong, A. (2006) Mutations in citizenship. *Theory, Culture and Society, 23*(2–3), 499–531.

Oppliger, P. (2008) *Girls Gone Skank.* Jefferson, NC: MacFarland and Company Press.

Orbach, S. (2009) *Bodies.* London: Profile Books.

Ouellette, L. (2002) Victims No More: Postfeminism, Television and Ally McBeal. *The Communication Review, 5*(4), 315–335.

Ouellette, L., and Hay, J. (2008) Makeover Television, Governmentality and the Good Citizen. *Continuum 22*(4), 471–484.

Paasonen, S. (2009) Healthy Sex and Pop Porn: Pornography, Feminism and the Finnish Context. *Sexualities, 12*(5), 586–604.

Papadopoulos, L. (2010) *Sexualisation of Young People Review.* London: Home Office Publication.

Parker, I. (1999) Critical Psychology: Critical Links, Radical Psychology. *A Journal of Psychology, Politics and Radicalism, 1*, 3–18.

Paul, P. (2005) *Pornified: How Pornography Is Damaging Our Lives, Our Relationships, and Our Families.* New York: Times Books.

Paulson, S., and Willig, C. (2008) Older Women and Everyday Talk about Ageing Body. *Journal of Health Psychology, 13*(1), 106–120.

Peterson, Z. (2010) What Is Sexual Empowerment? A Multidimensional and Process-Oriented Approach to Adolecent Girls' Sexual Empowerment. *Sex Roles, 63*(5–6), 307–313.

Phillips, M. (2011) These "Slut Walks" Prove Feminism Is Now Irrelevant to Most Women's Lives. The Daily Mail, June 13 [available at http://www.dailymail.co.uk/debate/article-2002887/Slut-Walks-prove-feminism-irrelevant-womens-lives.html#ixzz2jgy2tD7D].

Pierre, E. A. (1997) Methodology in the Fold and the Irruption of Transgressive Data. *International Journal of Qualitative Studies in Education, 10*(2), 175–189.

Plummer, K. (1995) *Telling Sexual Stories: Power, Change and Social Worlds.* London: Routledge.

Potts, V., and Parry, J. (2010) Vegan Sexuality: Challenging Heteronormative Masculinity Through Meat-free Sex. *Feminism and Psychology, 20*(1), 53–72.

Power, N. (2010) *One-Dimensional Woman.* Winchester: Zero Books.

Probyn, E. (2008) Silence Behind the Mantra: Critiquing Feminist Fat. *Feminism and Psychology, 18*(3), 401–404.

Radner, H. (1995) *Shopping Around: Feminine Culture and the Pursuit of Pleasure.* London: Routledge.

Radner, H. (1999) Introduction: Queering the Girl. In H. Radner and M. Luckett (Eds.), *Swinging Single: Representing Sexuality in the 1960's.* Minneapolis: University of Minnesota Press.

Raymond, J. (1980) *The Transsexual Empire: The Making of the She-Male.* London: Women's Press.

Read, J. (2009) A Genealogy of Homo-Economicus: Neoliberalism and the Production of Subjectivity. *Foucault Studies, 6,* 25–36.

Reason, P., and Riley, S. (2008) Co-operative Inquiry: An Action Research Practice. In J. Smith (Ed.), *Qualitative Psychology: A Practical Guide to Research Methods* (pp. 207–234). London: Sage.

Reay, D. (2010) Identity Making in Schools and Classrooms. In M. Wetherell and C. T. Mohanty (Eds.), *The SAGE Handbook of Identities* (pp. 277–295). London: Sage.

Reiss, T. J. (1983) Critical Environments: Cultural Wilderness or Cultural History? *Canadian Review of Comparative Literature 10*(2), 193–209.

Renold, E., and Ringrose, J. (2008) Regulation and Rupture: Mapping Tween and Teenage Girls' "Resistance" to the Heterosexual Matrix. *Feminist Theory: An International Interdisciplinary Journal 9*(3), 335–360.

Renold, E., and Ringrose, J. (2011) Schizoid Subjectivities: Re-theorising Teen-Girls' Sexual Cultures in an Era of Sexualisation. *Journal of Sociology (Special Issue on "Youth Identities, Cultures and Transitions"), 47*(4), 389–409.

Richards, G. (2002) *Putting Psychology in its Place: A Critical Historical Overview.* Sussex: Psychology Press.

Richardson, L. (2000) Writing: A Method of Inquiry. In N. K. Denzin and Y. Lincoln (Eds.), *Handbook of Qualitative Research* (2nd Ed.) (pp. 516–529). London: Sage.

Riley, S. (2002) Constructions of Equality and Discrimination in Professional Men's Talk. *British Journal of Social Psychology, 41*(3), 443–461.

Riley, S. C. E., and Cahill, S. (2005) Managing Meaning and Belonging: Young Women's Negotiation of Authenticity in Body Art. *Journal of Youth Studies, 8*(3), 261–279.

Riley, S., Morey, Y., and Griffin, C. (2010) The "Pleasure Citizen": Analysing Partying as a Form of Social and Political Participation. *Young (Special Issue on "Emerging Forms of Youth Engagement: Everyday and Local Perspectives"), 18*(1), 33–54.

Riley, S., and Scharff, C. (2013) Feminism vs Femininity? Exploring Feminist Dilemmas Through Cooperative Inquiry Research. *Feminism & Psychology, 23*(2), 207–223.

Riley, S. C. E., Thompson, J., and Griffin, C. (2010) Turn On, Tune In, But Don't Drop Out: The Impact of Neo-Liberalism on Magic Mushroom Users (In)Ability to Imagine Collectivist Social Worlds. *International Journal of Drug Policy, 21,* 445–451.

Ringrose, J. (2006) A New Universal Mean Girl: Examining the Discursive Construction and Social Regulation of a New Feminine Pathology. *Feminism and Psychology, 16*(4), 405–424.

Ringrose, J. (2007) Successful Girls?: Complicating Post-Feminist, Neo-Liberal Discourses of Educational Achievement and Gender Equality. *Gender and Education* *19*(4), 471–489.

Ringrose, J. (2011) Beyond Discourse? Using Deleuze and Guattari's Schizoanalysis to Explore Affective Assemblages, Heterosexually Striated Space, and Lines of Flight Online and at School. *Educational Philosophy & Theory*, *43*(6), 598–618.

Ringrose, J. (2013) *Postfeminist Education? Girls and the Sexual Politics of Schooling.* London: Routledge.

Ringrose, J., and Barajas, K. (2011) Gendered Risks and Opportunities? Exploring Teen Girls' Digital Sexual Identity in Postfeminist Media Contexts. International *Journal of Media and Cultural Politics*, *7*(2), 121–138.

Ringrose, J., and Renold, E. (2012) Slut-Shaming, Girl Power and "Sexualisation": Thinking Through the Politics of the International SlutWalks with Teen Girls. *Gender and Education (Special Issue: "Making Sense of the Sexualisation Debates: Schools and Beyond")*, *24*(3), 333–343.

Ringrose, J., and Walkerdine, V. (2008) Regulating the Abject: The TV Make-Over as a Site of Neo-Liberal Reinvention toward Bourgeois Femininity. *Feminist Media Studies*, *8*(3), 227–246.

Rose, N. (1996) *Inventing Ourselves: Psychology, Power and Personhood.* New York: Cambridge University Press.

Rose, N. (1999) *Governing the Soul: The Shaping of Private Life* (2nd Ed.). London: Free Association Books.

Rose, N., and Miller, P. (1992) Political Power Beyond the State: Problematics of Government. *British Journal of Sociology*, *43*(2), 173–205.

Rush, E., and La Nauze, A. (2006) *Corporate Paedophilia: Sexualisation of children in Australia.* The Australian Institute.

Russo, M. (1994) *The Female Grotesque: Risk, Modernity, Excess.* New York; London: Routledge.

Said, E. (1978) *Orientalism.* London: Routledge and Kegan Paul.

Schwyzer, H. (2011) Redeeming the Slut: A Response to Gail Dines. Blog post, May 9 [available at http://www.hugoschwyzer.net/2011/05/09/redeeming-the-slut-a-response-to-gail-dines/].

Scott, L. M. (2005) *Fresh Lipstick: Redressing Fashion and Feminism.* Hampshire: Palgrave Macmillan.

Segal, L. (1994) *Straight Sex: The Politics of Pleasure.* Berkeley: University of California Press.

Segal, L. (1998) Only the Literal: The Contradictions of Anti-Pornography Feminism. *Sexualities*, *1*(1), 43–62.

Segal, L., and McIntosh, M. (1992) *Sex Exposed: Sexuality and the Pornography Debate.* New Brunswick, NJ: Rutgers University Press.

Sherwin, A. (2011) The worst pop song of all time? – 10 million YouTube hits for Rebecca Black's "Friday". The Independent, March 18 [available at http://www.independent.co.uk/arts-entertainment/music/news/the-worst-pop-song-of-all-time--10-millio n-youtube-hits-for-rebecca-blacks-friday-2245353.html]

Skeggs, B. (1993) Two Minute Brother: Contestation Through Gender, "Race" and Sexuality. *Innovation: The European Journal of Social Sciences*, *6*(3), 299–322.

Skeggs, B. (1997) *Formations of Class and Gender: Becoming Respectable*. London: Sage.

Skeggs, B. (2005) The Making of Class and Gender Through Visualizing Moral Subject Formation. *Sociology, 39*(5), 965–982.

Skeggs, B., and Wood, H. (2004) Notes on Ethical Scenarios of Self on British Reality TV. *Feminist Media Studies, 4*(1), 205–208.

Smith, C. (2007) Designed for Pleasure: Style, Indulgence and Accessorized Sex. *European Journal of Cultural Studies, 10*(2), 167–184.

Smith, C. (2010) Pornographication: A Discourse for All Seasons. *International Journal of Media and Cultural Politics, 6*(1), 103–108.

Sonnet, E. (1999) Erotic Fiction by Women for Women: The Pleasures of Post-feminist Heterosexuality. *Sexualities, 2*(2), 167–187.

Sontag, S. (2003) *Regarding the Pain of Others*. London: Penguin Books.

Sontag, S. (2009) *Styles of Radical Will*. London: Penguin Classics.

Stacey, J. (1987) Desperately Seeking Difference: Desire between Women in Narrative Cinema. *Screen 28*(1), 48–61.

Stacey, J. (1994) *Star Gazing: Hollywood Cinema and Female Spectatorship*. London: Routledge.

Stainton-Rogers, W. (2011) *Social Psychology* (2nd Ed). Berkshire: Open University Press/McGrawHill.

Stallybrass, P., and White, A. (1986) *The Politics and Poetics of Transgression*. London: Methuen.

Statham, J., Mooney, A., and Phoenix, A. (2011) Summary of Regulatory Frameworks in Four Selected Countries, for the Bailey Review of Commercialisation and Sexualisation of Childhood. Childhood Wellbeing Research Centre, Working Paper No. 5.

Storr, M. (2003) *Latex and Lingerie: Shopping for Pleasure at Ann Summers Parties*. Oxford: Berg.

Tate, Shirley A. (2009) Black Beauty: Aesthetics, Stylization, Politics. Surrey: Ashgate.

Thompson, E. M. (2006) Girl Friend or Girlfriend: Same-Sex Friendship and Bisexual Images as a Context for Flexible Sexual Identity among Young Women. *Journal of Bisexuality, 6*(3), 47–67.

Tiefer, L. (2006) The Viagra Phenomenon. *Sexualities 9*(3), 273–294.

Tuck, G. (2009) The Mainstreaming of Masturbation: Autoeroticism and Consumer Capitalism. In F. Attwood (Ed.), *Mainstreaming Sex: The Sexualization of Western Culture* (pp. 77–92). London: I. B. Tauris.

Tunaley, J. R., Walsh, S., and Nicolson, P. (1999) "I"m Not Bad for My Age': The Meaning of Body Size and Eating in the Lives of Older Women. *Ageing and Society, 19*, 741–759.

Turner, G. (2004) *Understanding Celebrity*. London: Sage.

Tyler, I. (2008) Chav Mum, Chav Scum: Class Disgust in Contemporary Britain. *Feminist Media Studies, 8*(1), 17–34.

Tyler, I. (2009) Against Abjection. *Feminist Theory, 10*(1), 77–98.

Tyler, I. (2013) *Revolting Subejcts: Social Abjection and Resistance in Neoliberal Britain*. London: Zed Books.

Tyler, I., and Bennett, B. (2010) "Celebrity Chav": Fame, Femininity and Social Class. *European Journal of Cultural Studies, 13*(3), 375–393.

Vance, C. S. (1984) *Pleasure and Danger: Exploring Female Sexuality*. London: Routledge.

Vares, T. (2009) Reading the "Sexy Oldie": Gender, Age(ing) and Embodiment. *Sexualities, 12*(4), 503–524.

Vares, T., Potts, A., Gavey, N. and Grace, V. M. (2007) Reconceptualizing Cultural Narratives Of Mature Women's Sexuality in the Viagra Era. *Journal of Aging Studies* *21*(2), 153–164.

Villani, S. M. D. (2001) Impact of Media on Children and Adolescents: A 10-Year Review of Research. *Child and Adolescent Psychiatry*, *40*(4), 392–401.

Walkerdine, V. (2003) Reclassifying Upward Mobility: Femininity and the Neo-liberal Subject. *Gender and Education*, *15*(3), 237–248.

Walkerdine, V., and Ringrose J. (2006) Femininities: Reclassifying Upward Mobility and the Neo-Liberal Subject. In C. Skelton, B. Francis, and L. Smulyan (Eds.), *The SAGE Handbook of Gender and Education* (pp. 31–46). Thousand Oaks, CA: Sage.

Walkerdine, V., Lucey, H., and Melody, J. (2001) *Growing Up Girl: Psychosocial Explorations of Gender and Class.* London: Palgrave.

Walter, N. (1999) *The New Feminism.* London: Virago.

Walter, N. (2010) *Living Dolls: The Return of Sexism.* London: Virago.

Weekes, D. (2004) Where My Girls At? Black Girls and the Construction of the Sexual. In A. Harris (Ed.), *All About the Girl: Culture, Power and Identity* (pp. 141–154). London: Routledge.

Weeks, J. (1998) The Sexual Citizen. *Theory, Culture and Society*, *15*(3/4), 35–52.

Wetherell, M. (1995) Romantic Discourse and Feminist Analysis: Interrogating Investment, Power and Desire. In C. Kitzinger and S. Wilkinson (Eds.), *Feminism and Discourse: Psychological Perspectives* (pp. 128–144). London: Sage.

Whitehead, K., and Kurz, T. (2009) "Empowerment" and the Pole: A Discursive Investigation of the Reinvention of Pole Dancing as a Recreational Activity. *Feminism and Psychology*, *19*(2), 224–244.

Widdicombe, S., and Wooffitt, R. (1995) *The Language of Youth Subculture.* Brighton: Harvester.

Williams, A., Ylanne, V., and Wadleigh, P. M. (2007) "Selling the Elixir of Life": Images of Elderly in an Olivio Advertising Campaign. *Journal of Aging Studies*, *21*(1), 1–21.

Williams, L. (1989) *Hard Core: Power, Pleasure and the "Frenzy of the Visible."* Berkeley: University of California Press.

Williams, L. (2004) *Porn Studies.* Durham, NC: Duke University Press.

Williamson, J. (1985) *Consuming Passions: The Dynamics of Popular Culture.* London: Boyars.

Willson, J. (2008) *The Happy Stripper: Pleasures and Politics of the New Burlesque.* London: I. B. Tauris.

Wolf, N. (1990) *The Beauty Myth: How Images of Beauty Are Used Against Women.* London: Vintage.

Wolf, N. (2009, April 4) Is Porn Damaging Your Emotional Health? *The Times Online.* [retrieved April 10, 2009, from http://women.timesonline.co.uk/tol/life_and_style/women/relationships/article6027904.ece].